teach yourself®

photography

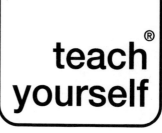

photography
lee frost

Launched in 1938, the **teach yourself** series grew rapidly in response to the world's wartime needs. Loved and trusted by over 50 million readers, the series has continued to respond to society's changing interests and passions and now, 70 years on, includes over 500 titles, from Arabic and Beekeeping to Yoga and Zulu. What would you like to learn?

be where you want to be with **teach yourself**

Orders: please contact Bookpoint Ltd, 130 Milton Park, Abingdon, Oxon OX14 4SB. Telephone: +44 (0) 1235 827720. Fax: +44 (0) 1235 400454. Lines are open 09.00–17.00, Monday to Saturday, with a 24-hour message answering service. You can also order through our website www.hoddereducation.co.uk

British Library Cataloguing in Publication Data: a catalogue record for this title is available from the British Library.

First published in UK 2008 by Hodder Education, part of Hachette Livre UK, 338 Euston Road, London NW1 3BH.

This edition published 2008.

Typeset by Transet Ltd, Coventry, England.
Printed in Great Britain for Hodder Education, an Hachette Livre UK Company, 338 Euston Road, London NW1 3BH, by Cox & Wyman, Reading, Berkshire.

The publisher has used its best endeavours to ensure that the URLs for external websites referred to in this book are correct and active at the time of going to press. However, the publisher and the author have no responsibility for the websites and can make no guarantee that a site will remain live or that the content will remain relevant, decent or appropriate.

Hachette Livre UK's policy is to use papers that are natural, renewable and recyclable products and made from wood grown in sustainable forests. The logging and manufacturing processes are expected to conform to the environmental regulations of the country of origin.

Impression number   10 9 8 7 6 5 4 3 2 1
Year   2012 2011 2010 2009 2008

contents

When I sat down to write the first edition of this book, I had no idea just how dramatically the world of photography would advance and change in 15 short years.

Looking through the original manuscript, I was shocked to discover how simple and straightforward everything seemed back then and how clever and complicated it is today.

In 1992 cameras were still predominantly manual focus with relatively basic metering. Auto focusing was considered to be emerging, prime lenses were said to be better than zooms. If you wanted to take photographs, you loaded a roll of film into your camera, exposed it, then either sent it away to a processing lab or did the job yourself in a darkroom – which a large proportion of enthusiast photographers had, even if it was only the cupboard under the stairs.

Today, in 2008, the digital age is well and truly upon us and photography has changed forever. Film is slowly being replaced by digital cameras and if you are coming into photography for the first time you may never have taken a photograph using film in your life!

Those wonderful darkrooms of old are now considered unnecessary because armed with a computer – which the vast majority of us now possess – suitable imaging software and a decent inkjet printer, it's possible to create photo-quality prints in both colour and black and white with ease.

Photography has never been more complicated in terms of the equipment or technology involved, but at the same time it has never been more accessible or versatile or enjoyable. The creative possibilities are endless today, and the opportunities to share your work with others in the form or prints, books, albums, email and websites has never been greater, adding to the satisfaction there is to be gained from picking up a camera and recording the world around you.

Photography as a hobby serves many important purposes. First and foremost it allows you to document your life. By taking pictures of your family and friends, home town, and the many places you visit, you are creating an important visual record that will tell a fascinating story to future generations, as well as bringing back many happy memories as the years roll by. Photographs are like visual time capsules. Places change and people change, but in your pictures everything remains the same.

Photography also makes you more observant and receptive to what's going on around you. The simple act of taking pictures forces you to look more closely at the world. You begin to see things that other people miss because they are blinded by familiarity, and this leads to a greater appreciation of your surroundings.

But most important of all, photography is a fascinating creative process that allows you to tap into the hidden depths of your imagination. And thanks to the wonders of modern technology, taking successful photographs is easier than ever. Digital cameras allow you to see the results instantly, which is invaluable as a teaching aid because you can spot mistakes and correct then immediately, instead of waiting days for a film to return from the processing lab – by which time it is too late to reshoot!

What technology has yet to harness is the artistic side of photography. Cameras may be able to focus automatically, sort out the exposure and provide a burst of electronic flash when light levels are low, but they can't tell you what to photograph, or how to compose a picture. Neither can they tell you when the light is perfect, or when to trip the shutter to capture a person's character.

These decisions – the most important decisions of all – will always have to be made by you. And the more your interest in photography develops, the more frequently you will have to make them because they hold the key to the creative success or failure of every picture you take.

This is where this book comes in. I'll be taking you through all aspects of photography, from the fundamentals such as choosing cameras and lenses, and mastering the intricacies of exposure and depth of field, to the importance of light, using flash and composing a picture. You will also find advice on digital technology – what you need and how to use it to enhance your images before producing perfect prints in the comfort of your home.

After that we will look at specific subjects such as landscapes, portraits, action, still life, nature, close-ups, architecture, holidays and travel, so you can put your new-found knowledge to good use.

If you are new to photography, absorbing all this information may seem like a daunting prospect. However, do not worry – we have all been there.

In the beginning you will make a lot of mistakes, and at times you will wonder why you ever became interested in photography in the first place. But this is all part of the learning process, and if you think carefully about what you are doing, confusion will quickly turn to elation as you discover the great joy to be derived from taking successful pictures.

Lee Frost
January 2008

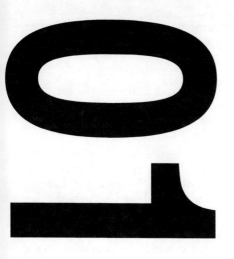

01

choosing a camera

In this chapter you will learn:
- which type of camera to buy
- the main features to look for
- how digital cameras work
- how to care for your camera.

In the last few years, a photographic revolution has taken place and the art of image-making will never be the same again. The reason for this can be summarized in two words – digital technology.

Manufacturers have been producing digital cameras for more than a decade now. However, the early efforts were not only very expensive but offered poor image quality compared to film cameras costing a fraction of the price. Not any more.

Digital cameras are still more expensive than their film equivalents, but the quality they are capable of makes the additional investment well worthwhile because the benefits digital capture offers over traditional film photography are incredible.

Not only do you get to see your pictures immediately, which means that you can correct mistakes and learn from them on the spot, but they are free. With no film or processing costs to worry about, you can shoot away to your heart's content and though the initial investment in a digital camera may be high, if you are a serious enthusiast who tends to take a lot of pictures, that investment will soon pay for itself in the money saved by not having to buy film or pay for processing.

Financial benefits aside, the practical and creative advantages of digital over film are also significant. Once the images are downloaded onto a computer, you can enhance and manipulate them, convert colour to black and white, join images to create panoramas, crop images to different shapes and formats, add filter effects, create special effects – all before making high quality prints using an inkjet printer.

Digital technology has not only made its easier to take high quality photographs and master photographic technique, but has also opened up all kinds of creative doors and made it much easier to share your work with others, be it via websites, email, digital slide shows, printed photo books or exhibited prints.

The biggest problem is actually deciding which camera to buy. Even if you are working to a specific budget there are more models to choose from than ever before, and if money is no object, the sky is the limit!

The thing to remember is at the end of the day a camera is only as good as the person using it. You can buy the most sophisticated model on the market and it won't necessarily make you a better photographer, but if you have a thorough grasp of exposure, light and composition you will be able to take stunning pictures with any camera.

Compact or SLR?

If you are in the market for a new camera today then you will almost certainly be looking at digital models. The first decision you need to make is whether to go for a digital compact camera or a digital SLR (single lens reflex).

If you need a camera mainly to take good quality pictures of family and friends and to record everyday life, then a compact will be the best choice.

Compact cameras, as the name implies, are small, so you can slip them into a pocket or handbag and never miss a photo opportunity. Many serious photographers invest in a compact for this very reason as it means they always have a camera to hand and can take pictures on a daily basis as they go about their lives.

The latest generation of digital compacts are capable of surprisingly good results, boasting not only a wide-ranging zoom lens, built-in flash and sophisticated metering, but a choice of exposure modes, variable ISO (to make the camera's sensor more or less sensitive to light) so you can shoot indoors and out, a good range of shutter speeds and many other handy features that could include the ability to record video clips as well as stills.

If you buy a model with a resolution of 6 mp (6 million pixels) or more you will also be able to output pin sharp prints up to A4 or bigger – the latest compacts offer a resolution as high as 12 mp!

Do not have a computer and printer? No problem – most processing labs will make enlargements for you from digital images while an increasing number have machines in-store when you can make your own prints from images stored on the camera's removable memory card.

The main drawback with most compact cameras is that they tend to be highly automated, so you have limited control over settings such as aperture and shutter speed. You are also limited to the focal length range of the integral zoom as the lens can't be changed, the built-in flash will have a relatively low output, and because compact cameras are small, the sensor they use to record an image is also small, which puts a limit on the image quality it can achieve. For example, a 7 mp sensor in a digital compact won't be capable of the same quality as a digital SLR with a 7 mp sensor simply because the SLR's sensor, and the pixels contained within it, is bigger.

Therefore, if your intentions are more serious – and the fact that you are reading this book suggests they are – you should invest in an SLR.

Pixel resolution

When I wrote the first edition of this book, digital technology was still a long way off and all photographers used film cameras.

The norm then was to start out with a 35 mm SLR then, depending on subject preference, maybe upgrade eventually to a medium-format camera so that better image quality could be achieved – on the basis that the bigger the film format, the better the image quality.

Today, in this digital age, it is the number of pixels a camera offers that tends to be the main deciding factor, and instead of upgrading to a different film format, digital photographers instead upgrade to a camera with more pixels – because more pixels means bigger, sharper pictures can be produced.

Here's how it works. To make a good quality print from a digital image you need to print at an output resolution of at least 240 dpi (dots per inch). Therefore, the maximum image size a digital camera is capable of without resorting to special software is based solely on how many pixels its sensor contains.

For example, a 10 × 8 inch print made to a resolution of 240 dpi will contain around 4.6 million pixels – (10 × 240) × (8 × 240) = 4 608 000 – which means that a camera with a pixel resolution of 4.6mp will be capable of producing high quality prints up to 10 × 8 inches. If you want to produce bigger prints you need more pixels – a 16 × 12 inch print contains around 11 million pixels, so you need a camera with a pixel resolution of 11 mp to achieve that. (See DVD 1.01 and 1.02.)

Pixel resolution is one of the main areas where digital cameras continue to improve because for most it is the main selling factor. Today, digital SLRs with a 10 mp sensor are affordable to a large proportion of enthusiasts and more than good enough to sustain you. In fact, unless you really need to make prints bigger than 16 × 12 inches there's no need to spend more money.

That said, if money is no object, there are some very desirable cameras out there. Canon's latest launch, the EOS 1ds MkIII, boasts a 21.7 mp sensor. But that's nothing compared to the Hasselblad H3DII 39 which has a 39 mp sensor. However, this kind of quality currently comes at a huge price – the Hasselblad costs around £20 000. But remember, it's not that many years since a 1 mp camera cost the same as a 10 mp model does today, so prices will inevitably fall and before long it will be perfectly normal for photography enthusiasts to be shooting with 20+ mp cameras.

Choosing a digital SLR

The main benefit of the digital SLR, like the 35 mm film SLR, is that it gives you access to a vast range of accessories that allow you to photograph every subject under the sun. You can use lenses from ultra wides to monstrous telephotos. You can shoot amazing close-ups, use electronic flash and studio lighting systems for all sorts of effects and experiment with filters and film.

Another advantage of the SLR over compact cameras is that you are actually looking through the lens when you raise the camera to your eye, so you can see pretty much exactly what's going to appear on the final picture. This makes accurate focusing and the use of accessories such as filters much easier, because you can see the effect they are having.

All in all, then, today's digital SLRs are the perfect cameras for all-round use. They give you the scope to take control over every aspect of the picture-taking process when you feel it is necessary, but will happily make all the decisions for you when there isn't time to think.

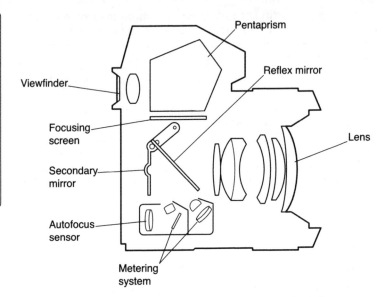

figure 1.1 This cross-section through a modern digital SLR shows the main features used in its design.

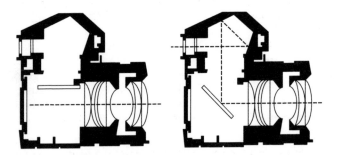

figure 1.2 When you press the shutter release on an SLR, the shutter opens and the reflex mirror flips up so light can reach the film or digital sensor inside – that is why the viewfinder blacks out while you are taking a picture. The mirror then returns to its normal position after the exposure is made.

Features to look for

Although pixel count is likely to be the main feature you look at initially, and your budget will in turn dictate how many pixels you can afford, there are many other features that make a digital SLR what it is.

Today, the range of models available is bigger than ever. However, the list of features they offer from brand to brand and model to model seems to be pretty standard so you can't really make a bad choice. There is no such thing as a poor quality SLR! All have a wide shutter speed range, a choice of metering patterns and exposure modes, an integral motordrive and so on.

The main differentiating factors are build quality and megapixels. Professional models are much bigger, heavier and more robust than SLRs aimed at the enthusiast market and also tend to boast a higher pixel resolution because pro photographers generally need more pixels than enthusiasts. However, in most other respects – metering, focusing, handling and lens quality – there is little to choose between the main marques.

Here are the main features to watch out for.

Viewfinder

This is the system which allows you to look directly through the lens at your subject. On most SLRs it provides useful information, such as the aperture and shutter speed set, a flash-ready light and so on. You will also see the focusing sensors and which one is active so you know what the lens is focusing on. Modern digital SLRs have bright, crisp viewfinders compared to older manual-focus film cameras.

Metering and exposure modes

Probably the most important feature of any camera is the metering system, because this determines how accurately exposed your pictures will be.

These days the type of metering used tends to be very similar across the board. Expect a selection of metering patterns that will include centre-weighted, multi-zone and spot metering plus a whole host of exposure modes (see page 114). All the latest systems are incredibly accurate and reliable. Metering has never been this good in the history of photography.

Shutter speed range

Until a few years ago the majority of SLRs boasted a shutter speed range from around 1–1/1000 sec, which is perfectly adequate for just about all picture-taking situations. Today a more common range is 30–1/4000 sec, although some models boast a top shutter speed of 1/4000 sec or 1/8000 sec.

These high speeds may sound impressive, but for all but the fastest action they are unnecessary. Longer shutter speeds are far more useful because they allow you to take pictures in low light where the camera is able to set the exposure time automatically.

Preview screen

The heart of any digital SLR is the preview screen because it not only allows you to check an image seconds after capturing it, but also to analyse the histogram and access menus to change the camera setting and custom functions. Generally, the bigger the screen the better – especially when it comes to previewing images. The latest digital SLRs usually boast a 3-inch screen, which is ideal.

ISO range

A great benefit of digital cameras is that you can adjust the ISO setting of the sensor as and when you like, so that pictures can be taken in a wide range of lighting situations. One minute you can be outdoors shooting at ISO 50 or 100 for optimum image quality, the next inside a dimly-lit room shooting handheld with the ISO set at 1600 or above. Although shooting at high ISOs does introduce issues such as noise (see below) and you should always shoot at the lowest ISO possible to minimize noise, being able to keep shooting no matter what the light does is a huge plus. ISO 100–1600 seems to be the typical range offered, though some digital SLRs go as low as ISO 50 and a growing number have an extended range to ISO 3200 and beyond.

Depth of field preview

This feature allows you to stop the lens down to the aperture you are using so you can reasonably assess depth of field – what is going to be in and out of focus in the final image. Not all digital SLRs have this facility, and it is not essential as you can always check that everything is sharp in a photograph by zooming into the image on the preview screen and scrolling from foreground to background.

Exposure compensation

Although camera meters are accurate and reliable most of the time, they can still be fooled by tricky lighting situations. For this reason, all digital SLRs have a facility to override the metering system and compensate the exposure to prevent error – usually up to +/–5 stops in one-third or half- and full stop increments.

Integral flash

Many digital SLRs aimed at the consumer market have a small flash unit built into the pentaprism which works in conjunction with the metering system to give perfectly exposed results. They're handy for snapshots or for fill-in flash outdoors, but the power output is quite low so they only work on subjects that are relatively close to the camera. This is a useful feature to have but by no means essential.

Motordrives and burst rates

All digital SLRs have an integral motordrive that re-cocks the shutter after each frame so you can continue shooting without taking the camera from your eye – ideal for sport and nature photography.

As a minimum there will be two settings – Single shot, where you need to release the shutter button after each shot in order to take another and Continuous, where the camera will keep firing whenever the shutter release is depressed.

The limiting factor with digital SLRs is the number of frames that can be recorded in a single burst before the buffer is full and the images have to be written to the memory card. The numbers vary but an average digital SLR would allow a burst of nine images to be captured in RAW (see below) at a rate of three frames per second. With some models it's lower and with others it's higher. Some digital SLRs are designed to operate at high speed and tend to sacrifice pixel count in favour of burst rate – the new Canon EOS 1d MkIII has a 10 mp sensor and can capture up to 30 images at a rate of 10 fps. In most cases this rate goes up if you shoot in jpeg mode instead of RAW and many digital SLRs can keep shooting until the memory card is full.

File formats

The most common file formats for digital images are RAW and jpeg. RAW is favoured by serious photographers because it is a pure, uncompressed format that contains all data recorded by the sensor – rather like a film negative. Jpeg is a compressed format so the file sizes are smaller and you can record more images on a memory card but some data is lost in compression. All digital SLRs allow you to use either file format, and an increasing number record each picture you take in both RAW and jpeg. A small number can also record in TIF format.

Sensor cleaning

Dust and dirt on the sensor is the bane of every digital photographer's life because it means time has to be spent retouching each photograph to get rid of ugly black spots and marks. The latest trend in digital SLR design is for cameras to have a vibrating sensor so that dust can be shaken off. Canon's latest flagship DSLR, the 1Ds MkIII, has this facility and early reports suggest that it works well – no more dust! More and more cameras are likely to adopt this feature.

Sensor size

Only a small number of digital SLRs in production at the time of writing – three to be exact – boast a full-frame sensor (24 × 36 mm, the same size as a 35 mm film frame). The remainder have a sensor that is smaller, though there is no standard here and the actual size varies from manufacturer to manufacturer. Consequently, a magnification factor has to calculate the effective focal length of a lens when it is used on non full-frame cameras. This can be anything from 1.3 × to 2 ×, though 1.5 × is about the norm.

Batteries

Digital cameras are far more battery dependent than film cameras ever were and, with all those fancy features, tend to drain batteries surprisingly fast. Fortunately, all models use rechargeable batteries and some of the pro-spec cameras can also be fitted with an adaptor that takes standard AA batteries so all is not lost if the rechargeable ones run out of steam when you are miles from an electricity supply.

Handling

One important factor than tends to be overlooked in favour of fancy features is the way a camera handles – how it feels in your hands, how accessible the controls are and how easy it is to use. Remember, once you buy a new camera you are likely to be stuck with it for years, so do not forget to pick it up and try it out before making a commitment to buy. This is especially important with the more expensive pro-spec digital SLRs which can be surprisingly big and heavy. You are also going to have to carry it, as well as hold it.

The case for film cameras

So now the world has gone digital, is it still worth considering buying a film camera? In a word, yes.

Film photography is different from digital photography, both aesthetically and psychologically. Digital images are perfect to the point of sterility. They lack character and individuality, and although that can be added later when the image is downloaded onto a computer and manipulated using software such as Adobe Photoshop, it's not the same as doing that the second you press the shutter release and let light flood into your lens.

Film has character. Every brand and variety of film has its own unique characteristics that are imprinted on every image – grain, sharpness, contrast, colour balance. That is why some photographers love Fuji Velvia while others swear by Kodak Ektachrome Elite Chrome 100, or for black and white Ilford HP5 Plus is favoured over Kodak Tri-x and vice versa.

There isn't the same differentiation with digital cameras beyond pixel count, which determines how big you can print an image.

Digital photography also removes any anticipation or surprise from the picture-taking process. You press the shutter release, take a picture, then look at it three seconds later on the screen. It's foolproof, because if the exposure is wrong, the picture unsharp or the composition not quite right you can simply reshoot and keep reshooting until you get everything right – and if you never manage to get it quite right you can always have another attempt when it's on your computer screen.

Of course, it is all these very same factors that make digital capture so popular and so amazing. As a learning aid, a digital SLR is unbeatable and if you want perfect pictures every time, then a digital camera wins hands down.

But despite the enormous popularity of digital imaging, film photography is alive and well and ironically, a growing number of photographers are reverting back to it having realized that digital capture isn't all it's cracked up to be.

Similarly, more and more people who came into photography via the digital route and found themselves bitten by the picture-taking bug are trying film for the first time and finding that they actually quite like it.

There is something intrinsically more real and more artistic about recording images by exposing silver-based materials to light. Negatives and transparencies are tangible; you can hold them and see them. They have a physical presence. Digital images on the other hand are nothing more than millions of coloured dots whizzing around in cyberspace!

An added bonus of shooting with film is that because so many enthusiasts are switching from film to digital, there has never been a better time to buy second-hand film cameras. There is also a growing movement towards retro and alternative photography, using vintage and novelty cameras to create images that are far from perfect, but beautiful as a result – and about as far removed from digital as you could possibly get. Below are just a few of them.

Medium-format

Medium-format cameras are the big brother of the 35 mm SLRs, producing a much bigger negative or slide which means that image quality is higher and photographs can be printed much larger with no loss of detail. The film type used is 120 roll film (220 is also available which is double the length) and a range of formats is available depending upon the camera model – 6 × 4.5 cm, 6 × 6 cm, 6 × 7 cm, 6 × 8 cm or 6 × 9 cm. Most models have interchangeable backs, so you can switch from one film type to another mid-roll.

Professional photographers favoured medium-format over 35 mm, especially for studio work, although the 6 × 6 cm and 6 × 7 cm formats have long been popular for landscape photography too.

A second-hand medium-format camera will match the quality of the best digital SLRs on the market, and cost just a fraction of the price. Check out models from Pentax, Mamiya, Bronica and Hasselblad.

Large-format

These are huge, heavy, slow to use and ancient-looking, but when ultimate image quality is required a large-format camera just can't be beaten.

The two most popular formats are 5 × 4 inch and 10 × 8 inch, though much bigger formats are available. The smaller of the two is a favourite among landscape and architectural photographers while 10 × 8 inch is mainly used for studio work. The images from both formats can be enlarged to phenomenal sizes and still remain pin sharp.

An additional benefit of large-format cameras is that they allow you to adjust the position of the lens in relation to the film plane – this is known as 'camera movements' – to control perspective and depth of field and correct converging verticals.

A sturdy tripod is essential for keeping the camera steady, and material costs are very high, but large-format photography is in a world, and league, of its own and continues to be popular.

Panoramic

Panoramic images can be created simply by cropping a photograph to a letterbox shape or, if you use a digital camera, by stitching a sequence of frames together (see page 200). Alternatively, you could use a purpose-made panoramic camera.

The most popular model ever is the Hasselblad xpan which produces 24 × 65 mm images on 35 mm film. Although no longer made, it is still readily available on the second-hand market. Models that use 35 mm film are also available from Noblex and Horizon, although unlike the xpan which has a range of three interchangeable lenses available (30 mm, 45 mm and 90 mm), they have a fixed focal length and use a rotating lens system to record a wide angle-of-view.

If you prefer medium-format, there are two main formats – 6 × 12 cm and 6 × 17 cm. The latter is the most popular simply because it is more elongated. Cameras are made in both formats by Fotoman, Linhof and Horseman, while the legendary Fuji Gx617 is available second hand and a budget 6 × 17 cm model is made by Widepan. (See DVD 1.04.)

Rangefinder

Rangefinder, or non-reflex, cameras work in the same way as compacts, where the viewing and taking systems are separate.

This can lead to what is known as parallax error, because what you see through the viewfinder isn't exactly the same as what the lens sees, but most models are corrected for parallax.

Many photojournalists prefer rangefinder cameras because they are smaller than SLRs. Also, with no reflex mirror to flip up they are much quieter to use, and the viewfinder doesn't black out during the exposure. The most famous make of rangefinder is the Leica. Most models have a coupled rangefinder so you can focus accurately on a specific point even though you are not looking through the lens.

Twin-lens reflex (TLR)

This is an old-fashioned type of medium-format camera which uses two lenses – one for viewing the subject and one for taking the picture. Parallax error can again be a problem at close-focusing distances. Using graduated and polarizing filters is also tricky because you can't see the effect obtained. The main benefit of TLRs is they can be picked up second hand at bargain prices and offer superb quality for a small investment. Most TLRs have a fixed 80 mm standard lens but later Mamiya models – the C220 and C330 – accept a range of interchangeable lenses from 55 mm wide-angle to 250 mm telephoto.

Instant cameras

Polaroid have been producing instant-picture cameras for almost 60 years and although only few consumer models are still made, vintage classics such as the Sx70 and 110B are widely available on the second-hand market, and many Polaroid instant films are still manufactured.

Instant photography is not only great fun – you get to see the results within minutes, so it's rather like a retro alternative to digital photography – but each type of Polaroid film has its own unique characteristics that can produce beautiful fine-art images when used with care and imagination. (See DVD 1.05.)

Pinhole cameras

The very first cameras didn't have a lens, but a tiny hole punched through a metal disc instead. This acted as both the lens and the aperture, projecting an image onto light-sensitive paper placed inside the camera. Today, many photographers around the world still work with pinhole cameras and despite their simplicity they are capable of stunning results.

Pinhole characteristics include an ultra wide field of view, endless depth of field and a wonderful soft image quality. Because the pinhole itself is tiny, exposure times are also long – anything from several seconds to several hours – so motion is recorded and this adds to the atmosphere of the final image.

Purpose-built pinhole cameras are available – the best-known brand is Hong Kong-based Zero Image. However, they are also relatively easy to make yourself and fascinating to use. (See DVD 1.06.)

Toy cameras

The Holga is a cheap, plastic, mass-produced 6 × 6 cm roll film camera from China that costs no more than the price of a few rolls of film. It has just one shutter speed – around 1/100 sec – plus B (bulb) and one aperture, f/11. Focusing is manual, aided by dubious distance symbols on the barrel of the fixed 60 mm lens. Aberrations such as barrel distortion and flare are guaranteed, along with vignetting at the image corners and possibly light leaks, and while the lens is actually quite sharp in the centre, it blurs badly towards the edges.

But it's all these things that make the Holga such a popular camera and it now has a worldwide cult following. The dubious lens quality produces images with a wonderful dream-like feel (see DVD 1.07) and the simplicity of the camera makes it incredibly liberating to use. You just point and shoot, hoping the wide exposure latitude of colour print film will yield a decent negative.

The popularity of the Holga is also repeated with other unusual cameras such as the Russian Lomo LCA compact, the Lomo Lubitel TLR, the Diana camera and its many clones, and vintage cameras such as the legendary Kodak Box Brownie. All are widely available on eBay and well worth trying out.

Caring for your camera

Cameras are delicate precision instruments – especially digital cameras – so if you want yours to have a long and happy life you need to treat it with reverence and care.

- If you are going to be taking pictures in wet weather, place your camera in a polythene bag to keep it dry and cut a hole for the lens to peep through.

- Beaches are unfriendly places for cameras – sand can find its way into the body and cause untold damage. To prevent this, keep your camera safely inside a bag or case when it's not in use, and never leave it lying around uncovered.
- If a fault develops, take your camera to the local dealer or a professional repairer. Never try to repair faults yourself.
- If your camera is going to lie unused for several months, remove the batteries to prevent corrosion and store it with sachets of silica gel to absorb damp.
- Never leave your camera for long periods with the shutter cocked – it places tension on the springs and shutter blades.
- Never touch the shutter curtain – it can easily be distorted and this will make the shutter speeds inaccurate.
- Take care when changing lenses as dust can easily find its way onto the sensor and will appear as black dots on all your photographs
- If you need to clean your camera's digital sensor, do so with care and only using the correct products otherwise you could cause irreparable damage (see page 97).

Keeping your camera steady

The way you hold your camera can make all the difference between taking a pin sharp picture and one that's ruined by camera shake.

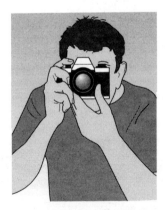

figure 1.3 1 Grip the camera body with your right hand, so your index finger falls naturally to the shutter release. Cup your left hand under the lens so you can support it.

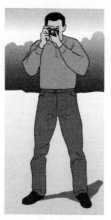

2 Stand with your legs slightly apart and your back straight. Do not lean forward or put your feet together as this reduces stability. Take the picture after breathing out, when your body is relaxed.

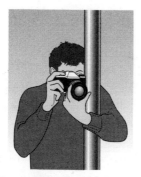

3 Leaning against a wall, lamp post or tree will help to stabilize the camera when using slower shutter speeds or heavy lenses.

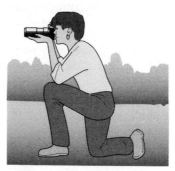

4 Adopting a crouching position with one knee resting on the ground is ideal when using long lenses. Rest your left elbow on your left leg to provide extra stability.

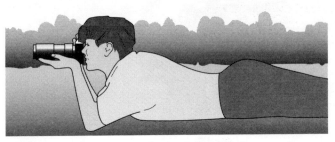

5 If you are using a long lens, stretch out on the ground and use your elbows or a backpack to support the camera and lens.

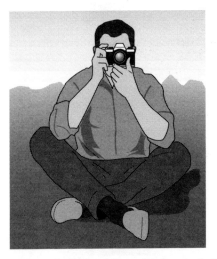

6 Sitting on the ground cross-legged is a stable position to use and will help keep your camera steady when using less than ideal shutter speeds.

You can also prevent camera shake by making sure the shutter speed you use is fast enough to hide any camera movement. As a rule-of-thumb, the shutter speed should at least match the focal length of the lens – 1/60 sec at 50 mm, 1/125 sec at 135 mm, 1/250 sec at 200 mm, 1/500 sec at 400 mm or 500 mm and so on.

Once the shutter speeds begin to drop below acceptable levels for handholding, some kind of support will be required, such as a tripod or monopod (see page 88).

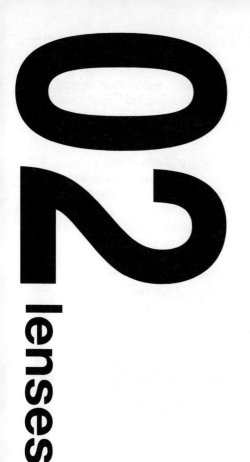

02

lenses

In this chapter you will learn:
- what features a lens has
- about focal length and 'angle of view'
- how to make the most of your lenses
- about lens care and common lens faults.

Buying your first SLR is an exciting moment – you can't wait to get it home, open the box and start taking pictures. But this initial purchase is just one of many that you will make over the years, because before long you will realize that in order to photograph a wide range of subjects you will need more than just the lens your camera came with. The burning question is which type of lens do you buy first? A wide-angle? A telephoto? A zoom?

With so many different lenses available today, with prices to suit all budgets, making that decision can be a real headache – unless you have an unlimited budget and can buy a whole system in one fell swoop, but few of us are so fortunate.

Throughout this chapter we will be taking a close look at lenses in all their shapes and forms, so by the time you've read it you will know exactly which ones to buy for the subjects you prefer to photograph, and how to make the most of them.

Before we go on to that, however, there are a few vital factors to consider...

Anatomy of a lens

The following illustrations show the components found on a typical prime lens:

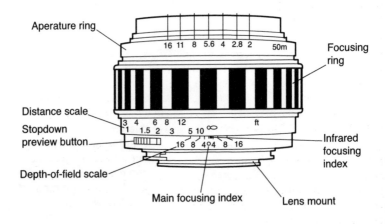

figure 2.1

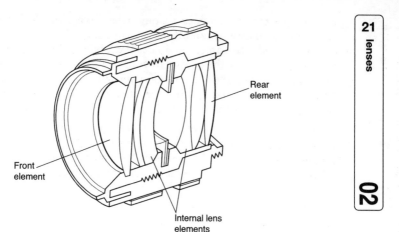

Rear
element

Front
element

Internal lens
elements

figure 2.2

Quality counts

An image is formed on film by light passing through the lens fitted to your camera. As the light enters each element the rays are bent and refracted, causing various optical aberrations which lead to unsharp or distorted pictures.

Modern lenses are designed to overcome these aberrations by using a carefully designed system of elements which correct any distortion. But if a lens is poorly designed, the aberrations aren't fully corrected so you end up with slightly unsharp or slightly distorted pictures (see Lens faults on page 36).

Over the past decade or so, optical technology has improved so much that nowadays there is no such thing as a poor quality lens. Nevertheless, you still get what you pay for, so if you buy the cheapest lenses available you cannot expect breathtaking quality, especially at the frame edges where a noticeable drop in sharpness may be noticeable – particularly when shooting at maximum and minimum aperture.

The mistake most photographers make is spending just about all their budget on an all-singing, all-dancing SLR then having to compromise when it comes to buying lenses. But this is counter-productive because the lens determines image quality, so if you fit a cheap lens to an expensive SLR you will still end up with poorer quality pictures.

A much better approach is to buy a less expensive SLR then spend as much as you can afford on top quality lenses. You can always upgrade the camera at a later date, but at least you won't have to compromise the quality of your pictures in the meantime. Alternatively, buy the camera of your dreams but instead of trying to equip yourself with two or three new lenses straight away, buy just one top quality lens.

Whichever make or model you buy, the general rule is that all lenses give their best optical performance when set to an aperture of f/8 or f/11. At the widest and smallest aperture settings, image quality will be lower – though not necessarily to a point where you can tell the difference without making huge enlargements.

Obviously, in many situations you will need to use a wider aperture such as f/4 to reduce depth of field or a smaller aperture such as f/16 to increase it, so do not feel that by doing so you will take poor quality pictures – far from it. It is just that where the choice of aperture isn't so crucial, f/8 to f/11 should be used.

Focal length

This term refers to a lens's magnification power and is measured in millimetres (mm). Focal length can be divided into three categories: standard, wide-angle and telephoto.

The standard focal length is roughly equivalent to the diagonal measurement of the image format – for 35 mm and full-frame digital SLRs it is 50 mm, for 6 × 6 cm medium-format it is 80 mm and so on. Any lens with a focal length less than the standard is considered a wide-angle lens, such as 24 mm or 28 mm in 35 mm and full-frame DSLR format, and any lens with a focal length greater than the standard is considered a telephoto, such as 200 mm or 400 mm.

The table below shows the focal lengths of popular lenses for 35 mm, medium-format and large-format cameras.

Film format

Lens type	35 mm	6 × 4.5 cm	6 × 6 cm	6 × 7 cm	5 × 4 inch
Ultra-wide	20 mm	35 mm	40 m	45 mm	65 mm
Wide-angle	28 mm	45 mm	50 mm	55 mm	90 mm
Standard	50 mm	75 mm	80 m	90 mm	150 mm
Short tele	85 mm	140 mm	150 mm	180 mm	270 mm
Med tele	200 mm	300 mm	350 mm	420 mm	560 mm
Long tele	300 mm	450 mm	500 mm	600 mm	800 mm

Magnification factors

The majority of digital SLRs use a sensor that's smaller than full-frame 35 mm (24 × 36 mm). This means that the focal length of the lens you use on those cameras is effectively increased. The amount of increase can be calculated using a magnification factor (MF) and this is governed by the size of the sensor in the camera. Most digital SLRs require an mf of 1.5 ×, but for some it is 1.6 × and for a few it is 2 ×.

Below is a conversion chart to show how focal length changes when lenses are used on digital SLRs with sensors smaller than full-frame.

For 35mm/ full-frame	For 1.5 × MF	For 1.6 × MF	For 2 × MF
17 mm	26 mm	27 mm	34 mm
20 mm	30 mm	32 mm	40 mm
24 mm	36 mm	38 mm	48 mm
28 mm	42 mm	45 mm	56 mm
35 mm	52 mm	56 mm	70 mm
50 mm	75 mm	80 mm	100 mm
70 mm	105 mm	112 mm	140 mm
100 mm	150 mm	160 mm	200 mm
135 mm	200 mm	216 mm	270 mm
200 mm	300 mm	320 mm	400 mm
300 mm	450 mm	480 mm	600 mm
400 mm	600 mm	640 mm	800 mm
500 mm	750 mm	800 mm	1000 mm
600 mm	900 mm	960 mm	1200 mm

Depending on the subjects you shoot, these magnification factors can be a blessing or a nuisance.

Landscape photographers tend to dislike them because they generally work with wide-angle lenses, and the MF increases focal length so even wider lenses are required. For sport, nature and other subjects requiring telephoto lenses, however, the focal length increase is seen as a huge benefit.

Another factor to consider is that lenses are at their sharpest in the centre and at their softest towards the edges. Cameras with sensors smaller than full-frame 24 × 36 mm therefore get the best from the lens because they use the sharper central area of lens's 'image circle'. At the time of writing, there are only three digital SLRs with a full-frame sensor – the Canon EOS 5D and 1DS MKIII and the Nikon D3, though this will undoubtedly change with time.

Lenses for digital SLRs

An increasing number of lenses are being manufactured specifically for digital SLRs.

Digital-specific lenses use a telecentric design which allows light to hit the sensor inside the camera at an angle very close to 90° and in doing so gives optimum image quality.

Some ultra wide-angle lenses and ultra wide-angle zooms are also designed specifically for digital SLRs that do not have a full-frame sensor. They utilize a smaller 'image circle' which is not big enough to cover the full area of a 24 × 36 mm sensor so if you use them on a full-frame digital SLR, vignetting will occur.

As it isn't always obvious that a lens is digital specific or designed for smaller sensors, you should always check before buying.

Angle of view

This term, measured in degrees, refers to how much a lens actually 'sees' and is directly related to focal length. The standard focal length in any film format is said to have a similar angle of view to the human eye. Wide-angle lenses have a greater angle of view and therefore allow you to include much more in a picture, whereas telephotos have a smaller angle of view and make distant subjects bigger in the frame.

The illustration shows the angle of view of common focal lengths for the 35 mm and full-frame digital format. As you can see, as focal length is reduced, angle of view increases and as focal length increases, angle of view becomes smaller.

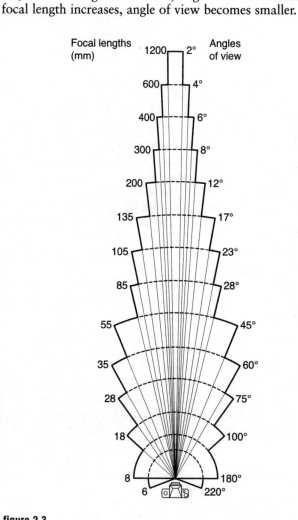

figure 2.3

Lens speed

When photographers talk about a lens they usually refer to it as a 70–200 mm f/2.8, 300 mm f/4, 50 mm f/1.4 and so on. The first half of this is the focal length, the second half is the lens's maximum aperture, and this gives an indication of its 'speed', or how 'fast' it is. Lens speed is important because it determines the fastest shutter speed you can use in any given situation.

It works like this: the vast majority of lenses have a variable aperture scale. Each aperture is given an f/number, which denotes the physical size of the hole in the lens through which light passes. Large apertures have small numbers, such as f/1.8, while small apertures have big numbers such as f/16.

The aperture scale on all lenses follows a set pattern of f/numbers. But it's where that scale begins that's the most important because the bigger the maximum aperture is, the more light will be admitted, allowing you to use faster speeds. Get the idea? Also, the larger the maximum aperture is, the brighter the viewfinder image, which makes focusing easier – especially in low light.

Lenses with a maximum aperture that is wider than the norm for their focal length or focal length range are considered 'fast' lenses. They are also usually bigger, heavier and significantly more expensive that their 'slower' counterparts.

For example, a 70–200 mm f/2.8 zoom is considered fast compared to a 70–200 mm f/4-5.6. Similarly, a 300 mm f/2.8 lens is fast compared to a 300 mm f/4.

Is it worth spending the extra on a 'fast' lens? Well, that depends. If you regularly photograph subjects that require you to handhold or use fast shutter speeds, such as sport/action and wildlife or travel/documentary photography, then yes, the extra investment is worthwhile. (See DVD 2.01.) For general use, however, the slower and cheaper versions of those lenses are just as good. In many cases they offer the same excellent image quality, but save on weight, bulk and cost, and if the range you are looking at includes lenses with image stabilization, as Canon, Nikon and Sigma do, then the extra speed from a fast lens isn't so important because the image stabilization will allow you to handhold at slower shutter speeds without worrying about camera shake.

Prime or zoom?

The popularity of zoom lenses has increased enormously in recent years, but when you look at the benefits they offer it's not difficult to see why.

The main feature of a zoom lens is its variable focal length, which allows you to make your subject bigger or smaller in the frame at the flick of a wrist. One or two zooms can also replace a whole bagful of prime (fixed focal length) lenses, cutting down on weight and bulk considerably without reducing your optical options. A 24–70 mm and 70–200 mm zoom, for example, will replace a 28 mm wide-angle, 50 mm standard, 85 mm portrait lens, plus 135 mm and 200 mm telephotos and cover all your needs for general picture-taking.

Even better, with a zoom you can make minute adjustments to focal length so your pictures are precisely composed. There's nothing to stop you shooting at 128 mm, or 37 mm or 167 mm; focal lengths that just aren't available on prime lenses. (See DVD 2.12.)

The two zooms mentioned above – the 24–70 mm and 70–2000 mm – or other models with similar focal length ranges are ideal for general use, but if you are a wide-angle lens fan you could go for something wider, such as a 17–35 mm. In recent years a generation of super-wide zooms have appeared with focal length ranges of 10–22 mm or 12–24 mm. Some are designed only for use with digital SLRs that do not have full-frame sensor, so the focal length range will be increased according to the magnification factor of the camera, but some are full-frame optics and also corrected for distortion, so you really can shoot at a focal length of just 12 mm! Similarly, if you use telephoto lenses more you could buy a 75–300 mm or 100–400 mm instead of the popular 70–200 mm. (See DVD 2.13.)

What you shouldn't do is let your zoom turn you into a lazy photographer – you should still use your feet to get closer to your subject and find the best vantage before zooming away.

The only other thing you need to be aware of is that a zoom's maximum aperture is usually a stop or two smaller than it would be on prime lenses in the same focal length range – f/4–f/5.6 is common for a 70–200 mm zoom. This means you won't be able to use such fast shutter speeds, so take care in low light and if the shutter speeds start to get slow use a tripod to prevent camera shake.

Despite the popularity of zooms, prime lenses are still worth considering for certain uses. A 50 mm standard lens makes a welcome addition to any photographer's kit, for example, because as well as being small and light, it also boasts a very fast maximum aperture – usually f/1.8 or f/1.4 – so you can take handheld shots in low light and still maintain a safe shutter speed.

Macro lenses also have a fixed focal length (see page 32) and if you do a lot of portrait photography it's worth investing in a 'portrait' lens with a focal length of 85 mm, 100 mm or 105 mm and a wide maximum aperture of f2.8 or even f/1.8.

Maker's own or independent?

One of the biggest decisions you have to make when buying lenses is whether you go for your camera-maker's own, or independent models.

In years gone by the answer was simple – if you wanted the best, stick with the camera manufacturer's lenses. But today that's no longer the case, because independent manufacturers such as Sigma and Tamron are producing lenses that are equally as good as those from the likes of Nikon and Canon.

Sigma, in particular, has been active in developing and improving its range, which is now more extensive than those from many camera makers and includes everything you are likely to need from zooms to macro lenses to fast telephotos. Prices are generally lower too.

If money is no object you will probably want to put Nikon lenses on your Nikon SLR and Canon lenses on your Canon EOS. But do not think that by doing that you will always get better quality.

Lenses and perspective

Many photographers are misled into thinking that telephoto lenses record perspective differently from wide-angle lenses, but this is only half true. If you stand in one spot and photograph the same scene with a 28 mm wide-angle lens, then a 300 mm telephoto, perspective will remain exactly the same. This can be proven by enlarging a small section of the wide-angle shot so it covers the same angle of view as the telephoto shot – perspective on both will be identical.

Perspective only changes if you move the position so your main subject is the same size in the frame when you photograph it through different lenses. (See DVD 2.02–2.04.)

Wide-angle lenses seem to 'stretch' perspective so the different elements in a scene appear much further apart. Telephotos do the opposite – they make everything appear to be crowded together and much closer to the camera. Once you are aware of this you can use perspective to produce stunning results.

Using your lenses

Wide-angle lenses

Peering through your camera's viewfinder for the first time with a wide-angle lens fitted is like looking out on another world. Suddenly you can see considerably more than is possible with the naked eye, and the initial reaction is one of amazement and excitement. Nearby features loom large in the frame, while everything else seems to rush off into the distance. Lines and shapes are distorted, perspective is exaggerated, and even the most ordinary subjects and scenes can be turned into dynamic compositions.

Any lens with a focal length less than the standard is considered a wide-angle. In 35 mm and full-frame digital format that is anything from a 35 mm down, although many photographers use a 35 mm as standard. Generally, 24 mm and 28 mm optics are considered 'normal' wides, and are the best choice for regular use, while anything from 12 mm to 21 mm is classed as 'ultra' wide.

Confusingly, some ultra-wide lenses and zooms are corrected for rectilinear distortion so straight lines come out straight, even when the focal length is as small as 12 mm. However, uncorrected lenses with a focal length of 16 mm or less fall into the fisheye category (see Specialist lenses on page 31).

Of course, there is much more to wide-angle lenses than their ravenous angle of view. For a start, they have a habit of distorting things. Features close to the edges of the picture area bend and lean, particularly with ultra wides, and if you move in really close to your subject its whole shape will be distorted.

Something else you will notice once you start using wide-angle lenses is they seem to exaggerate perspective. Suddenly elements in a scene that appear close together in reality are miles apart.

This characteristic is great for subjects such as landscape photography because you can make nearby features like rocks or a river dominate the foreground of your picture. (See DVD 2.05.) The result is a dynamic, sweeping composition that carries your eye through the scene and creates a strong feeling of depth and scale. (See DVD 2.06.)

Wide-angle lenses also give extensive depth of field at small apertures such as f/11 and f/16 – the wider the lens, the greater it is. This means you can keep everything in sharp focus from a few feet, or even a few inches in front of the camera to infinity; a real bonus when you are shooting landscapes or architecture.

A further advantage is that you do not have to worry about focusing accurately. If you are shooting candids in a crowd from close range, say, you can just set the aperture to f/8, the focus to 2 m and fire away with the camera at your hip so no one realizes what you are doing. The depth of field will be large enough to ensure your subject is sharp.

The main drawback with wide-angle lenses is that they need to be used carefully – particularly the wider focal lengths – otherwise you can easily end up with a tiny subject surrounded by acres of empty space, and this leads to very empty, boring pictures. The key is to think carefully about the composition. Go in close for impact, and if you do not want your subject to distort keep it away from the frame edges. (See DVD 2.07.)

Telephoto lenses

Any lens with a focal length greater than the standard is considered a telephoto – in 35 mm format that is anything over 50 mm. The obvious advantage of telephoto lenses is that they magnify everything. This means you can fill the frame with subjects that are far away – like wildlife – or isolate your subject from its surroundings, such as a person standing in a crowd.

Just as wide-angle lenses exaggerate perspective, telephotos flatten it. (See DVD 2.08.) If you photograph a line of people with a 300 mm lens they will appear to be touching each other. The longer the focal length, the greater this effect – known as 'foreshortening' – is. Telephotos also reduce depth of field considerably, particularly at wide apertures such as f/4 or f/5.6. This is a great benefit when you want to make your main subject stand out, because by focusing carefully on it, the background and foreground will be reduced to a fuzzy blur. The effect, known as fall-off, becomes more pronounced as focal length increases.

The most popular telephoto lenses have a focal length between 80 and 200 mm. The bottom end of this range, up to 135 mm, is ideal for portraiture because the slight foreshortening or perspective flatters the human face – most people photographers use an 85 mm or 105 mm as their standard.

Telephotos from 135 to 200 mm are handy for all sorts of subjects, from candids and landscapes to architecture and abstracts, so they are well worth using. (See DVD 2.09 and 2.10.)

If you are interested in sport or nature photography then you will need something longer. A 300 mm is a nice focal length to work with, but really you need to be looking at a 400 mm or 500 mm if you want to fill the frame with distant subjects.

The physical size and weight of telephoto lenses makes camera shake a real danger if you are handholding. As a rule of thumb, make sure the shutter speed you use at least matches the focal length of the lens – l/250 sec for a 200 mm, 1/500 sec for a 400 mm and so on. Even better, use a tripod or other support so camera shake won't be a problem at all.

Lastly, because depth of field is shallow when using telephoto lenses at wide apertures, accurate focusing is vital. If you rush it, nine times out of ten your main subject will come out unsharp, so take your time, take care and problems will be avoided.

Specialist lenses

Tilt and shift lenses

If you take a picture of a building, and tilt the camera back to include it all in the frame, converging verticals will result, making the building look as through it is toppling over. (See DVD 2.14.)

To prevent converging verticals the back of your camera must remain parallel to the building. Tilt and shift, or perspective control (PC), lenses make this possible because they contain adjustable elements which move up and down so you can include all the building in your picture without tilting the camera. (See DVD 2.15.)

Shift lenses tend to have wide-angle focal lengths such as 35 mm, 28 mm or 24 mm so large buildings can be photographed from close range, although longer focal lengths such as 45 mm and 90 mm are also available.

Modern PC lenses often have a 'tilt' facility too which means you can tilt the front section of the lens down so the plane of focus is more in line with the plane of the film or sensor. Doing so increases depth of field without having to set a smaller aperture. By tilting the wrong way you can also reduce depth of field to almost nothing and achieve unusual effects where only a tint area is recorded in sharp focus and everything is blurred beyond recognition.

These lenses are very costly, so unless you need their specific characteristics they are not worth the expense.

Macro lenses

A range of accessories can be used for close-up and macro photography (see Chapter 23), but for convenience nothing beats a proper macro lens.

Physically, they're just like a normal lens, but the major difference is they can focus much closer, allowing you to fill the frame with tiny subjects like insects and butterflies. They are also specially designed for use at close focusing distances, so the optical quality is superb.

The focal length tends to be either 50/55/60 mm or 90/100/105 mm. Both are useful, but the longer focal lengths are more suited to nature photography because you can take powerful close-ups up to life-size (1:1) from further away, reducing the risk of scaring your timid subject. They also double as perfect portrait lenses. The shorter lenses can usually manage just half life-size reproduction (1:2) without the addition of attachments to increase magnification. (See DVD 2.16.)

Fisheye lenses

So named because their bulging front element looks like a fish's eye, these lenses have an amazing 180° angle of view which swallows up everything in front of you and distorts anything near the edge of the frame considerably. (See DVD 2.17.)

There are two types of fisheye lens available: circular and full frame. The former produces a circular image in the middle of the frame and tends to have a focal length around 8 mm, whereas the latter fills the whole picture area and has a focal length of 15 mm or 16 mm.

If you are thinking of buying a fisheye lens, choose the full frame type – they cost less than the circular type and are more versatile for general use because the effect isn't as extreme.

Teleconverters

Teleconverters fit between your camera body and lens and increase the focal length of that lens. This means you can literally double the scope of your lens system in one fell swoop.

The most common model is a 2 × converter which doubles focal length – turning a 70–200 mm zoom into a more powerful 140–400 mm. There are also 1.4 × converters which increase focal length by 40 per cent, turning a 70–200 mm zoom into a 100–280 mm. In both cases, the minimum focusing distance of the original lens remains the same, so you can get really close to your subject.

There are drawbacks to using teleconverters, of course. With a 2 × model you lose two stops of light, so a 200 mm f/4 lens becomes a 400 mm f/8 and with a 1.4 × you lose one stop. This also darkens the viewfinder image, making focusing trickier – though modern AF systems will overcome this easily. The optical quality of the lens is reduced so your pictures won't be quite as sharp. To minimize this buy the best model you can afford – seven-element converters are better than the cheaper four-element types – and stop your lens down to a smallish aperture such as f/8 or f/11.

Teleconverters could never replace a prime lens, but if you want to take long telephoto shots occasionally and can't justify buying the real thing, they provide an ideal back-up. They also save carrying lots of lenses around, which can be a real advantage when you need to travel light, and combined with the magnification factor of many digital SLRs, can really expand your lens range. For example, a typical 70–200 mm zoom effectively becomes 105–300 mm when used on a digital SLR with a MF of 1.5, so if you then add a 1.4 × teleconverter you end up with a focal length range of 150–420 mm; ideal for nature and sports photography.

Building a system

With so many different types of lens to choose from, deciding which you will need for your own brand of picture-taking will be a subject of much personal debate.

Before zoom lenses became popular, it was normal to start out with a 50 mm lens, then once funds allowed, to add a 24 mm or 28 mm wide-angle for scenic photography and a 135 mm telephoto for portraits. Today, zoom lenses have changed things considerably and it is now common practice to buy an SLR body with a 'kit lens' such as a 28–80 mm or a 35–105 mm zoom and to then invest in a 70–200 mm or 75–300 mm telezoom later.

Whichever route you take, these initial investments will provide a good system for all-round use, and you will find that lenses from 24 mm to 200 mm will cover perhaps 90 per cent of your picture-taking needs. Any further additions can then be made once you begin to specialize in certain subjects.

If you are interested in sport or nature photography, for example, a 300 mm, 400 mm or 500 mm lens – or zoom covering that kind of range – will be invaluable for capturing distant subjects.

For landscape, architecture and general scenic photography, wide-angle lenses from 17 mm to 35 mm are more useful. So you may decide to cover that whole range with a 17–35 mm zoom.

The main thing to bear in mind is that the lenses you use dictate the sharpness of your pictures, so always buy the best you can afford.

Caring for your lenses

Your lenses will only give their best performance and provide years of trouble-free service if you treat them with care. Here are a few hints on how you can avoid trouble.

- Do not get your lenses wet. If you are going to be taking pictures in the rain, or near splashing water, place your camera and lens inside a polythene bag for protection. Cut a hole in the bag and tape the edges to the end of the lens barrel.
- In dusty or sandy areas – particularly beaches – keep your lenses in a closed gadget bag when they are not in use. Fine particles of sand can easily find their way inside your lenses, causing irreparable damage.
- Fit a clear skylight or UV filter to the front of each lens. This protects the front element from accidental scratching, and

reduces the need to clean the element on a regular basis. It is far cheaper to replace a damaged filter than a whole lens.

- Keep the front and rear lens caps in place at all times when your lenses are not in use. This protects the front and rear elements from dirt and reduces the risk of damage.
- Buy a set of small jeweller's screwdrivers so you can tighten any loose screws on the lens mounts.

Cleaning your lenses

Dust, dirt and greasy fingerprints on your lenses degrade their optical quality and reduce the sharpness of your pictures, so it is vital you keep them spotlessly clean at all times.

Following the steps outlined above should minimize the need to clean your lenses on a regular basis, but every once in a while they will need a good dust down. When you do this, you should take extreme care because damage can easily be done, particularly to the delicate front and rear elements.

- Remove any loose dust and hairs with a soft brush, then clear remaining particles with a blast of canned air or a blast of air from a lens blower.
- Wipe away fingermarks or greasy smears with a lens tissue or micro-fibre lens cloth. Breathing lightly on the lens will help to moisten any marks and make them easier to remove. Alternatively, use a special lens cleaning fluid. Place a couple of drops of fluid on a cleaning tissue or cloth then wipe the lens gently. Wipe in a circular motion, starting at the centre and working your way out.
- The rear element of telephoto and zoom lenses is often recessed in the lens barrel, making it difficult to reach. To clean it wrap a lens tissue around a cotton-wool bud, moisten it with lens fluid then wipe very gently in a circular motion.
- Remove dust and dirt from the lens barrel with a stiff but soft brush, then use a moist cloth to get rid of stubborn marks.
- If the focusing action on your lenses becomes stiff it means the lubricants are drying out. This needs the attention of a professional camera technician, so do not try to repair it yourself.

Lens faults

Despite advances in optical technology, some lenses still suffer from common aberrations which lead to a reduction in image sharpness and may even cause visible distortion. Here are the most common problems and the kind of effects they create.

Chromatic aberration

Different wavelengths of light focus on different points, causing a loss of sharpness. This problem is controlled in modern lenses, and can be minimized by working at a small aperture such as f/11. Apochromatic (Apo) lenses are designed to reduce chromatic aberration by focusing all light rays on the same point.

Spherical aberration

Light rays passing through the edges of the lens focus on a point in front of the rays passing through the lens axis, leading to uneven sharpness across the frame. All lenses suffer from this problem, but not to the extent that it is clearly noticeable. Stopping down to a small aperture like f/8 or f/11 reduces it.

Barrel distortion

This is caused by image points at the outer area of the lens being displaced so straight lines near the edge of a picture appear to bend inwards. Although mostly corrected, it is still noticeable on some zooms.

Pincushion distortion

This is the opposite to barrel distortion. Image points are displaced outwards so lines parallel and close to the edge of the frame bend outwards.

Rectilinear distortion

This is the inability of a lens to record straight lines straight. It is common in wide-angle lenses and mainly noticeable at the edges of the picture area. Some wide-angle lenses are corrected for this so distortion is avoided.

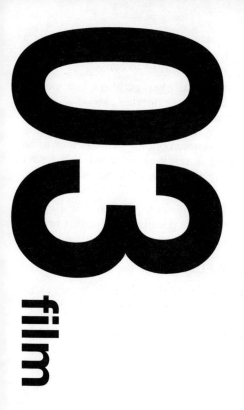

03

film

In this chapter you will learn:
- about film speed
- how different brands give different results
- about uprating and push-processing film
- about film care and common film faults.

Despite the fact that digital imaging has turned photography on its head in the last few years, film is far from dead and looks set to find continued support for a long time to come.

Many enthusiast and professional photographers continue to favour film over digital, while a large number choose to keep a foot in both camps and select one or the other as and when they see fit. Black and white film is also being buoyed by a growing number of obscure and lesser-known brands that continue to be made to support the die-hard traditionalists out there who prefer to make images as they always have – by exposing silver-based materials to light.

No one can deny that film sales have dropped dramatically and, as a consequence, many of the less popular or specialist brands of film have sadly gone out of production. But the main players – Kodak and Fujifilm – are still there in force and all the major film types are still widely available, as are the facilities to have them developed and printed.

If you have come into photography via the digital route you may well be wondering what the point of film is when digital images cost nothing to take and you get to see the results immediately. However, film has character and individuality; something than digital images lack unless it is added later. The anticipation of shooting film then waiting for the results to come back from the processing lab is also part and parcel of the picture-taking process – and an enjoyable one at that.

So maybe it's time you dusted down the old family film camera that has been sitting at the back of a cupboard for ages and see what all the fuss is about. You never know, you might even enjoy it!

Film speed

The first factor you need to consider when choosing film is the actual speed of the film, which is now universally referred to as an ISO number (International Standards Organisation). This is important for two reasons.

First, the ISO rating of a film gives an indication of its sensitivity to light, and in turn the amount of exposure it needs to create an image. Film with a low ISO rating such as 50 – known as 'slow' – is not very sensitive so it needs to be exposed for longer than a 'fast' film such as ISO 400, which is much more sensitive.

Slow films are therefore useful in situations where there is lots of light around or you do not need to use fast shutter speeds, whereas faster films are better in lower light and when fast shutter speeds are vital.

Second, film speed is also directly related to image quality. Slow films (ISO 50–100) offer finer grain, richer colour saturation and superb sharpness, but as the film speed increases this quality begins to tail off – grain becomes coarser and more obvious, colours lack the same depth, contrast is lower and sharpness reduced.

Bearing these two points in mind, the first step in film selection is deciding whether speed or image quality is most important. The ideal compromise is to use the slowest film you can get away with, so you gain maximum benefits on both counts.

Here's a brief guide to different film speeds and their uses:

Slow film (ISO 50–100) Perfect general-use film and the standard choice for most photographers. Image quality is superb, with extremely fine grain, vibrant colours and superb resolving power. A tripod will still be necessary when shooting in low light, but handholding is possible when shooting outdoors in good light. (See DVD 3.01.)

Medium-speed film (ISO 200–400) Films in this category offer a useful compromise between speed and image quality and can be used in a wide variety of lighting situations. This makes them ideal for general use – especially in compact cameras that offer little exposure control and are often fully automatic. (See DVD 3.02.)

Grain becomes more obvious at ISO 400 but quality is still very high and if you are shooting fast action in dull light, or you want to take pictures indoors without using a flash or a tripod, they are invaluable.

Ultra-fast film (ISO 800 and above) These films are ideal for taking pictures in low light – indoor sports, for example – but the coarse grain and poorer colour rendition is a major disadvantage. Best used as a last resort, or for subjects where the coarse grain is to be used for creative effect. (See DVD 3.03.)

Print or slide?

Whether you shoot print or slide film will mainly depend on what you intend to do with your pictures.

In terms of convenience, print film wins hands down. Prints are far easier to look at – you can just pass them around in an album – and enlargements are cheaper to make from negatives. The quality of colour print film has also improved immensely over the years, and most high streets have at least one lab where you can drop off your film then pick up the prints an hour or so later, whereas fewer labs process slide film so you may need to use a mail order service.

A further advantage of print film is that its tolerance to exposure error is high – you can under- or overexpose a picture by up to three stops and still get an acceptable print because the error can be corrected at the printing stage. This is particularly handy if you use a fully automatic camera which gives little or no control over the exposure.

That said, the colour saturation and sharpness of a perfectly exposed colour slide is still greater than that of a print because there is no intermediate stage where errors can be introduced. This is why serious enthusiasts and the majority of professional photographers – myself included – insist on using slide film.

Having prints made commercially from colour slides is more expensive than normal prints, but these days so many photographers own or have access to scanners and inkjet printers that lab-made prints are far less popular. It is also easier to scan colour slides rather than colour negatives as they are positive images. Slides are also preferred for publication – though in truth, images supplied in digital form are the first choice for publication these days.

If you decide to shoot slide film you need to take care because it can only tolerate around half a stop of over- or underexposure before the highlights begin to blow or the shadows block up. For this reason it is best used in cameras which give you control over the exposure set, so the chance of getting the exposure perfect is increased.

Colour or black and white?

The vast majority of pictures taken on film, especially by enthusiast photographers, use colour film. But then that's hardly surprising; it's a colourful world we live in, so why not take pictures that capture it in the most truthful way? Most photographers use their camera to record family, friends, special occasions and holidays, so colour is the natural choice and black and white is seen as rather old fashioned simply because it is not realistic.

Once you become more serious about photography, however, the benefits of black and white become more obvious. It is seen as a more artistic medium, and by removing colour and reality from an image you can concentrate on the basic elements such as texture and form and the play of light and shade – things that are so easily overlooked in colour photography (see Chapter 12). (See DVD 3.04.)

There's an old school of thought that suggests it is easier to learn the fundamentals of photography by starting out in black and white, because you do not have colour getting in the way. In reality we feel the opposite applies, and that it makes more sense to start out using colour film, and then explore black and white once you have enough experience to appreciate the creative benefits of the medium.

Brand differences

Although you might think that one colour film is like any other with the same ISO rating, you'd be wrong – brand differences can be quite significant, and some films are created to behave in a certain way.

Knowing how different films behave is useful because you can then put their characteristics to good use. If you are shooting portraits or nudes, for example, you may prefer a film that accurately captures skin tones, whereas if you are shooting abstracts or landscapes a well-saturated film with contrast will be more suitable.

Fuji film Velvia is perhaps the most popular colour slide film available thanks to its vibrant colours, super-fine grain and amazing sharpness. But for portraits Velvia is a poor choice because it makes skin tones appear too warm, and a more faithful alternative such as Fujifilm Astia or Provia is better.

The key is to experiment with a range of different films so you get to know how they respond in different conditions.

Uprating film

Occasionally you may find yourself in a situation where the film you have is too slow to allow you to continue taking pictures.

You could be shooting something like motor racing, for example, when suddenly the light begins to fade and even with your lens set to its widest aperture the fastest shutter speed available isn't fast enough to freeze the action.

If you have some faster film at hand then this can be used. If not, the alternative is to 'uprate' the slower film you do have so the required shutter speed can be used. This involves setting the film speed to a higher ISO, so you are effectively underexposing the film, then increasing the processing time to compensate. Prolonged development is known as 'push processing' or 'pushing'. If you uprate ISO 100 film to ISO 200, for example, you need to push it by one stop; if you rate it at ISO 400 you need to push it by two stops. (See DVD 3.05.)

The main drawback with push processing is contrast and grain size increase, so you should only do it when you really need to. That said, you can use these characteristics to your advantage. By rating an ISO 400 film at ISO 1600, for example, then push processing it by two stops, you can create gritty, grainy images. Also, ultra-fast black and white films can be uprated to really high speeds, such as ISO 6400, ISO 12 800, or even ISO 25 000, so you can shoot in extreme lighting conditions.

Colour slide film and black and white film are the easiest to uprate because most labs offer a push processing service, often at no extra cost. You can also buy special developers which are designed for pushing black and white film yourself. Very few labs will push process colour negative film though, so avoid uprating it.

Cross processing

If you want to try something different with your colour film, cross processing is a great technique to experiment with.

All you do is shoot a film as normal, then have it processed in the wrong chemistry – you have colour print film processed as slide film (E6 process instead of C41), or colour slide film processed as print film (C41 instead of E6). Doing this changes the film's characteristics and you can get some weird and wonderful effects. (See DVD 3.06.)

Cross processing colour slide film in C41 chemistry works best because the results are not totally unreal, but you get really intense colours, deep shadows, crisp highlights and lots of contrast – ideal for abstracts, architecture, flower close-ups, unusual portraits and so on.

Any colour slide film is worth trying, though Fuji films such as Velvia and Provia are especially good. Outdated or out-of-production slide films can also be found on eBay and purchased for bargain prices, so it is worth checking.

One good thing about cross processing slide film is that you do not have to change the ISO, and there is no need to bracket exposures because by treating the film as a print film you get lots of exposure latitude, just like you do when using negative film.

Having shot the film, put a label on the cassette saying 'Process C-41' and take it to your lab. High street labs may refuse to cross process film, but professional labs will be happy to do so – just make sure they know what you want!

Infrared film

Being sensitive mainly to infrared radiation rather than visible light, this film records the world in a totally different way from how we see it: skin tones go a ghostly pale shade, foliage turns white and blue sky and water goes jet black. (See DVD 3.07.)

The most effective infrared film is Kodak High Speed Infrared (HIE) as it is highly sensitive to infrared radiation, fast (ISO 400) and produces very stark, grainy images. It is prone to fogging though and must be handled in complete darkness – which means loading and unloading the camera using a changing bag if you are on location and also loading exposed film in the development tank in complete darkness.

The other options – Ilford SFX and Rollei IR820C – are not as sensitive to infrared but still need to be handled carefully and loading/unloading in complete darkness is recommended though subdued light would probably suffice.

The effects created by IR films are most noticeable on scenes that contain a lot of foliage, particularly if you shoot in bright, sunny weather. Woodland scenes and landscapes are perfect for infrared photography, and you can create some incredibly evocative images by photographing old buildings such as castles and churches covered in ivy or hidden by thick undergrowth.

For the best results, expose the film through a deep red filter – any brand will do – or a special infrared-transmitting filter (Kodak Wratten 87 or 88A or Hoya R72) which only admits infrared radiation.

Getting the exposure right with infrared film is tricky because it does not have an accurate ISO rating – just a guide speed which changes depending on the weather conditions and the level of infrared radiation in the atmosphere. Kodak and Rollei films should be rated at ISO 400 and Ilford SFx at ISO 200 if you meter through a deep red filter or ISO 50 and ISO25 respectively if you use a handheld meter. It is also a good idea to shoot one frame at the metered exposure then a second at +1 stop and a third at +2 stops. One of those three negatives should print well – although to get the most from infrared film you often need to print hard at grade IV or V.

Tungsten-balanced film

If you use normal daylight-balanced film under domestic tungsten bulbs or tungsten studio lighting, your pictures will come out with an obvious yellow/orange cast. To prevent this you can either use a blue 80A or 80B colour conversion filter (see page 68) or load your camera with tungsten-balanced film, which is designed to record colours naturally in tungsten light. Kodak and Fuji both manufacture ISO 64 tungsten-balanced slide film, although there is no longer a tungsten-balanced colour negative film available. (See DVD 3.08 and 3.09.)

This film can also be used to create unusual effects. Used in daylight it takes on a strong blue cast which is ideal for giving your pictures a cold, eerie feel.

Reciprocity Law Failure

Photographic film is designed to give the best results within a certain range of exposure times – usually 1–1/10 000 sec. Once you start using exposures outside this range – particularly long exposure – the film's ISO rating is no longer accurate and the exposure needs to be increased to prevent error. This is known as Reciprocity Law Failure (RLF) and it is a real problem for photographers who take a lot of pictures in low light – outdoors at night, or inside poorly lit buildings.

As a guide, if your camera meter suggests an exposure of one second, increase it to one-and-a-half seconds; if ten seconds is suggested increase it to 20 seconds; if 30 seconds is suggested increase it to 60. These increases are only guides though, because different films respond to RLF in different ways, so it is always a good idea to bracket your exposures under and over the exposure you think is 'correct', just to be on the safe side.

Reciprocity Law Failure can also cause the colour balance of film to alter so your pictures come out with a colour cast. This can be corrected using filters, but most of the time the strange colours actually look effective, so it is not worth trying to avoid them.

Film care

If you want to get the best results possible from your film you need to look after it. Here are a few useful hints worth bearing in mind.

- Always keep unused 35 mm film in its plastic canister to prevent dirt and grit collecting on the felt light trap – this can lead to scratches down the whole roll.
- Store unused film in a cool place – preferably a refrigerator – in a sealed container. Remove several hours before use and leave to warm up to room temperature.
- Never leave film in direct sunlight or the glove compartment of a car – the high temperature can cause colour shifts.
- Never buy film that has been stored on a shelf in direct sunlight for long periods.
- Process used film as soon as possible.
- Always try to use your film before the expiry date – unless it has been stored in a fridge, in which case it will last for two or three years beyond the expiry date.
- For long-term storage of film, use a deep freeze. This will halt the aging process and means that the film will last indefinitely. Allow 24 hours for it to thaw before use.
- When you are travelling, keep all film in your hand luggage. The x-ray machines used to scan hand luggage are film safe but the more powerful x-rays used to scan checked luggage are not, so film placed in checked luggage may be fogged.

Common film faults

Occasionally you may receive a batch of pictures back from the processing lab that suffer from various faults. Sometimes these are caused by user error; sometimes they may have been introduced by the lab itself.

Below is a list of common film faults to help you identify and solve any problems. Most of them can be solved by scanning the offending slide or negative and using tools such as the Healing Brush or Clone Stamp in Photoshop.

Tramlines Parallel scratches, usually down the full length of the film, caused by grit in the felt light trap of the film cassette, grit on the pressure plate in the camera back or a processing fault.

To avoid, store film in tubs, take care when loading film and keep the camera's pressure plate clean.

Drying marks/chemical stains Appear as blotches and stains of varying size on negatives, slides and prints and are caused by insufficient washing of the film or print after processing.

To avoid, use wetting agent in your final rinse if you are processing and printing at home, or change labs. Offending marks can usually be wiped away with a damp cloth.

Fogging Ghostly patches or streaks on film and prints, created when film or printing paper is accidentally exposed to light before or during processing. Opening the camera back by mistake, loading and unloading film in bright light or a light leak in the processing tank/darkroom blackout are common causes.

To avoid fogging, load and unload film in subdued light and check your darkroom for light leaks. Fogged film cannot be rectified, but a fogged print can be re-made if the negative or slide is okay.

Colour casts Can be caused by several things: deterioration of the film due to exposure to heat, damp or chemicals, the automatic printing unit at the lab trying to correct a colour cast by dialling in extra filtration and so on.

To avoid problems use fresh film stock, avoid storing film in hot places – such as the glove compartment of your car – and inform the lab if you use coloured filters on colour negative film, so they do not try to cancel it out.

Blank film Black slides or clear negatives indicate either gross underexposure if it is just the odd frame or, if it is the whole roll, the film probably never went through the camera.

To avoid problems take care when loading the film and keep your fingers away from the shutter unless you are about to take a picture.

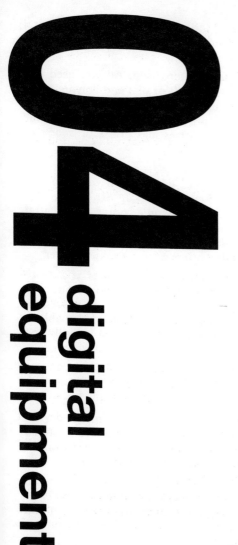

04

digital equipment

In this chapter you will learn:

- about memory cards and portable storage devices
- about choosing and using software
- about peripherals such as card readers and graphics tablets
- how to manage your images.

A major difference between film photography and digital capture is the amount of additional equipment required for digital imaging.

Film photography is simple in comparison. All you need is a camera, a lens or two and a few rolls of film and you are ready to go. Once the film has been exposed, you can drop it off at your local processing lab, then hours or days later, collect the results – either a wallet of negatives and prints or a box of mounted colour slides.

Digital photography, on the other hand, is much more involved. Once a series of images have been captured on your camera's memory card, they should be copied onto an external storage device for safekeeping, then at some point soon after downloaded onto a computer where the image files can be processed, enhanced, manipulated and eventually, if you so choose, output as high quality prints using an inkjet printer.

From a positive perspective, digital imaging puts you much more in control of the whole picture-taking process because you are involved at every stage – from image capture to processing to printing. However, it also means that as well as being able to use a camera you have to develop computer-based skills and invest a significant amount of money in additional equipment.

Memory cards

These are the digital equivalent of film – small storage devices that are loaded into the camera and used to record captured images. When the card is full, it is replaced by an empty one in the same way that you would load a new roll of film.

The main difference between memory cards and film is that you can copy the images from a memory card onto a computer or alternative storage device, erase the images from the card and use it over and over again.

There are numerous card formats available. Digital SLRs and many compacts use either Compact Flash (CF) or Smart Media (SM) cards, although others are available such as Memory Stick and Memory Stick Pro Duo.

All types of card come with different levels of storage capacity. The smallest is usually 256MB (megabytes – see glossary) and the biggest available is now a whopping 16GB (gigabytes – see glossary). Such high capacity is becoming more common as the pixel count of digital cameras increases and image files become bigger.

That said, it is important to remember that memory cards are not 100 per cent reliable and until the images on the card are copied onto a permanent storage device they are vulnerable. It is not uncommon for memory cards to develop faults that render them unreadable. Consequently, any images stored on the card could be lost forever and the more storage the card offers, the more images there are likely to be on it.

To minimize the risk of losing images, it makes sense to work with several cards of lower capacity – 1, 2 or 4GB – so if one card fails, all is not lost. You should also stick to reputable brands – cheap cards are often less stable.

A final consideration is the write speed of the card – the higher this is, the faster images will be recorded once taken, which is becoming more significant as pixel count increases and image files become bigger.

Portable storage devices

To reduce the risk of images being lost if a memory card develops a fault, it is a good idea to copy or back them up onto a more permanent storage device as soon as possible.

If you are working indoors or in a studio, a laptop computer is a practical solution because you can also preview the images on the screen, process RAW files, work on individual images and, if necessary, make additional copies of the images to an external hard drive or CD/DVD.

In the field or when travelling, however, laptops are less practical due to their size and weight and a smaller portable storage device is a better solution.

There are many different devices on the market today, with prices to suit all budgets and storage capacities from 20–160GB. All are similar in that they allow you to insert a memory card and copy the data from it. Many also have a preview screen so you can check the images as well, and they have high capacity batteries so that you can use them on location for hours on end.

Once the data from a memory card has been copied onto a storage device, it is tempting to wipe it clean and reuse it. However, ideally you should leave all the images on the cards until they have also been backed up onto a computer hard drive,

CD or DVD – which may means waiting until you return home if you are travelling.

An alternative – or complementary – means of back-up is to use a portable DVD burner to copy image files to DVD. These devices do not allow you to view the images, but DVDs provide a more stable means of storage than portable storage devices, which can easily be damaged by impact or moisture.

Computers

Whichever way you decide to store a back-up of your digital images, eventually they will all end up in the same place – on a computer where you can process the files, enhance and manipulate them, create image presentations, upload images to websites, email them to friends and maybe output your favourites as prints. The computer therefore forms the heart of any digital workstation.

There are two options when it comes to computer choice – PC or Apple Macintosh. The former is by far the most popular choice, though 'Macs' are considered the industry standard in the world of photography and design and are now finding their way into many more homes.

The one you choose will depend on taste, budget and what you are used to. The way Macs and PCs operate is very similar today, although if you have spent years working with one, switching to the other can be a little daunting. The choice of Macs is very limited compared to PCs, which are more widespread. PCs are also more modular so they can be upgraded with ease whereas with Macs, what comes out of the box is basically it. PCs are also available for much lower prices than Macs because so many models are available and competition is strong, and you can pick up some great package deals.

Whichever type you choose, you need to accept that before long it will seem slow and outdated compared to the latest model – which annoyingly costs less than what you paid for yours. That said, if you buy the best you can afford at the outset, it will sustain your for years, simply because advances in computer hardware are slowing down and we are reaching the stage where more memory and greater operating speed simply isn't necessary.

Here are the main features you need to consider when shopping for a computer:

Processor

The speed at which the computer operates is governed by the processor it uses. Intel is the best-known brand, being widely used in both PCs and the latest Macs. They do vary, but the norm these days seems to be a dual-core or quad-core processor with an operating speed of 2.4–2.6Ghz. Top-level machines have 8–core, 3Ghz processors, but such performance is only required by professionals.

RAM

RAM, or Random Access Memory, is used by the computer to process applications and actions, so when you open and run software, open and work on images and perform other tasks, they will all eat up the computer's RAM. Consequently, the more you have, the better – especially if you work with large image files such as scanned transparencies which can be 200MB or more. You can manage quite adequately with 1GB of RAM but memory is inexpensive to buy so the more you have the better. About 3–4GB will be ideal, although the latest computers can have as much as 16GB.

Hard drive

All data is stored on the computer's hard drive (HD) so the bigger it is the better. Today's Macs and PCs may offer up to 360GB of storage, which may seem like a phenomenal amount, but given that digital images files are getting bigger, software packages are taking up more memory and computers are also used for home entertainment, it is surprising how quickly your HD will fill up. So think of it as a temporary storage measure and be prepared to add external drives to provide more permanent storage (see below).

Interfaces

Any accessories you buy for your computer, such as scanners, printers, card readers, external drives, will all connect to it via an interface. The most common is USB (Universal Serial Bus) and there are two types – USB1 and USB2, the latter transferring data at a faster rate. The other main interface is Firewire, which is faster than USB2 and the preferred choice of photographers.

All computers tend to have one or other USB ports while many have both USB and Firewire. Check this out before buying and also establish how many ports are available on the computer – there may only be two of each, in which case you will need to purchase multi-port hubs that allow you to connect several peripherals to the computer via just one port.

DVD reader/writer

An easy, practical and inexpensive way to back up digital images is by copying the image files to writeable DVD – DVD/R. Each disc will hold 4.7GB of data and yet takes up very little space, so you could back up your whole archive and store the discs at a different location from your computer, or in a fireproof safe so you can rest assured that if your computer suffers a catastrophic crash or your external hard drives fail, at least you will have a copy of all your images elsewhere.

Monitors

While the computer handles storage and software, it is the monitor that brings your images to life and allows you to see exactly what they look like and what happens when you perform certain actions – be it adjusting colour and contrast, cropping, or creating special effects. To do the job efficiently and effectively you therefore need to make sure the monitor you choose is suited to the job and gives an accurate rendition of what the image is really like.

Modern monitors tend to be LCD flat screens which are sleek and slim and occupy little desk space. They are available in sizes from 15 to 30 inch, although the bigger sizes are very expensive and for photographic work a screen around 19 to 22 inches is more than adequate. If you need more screen space, it may be less costly to buy two smaller monitors and run them side-by-side. A pair of 19-inch monitors will cost far less than a single 30-inch one, for example, and you can use one to view images and the other for tools and dialogue boxes.

LCD flatscreens are easy to work with because they do not pick up reflections like older CRT (Cathode Ray Tube) monitors and they provide a flicker-free image. That said, some photographers prefer working with CRT monitors because they find them easier to calibrate (see below) and they cost less.

Ultimately, the type you choose is down to personal preference, though flatscreens are far more popular and tend to be offered as standard as part of a computer package. In all cases, make sure the monitor can display millions of colours and that screen resolution is a minimum of 1024 × 768 pixels.

Software

In order to work on digital images you will need suitable software, and by far the most popular package used is Adobe Photoshop. It has been the industry standard ever since digital imaging became accessible to the masses and with each new version (the latest is CS3) it becomes more intuitive, more user-friendly and more sophisticated, allowing you not only to make technical adjustments and corrections to an image, but also to create a myriad of creative and special effects, combine whole images or elements from many different images, stitch images to create panoramas and so on.

The full version of Photoshop is expensive and contains many features you will never use, so initially you could work with the more basic Photoshop Elements. It contains all the main features you are likely to need but costs much less and is often included for free with digital cameras and scanners. If you like it, you can always upgrade to the full version later.

In addition to Photoshop there are many other graphics packages as well as plug-in devices that allows you to perform specific tasks such as adding unusual borders to your image or mimicking the effects of certain films.

Image management software such as Adobe Lightroom (see below) will also do most of the things that Photoshop can do, for a fraction of the price, as well as allowing you to manage your growing image collection.

Peripherals

Card readers

Though it is possible to connect a digital camera direct to your computer via a USB or Firewire port to download images from the memory cards, it is much easier to remove the card from the camera and insert it into a card reader – which is basically like a small disc drive. Some readers are made to handle one type of memory card, such as Compact Flash, but there are also multi-slot readers available that will handle all card types.

Graphics tablets

If you do a lot of intricate work on digital images, such as selecting detailed areas so you can work on them independently, then a graphics tablet will make life much easier. They basically consist of a flat tablet like a mouse mat and a pen-like stylus which you can use to work on an image with far greater precision than a mouse.

External hard drives

As already mentioned, no matter how capacious your computer's integral hard drive is, it is only a matter of time before it fills up and you need to find an alternative place to store images and data.

External hard drives provide an inexpensive and practical solution. They simply plug into the computer via a USB or Firewire port and appear on the computer's desktop as a separate icon.

Even if you have plenty of space on the computer's integral hard drive, it is worth investing in an external drive which you can use to copy everything that is on the main hard drive. Better still, have two external drives and copy everything onto both – the chance of three separate hard drives crashing and losing data is very slim.

The storage capacity of external drives now exceeds 1000GB (1 terabyte). However, 160–250GB drives are more than sufficient and also reduce the risk of large numbers of images being lost if a drive ever malfunctions.

Printers

Having recorded an image with your digital camera, downloaded it onto a computer, processed the file, enhanced and manipulated it, the final stage is usually to create a photo-quality print.

Until a few years ago, the only way to do this and achieve a high-quality result was by sending the image away to a printing studio, but thanks to huge advances in inkjet printing and ink technology it is now possible to produce your own prints for a relatively small investment – and they are every bit as good as those from a professional lab.

Canon, Epson and Hewlett Packard are the main names in inkjet printing and all produce a range of models to suit every conceivable budget and need, from compact and inexpensive A4 colour printers to A3 and A3+ models. Epson also manufactures a range of professional printers in 17-inch, 24-inch, 36-inch, 48-inch and even 64-inch width!

For the majority of photography enthusiasts, A3+ is more than big enough, allowing you to generate prints up to 13 × 19 inch and in most cases load paper rolls so you can print panoramas up to 13-inch deep and as long as you like! Beyond A3+ the printers are big, heavy, expensive to buy and expensive to run, so unless you need to produce prints bigger than 13 × 19 inch on a regular basis, they are unnecessary.

The latest pigment inks used in inkjet printers are much more stable and consistent than earlier inks and, combined with a huge range of inkjet papers in different weights and surface finishes, they allow you to produce prints that have the same quality and archival permanence as traditional silver-based prints. See Chapter 16 for information on digital printing.

Colour management

If you want to produce the best possible results when working digitally, your computer monitor and printer must both be set up so that the prints faithfully reproduce the colours you see on the screen. If you ignore this then you will waste a lot of time, paper and ink trying to adjust images on-screen so that the prints from them are acceptable to you, but never quite knowing if the monitor is at fault, the printer or both.

Fortunately, it doesn't have to be that way because if you calibrate your monitor on a regular basis so the contrast, brightness and colour balance are correct, what you see on the screen will accurately reflect what the image really looks like.

Similarly, if you use ICC profiles for your printer, to optimize its settings when using specific inks and papers, your prints will not only look exactly the same as the image on the screen but print quality will also be at its highest.

The easiest way to calibrate your monitor is by investing in a hardware-based calibration unit which hangs in front of the monitor so a sensor in the unit can assess the colour output. Software then adjusts the colour channel and a custom profile is created which is then embedded in the monitor preferences so that every time you turn the computer on, the monitor settings are controlled by the profile to ensure consistency.

Similarly, with printers you can use custom profiles to colour manage when outputting on certain papers. The paper manufacturers tend to put these profiles on their websites so you can download and install them onto your computer. Alternatively, you can have profiles written for you for use with specific ink and paper combinations.

By calibrating your monitor and profiling your printer, you should be able to manipulate images on-screen with confidence and output top-quality prints every time.

Image management

In the good old days of film photography, managing a growing photo collection was relatively straightforward. Colour slides were generally mounted on individual card or plastic mounts, then stored in transparent sheets that could be placed in filing cabinets or ring binders. Negatives were placed in strips in sleeves then filed in a similar way, while prints could be placed in portfolio cases and presentation boxes.

With digital images, things are not quite so straightforward because the images exists in a virtual world – cyberspace! Consequently, unless you formulate some kind of logical system of organizing and filing batches of images as you shoot them, being able to locate specific images from the many thousands you end up with could take forever.

Software packages such as Adobe Lightroom and Apple Aperture can make image management much easier because they allow you to organize your collections and access them in many different ways. This is all based on key wording each image. For example, a beach scene shot at sunset on Ko Samui could have the following keywords: Asia, Thailand, Ko Samui, Sunsets, Beach, Sand, Water, Orange and so on. So, if you were searching for images in the future and you entered any one of those keywords, the image would be called up along with any others that matched the same keyword. Images can also be organized by subject, or you can have folders for favourites, or give images a star rating and so on.

In addition to file management, these software packages also have powerful RAW conversion tools, so that when you download images into the application you can convert the RAW files, enhance the images by adjusting colour balance, exposure and contrast, convert to black and white, tone images, crop them and organize them, all in the same place. Even better, the changes made to each image are saved as a series of actions so they are non-destructive, the original image file remains unchanged and consequently, far less memory is used.

It is much easier to use a system like this if you start it when your image collection is quite small. Wait until you have hundreds or thousands of images and it will take an age to input them into the system.

The main downside you need to be aware of is that if the system crashed you could lose every image contained in it, so regular backing up is crucial.

Scanners

Of course, you do not have to use a digital camera to create digital images – slides, negatives and prints can all be scanned and converted to digital form, and even though you may now shoot with a digital camera, it may still be worth buying a scanner so you can digitize your analogue collection as well.

There are two main types of scanner – flatbed and film. Flatbed scanners are the most versatile for general use because as well as scanning negatives and slides of any size up to the actual size of the glass bed, they can also scan flat artwork such as prints, paintings, documents and even 3D objects such as flowers and seashells. Film scanners, as the name implies are designed only for scanning negatives and slides and the bigger the film format they can handle, the more expensive they become.

Film scanners do tend to produce better results than flatbed scanners, so if you only need to scan 35 mm originals then a dedicated 35 mm film scanner from a manufacturer such as Nikon will be your best bet.

If you need to scan medium-format images, the cost of a film scanner will treble, while film scanners for 5 × 4 inch large-format and panoramic formats such as 6 × 17 cm cost at least ten times that of a 35 mm-only film scanner. Therefore, if you have a mixture of different film formats, a flatbed scanner with a film holder will be far more affordable and the latest models from manufacturers such as Epson are capable of stunning results.

The main factor that dictates scan quality is the optical resolution of the scanner because the more pixels it records, the larger the image can be printed. Scanner resolution is expressed as Pixels per inch (ppi). Make sure the one you choose offers a minimum of 4000ppi. Bit depth is another term you will come across. Scanners offering 8bit output will produce perfectly good results. But ideally choose a model with 16bit output as you will achieve better quality scans with a wider range of tone and colour. When scanning colour images, this bit depth will apply to the three separate colour layers that make up the RGB image (red, green and blue). Therefore, you may see bit depth expressed as 24bit (which is effectively 3×8 bit) or 48bit (3×16 bit).

A third factor to consider is dynamic range. Colour slide film has a dynamic range up to 3.6 so if you buy a scanner with a dynamic range lower than that, you are not going to capture the full range of detail in the shadows and highlight when you scan it. Fortunately, the majority of mid-priced scanners have a dynamic range of 4.0 or above, which is more than sufficient for scanning both slides and negatives.

In addition to the scanner you will also need scanning software. All scanner manufacturers have their own software and it is usually included with the scanner. However, third-partly software can also be used, such as Silverfast or Viewscan.

05

filters

In this chapter you will learn:
- about different filter systems
- about filters and exposure
- how to use the most popular filters
- how to care for your filters.

Filters are a crucial part of photography, playing both a creative and technical role and enabling us to produce the very best pictures in all situations. They help us control contrast and colour balance, enhance scenery so our shots look better than the real thing, and add countless effects that reflect our creative vision.

The big question is, which filters should you buy? With so many to choose from, it is no surprise that newcomers to photography get very confused over filters. But even if you do know which ones to buy, you still need to learn what they do and how to use them if they are ever to become regular fixtures on your lenses rather than white elephants gathering dust in the bottom of your gadget bag.

The aim of this chapter is to solve all the problems and answer all the questions you have ever had about choosing and using filters.

Filters with digital cameras

Many photographers shooting with digital cameras do not bother using any filters, for the simple reason that they feel the effects can all be created afterwards once the images are downloaded onto a computer.

To an extent this is true, and as any optical accessory placed in front of a camera lens will reduce its image quality, it makes sense to do that only when absolutely necessary.

At the same time, however, if you use filters at the point a picture is taken, especially filters that have technical rather than creative applications, it will save time spent at the computer later – which can be significant when you have hundreds of new image files to process.

Choosing a filter system

Before investing in specific filters, the first and most important decision you need to make is which filter system best suits your needs and budget.

Many photographers think about this too far down the line, and end up with an expensive mixture of filters in different sizes, from different manufacturers, that are not compatible and cause all kind of headaches. However, if you consider the pros and cons of each system on offer you will save a small fortune long term and have a collection of filters that can be used on all your lenses and even across different film formats.

Here are the main factors you need to consider:

Round or square?

Filters come in two main forms: either the round type that screw directly onto the front of your lens, or the square/rectangular variety that slot into a special holder which fits to your lens via adaptor rings.

In terms of versatility, the slot-in systems are infinitely better. All you need is one holder and a selection of adaptor rings to fit each lens in your outfit. You can also use two, three or sometimes even four filters (not that you would want to very often) in the holder at once to combine different effects.

The problem with round filters is they are made to fit lenses with a specific filter thread. That is fine if all your lenses have the same thread, but to use them on larger or smaller lenses you will need stepping rings to adapt their sizes. All filters will also have to be bought to fit your biggest lens, which could make the cost of a basic kit high if you have a lens with a 77 mm or 82 mm filter thread. Most important of all, the depth of the filter mount itself also means that if you use two or more together there is a risk of vignetting (darkening of the picture edges) especially with wide-angle lenses.

Size matters

The thing you need to be careful about is which square system you buy, because there are numerous ones to choose from, in different sizes and with vastly different price tags. The smallest are the Cokin A size systems which take 67 mm-wide filters. They are fine for digital SLRs with lenses as wide as 28 mm, but any wider and you will get vignetting because the sides of the filter holder encroach on the lens's field of view.

A more sensible option for anyone investing in a new filter system is the next size up – 85 mm. The most popular system in this size is Cokin P, though others such as Hitech 85 exist. They will work fine on lenses as wide as 18–20 mm (that's effective focal length, after applying a magnification factor for digital cameras with smaller sensors), and the inexpensive plastic holders can easily be adapted to work on lenses down to 17 mm without causing vignetting (by basically cutting off the front slot with a hacksaw!).

Beyond that you get into more expensive professional systems from the likes of Lee Filter, Hitech and Cokin Z-Pro, which are based on 100 mm-wide filters, or Cokin X-Pro which is even bigger at 130 mm wide.

They are a good choice if you use ultra wide-angle lenses with your digital or 35 mm SLR, as you can take pictures without fear of vignetting on lenses as wide as 17 mm. Ultra wide-angle zooms are becoming very popular now, with focal length ranges starting at just 10 mm or 12 mm on some models, so it is worth considering a 100 mm system straightaway. You pay dearly for this, because even items such as filter holders and adaptor rings can be ridiculously expensive for what they are, but long term you will be glad you made the investment.

Cross compatibility

Some filter systems are compatible with each other, which may be worth considering. If you buy a Cokin P system holder, for example, you can use Hitech 85 filters in it as well, and vice versa. Similarly, Hitech 100 filters will fit in a Lee 100 holder. You can also adapt the Lee filter holder to take Cokin P and Hitech 85 systems, but its own filters are too thick to fit in the holders of other manufacturers.

Filters and exposure

Many filters reduce the amount of light entering your lens, so you may need to compensate the exposure when using them to prevent your pictures coming out too dark. Each filter is given a 'filter factor' which indicates how many times the initial exposure needs to be multiplied by to make up for this loss. A factor of ×2 indicates an exposure increase of one stop, ×4 two stops, ×8 three stops and so on. The filter factor is usually printed on the filter mount or box.

Modern SLRs with TTL metering – which includes every digital and 35 mm film SLR on the market these days – will take this into account automatically, so you needn't worry about it. However, if you take an exposure reading without the filter in place, or use a handheld meter to determine correct exposure, you must increase the exposure accordingly based on the filter factor.

The table below shows the filter factors for some common filters.

Filter	Filter factor	Exposure increase
Polarizer	×4	2 stops
81A warm-up	×1.3	one-third stop
81C warm-up	×1.5	half stop
Blue 80A	×4	2 stops
Orange 85B	×3	one-and-a-half stops
Yellow	×2	1 stop
Orange	×4	2 stops
Red	×8	3 stops
Skylight	×1	None
Soft focus	×1	None

Skylight and ultra-violet (UV) filters

Both these filters reduce atmospheric haze and cut out the blueness found in the light at high altitudes, so they are ideal for scenic pictures taken in mountainous regions. However, because the effect they have on a photograph in normal shooting conditions is negligible, they tend to be used mainly to protect a lens's delicate front element.

When you buy a new lens, it is worth spending a little extra on a screw-in skylight or UV filter as it is far cheaper to replace a damaged scratched or broken filter than a damaged lens.

How to use a polarizing filter

The polarizer is the most versatile filter available. No other filter can make such a massive difference to the impact of a picture, or spend so much time on your lens, so make sure it is one of your first buys. The effect created cannot be mimicked digitally either, so even though you may shoot with a digital camera, a polarizer is still worth using.

It works by blocking out polarized light, and in doing so offers three distinct benefits:

1 Blue sky is deepened.
2 Glare is reduced on non-metallic surfaces such as foliage so colour saturation is increased.
3 Reflections are reduced or eliminated in water, glass and other surfaces.

The best part about using a polarizer is that you can see exactly what it is doing and therefore control the effect. This is done by placing it on your lens, then rotating it slowly while looking through the camera's viewfinder. You will see the sky darken then lighten as you rotate, glare disappear then reappear, and when you are happy with the effect you simply stop rotating. (See DVD 5.01 and 5.02.)

If you use an autofocus camera and the front end of the lens rotates as focus changes, focus first then adjust the polarizer, or hold the polarizer in place as you focus so its position does not change.

For the strongest effect when deepening blue sky, the sun should be perpendicular to the lens axis. In plain English that means keep the sun on one side of the camera. By doing so you will be looking towards the area of sky where maximum polarization occurs. (See DVD 5.04.) If you shoot with the sun to your back, the effect on the sky will be noticeable but not brilliant, and you will get no noticeable effect on the sky in dull weather.

Take care when using lenses wider than 28 mm, too, as polarization is uneven across the sky so you can end up with a picture where the sky is a darker blue on one side – especially if you are shooting with the sun just out of shot.

The reduction of glare can be clearly seen when shooting landscapes – the colour of grass and foliage suddenly seem much richer as maximum polarization is achieved.

To reduce or eliminate reflections with a polarizer, the angle between the reflective surface and your lens axis should be around 30° for the best results, although you needn't be too precise about this.

A polarizer will work on all non-metallic surfaces such as glass, plastic, paintwork and car body work. It is also ideal for getting rid of surface reflection in calm water so the true reflections of the surrounding scenery are enhanced. (See DVD 5.05.)

The main thing you need to watch when using a polarizer is that its two-stop light reduction doesn't make shutter speeds too slow for handholding – ISO 100 effectively becomes ISO 25 when you have a polarizer on your lens so even in bright sunlight exposures are going to be down to 1/30sec at f/11.

Although polarizers work best in sunny weather, they can be used in dull conditions to cut through the glare on wet foliage – autumnal woodland scenes can benefit from the use of a polarizer to make the warm colours really glow. (See DVD 5.05.)

There are two types of polarizing filter – circular and linear. Both do exactly the same job and give exactly the same effect, but the type you will need will depend on what camera you use. The basic rule to remember is if you use an autofocus camera, or a camera with spot metering, you need a circular polarizer. A linear polarizer will be fine with all other cameras. If you use a linear polarizer with an autofocus camera, underexposure is likely because the metering system will be fooled.

Graduated filters

There are two main types of graduated filter – neutral density (ND), which darken the sky without changing its natural colour, and coloured grads, which darken the sky and colour it at the same time. (See DVD 5.06.)

ND graduates are by far the most useful type of grad filter and along with a polarizer should be part of every photographer's kit. Their main use is to control the difference in brightness between the sky and the landscape. When shooting landscapes, this difference is often too great for film or digital sensors to record, so if you expose the landscape correctly, the sky is overexposed and records as a wishy-washy colour, with no depth and little detail – flashing highlight warnings are likely with digital cameras. Similarly, if you expose the bright sky correctly, the landscape will come out too dark. ND grads allow you to overcome this by darkening the sky to a point where it needs the same amount of exposure as the landscape. By doing this, the sky records as you remembered it. (See DVD 5.07 and 5.08.)

Different densities are available so you can darken the sky by a precise amount – a 0.3 ND grad will give a one-stop reduction in sky brightness; 0.6 two stops; 0.9 three stops. The most useful are 0.6 and 0.9 – 0.6 for general use during the day and the 0.9 at dawn and dusk when the sky is much brighter and there is no direct sunlight on the landscape so contrast is greater. (See DVD 5.09 and 5.10.)

To use an ND grad, slide it down into the filter holder on your lens until the dark part of the filter is covering the required amount of sky. You can do this by eye, although pressing your camera's depth of field preview so the viewfinder darkens makes accurate alignment easier. You may feel as though you cannot see any change when you first do this, but you will soon master grad alignment!

Because modern metering systems are so clever, you can meter with the grad filter in place and the results should be perfectly exposed, so once the grad is in place you can fire away. If you are shooting digitally, check the preview image and histogram to check that the grad has had the desired effect.

Digital sensors do not seem to be able to handle contrast as well as film, so you may find that you need to use a stronger grad than expected. However, you should rarely, if ever, need to use anything stronger than a 0.9ND grad during the daytime. In extreme situations, two grads can be combined to give a stronger effect.

Coloured grads work in the same way as ND grads, but their main purpose is to colour the sky. They can produce attractive results – a coral or pale pink grad is ideal for dawn or dusk shots, for example, or to add a little colour to a dull sky. Similarly, blue and purple grads can enhance the sky at twilight. They need to be used carefully, however, as the effect can look very unnatural.

Neutral density filters

Occasionally you may want to take a picture using a slow shutter speed, only to find that light levels are too high to allow it, even with your sensor set to its lowest ISO and your lens stopped down to its smallest aperture. (See DVD 5.11.)

Neutral density (ND) filters solve this problem by cutting down the light entering your lens, without changing the way colours or tones record, so a slower shutter speed can be used (or a wider aperture if necessary).

The amount by which the exposure must be increased depends on the density of the filter:

Filter density	Exposure increase
0.3	One stop
0.6	Two stops
0.9	Three stops
1.2	Four stops

Colour balancing filters

Photographers often get confused about this range of filters, but they are basically designed to help colour film record a scene or subject in a way that looks normal to the naked eye.

This is necessary because the colour of light changes, and while our eyes adapt automatically to those changes so everything looks normal, photographic film and digital sensors cannot and therefore record variations in the colour of light. Tungsten light bulbs give off a yellow/orange light, for example. We do not see this, but film does – which is why pictures taken in room lighting without flash have a yellow/orange colour cast.

There are three categories of balancing filter: colour correction, colour conversion and colour compensation. If you shoot digitally you do not really need to use any of them because most colour casts can be eliminated by adjusting your camera's white balance, or by adjusting colour balance when the images are downloaded and processed – this is especially easy if you shoot in RAW capture mode.

Colour correction filters

This category is split into two types: the 81 series of straw-coloured 'warm-up' filters, and the 82 series of pale blue 'cool' filters. Both are designed to balance slight changes in the colour of light. (See DVD 5.12 and 5.13.)

Warm-up filters are by far the most useful as they neutralize the slight blue cast found in the light in dull, cloudy weather, around noon in bright sunshine or in the shade under a blue sky. They are also ideal for making warm sunlight early and late in the day even warmer, and for making skin tones look more attractive when shooting portraits.

The weakest filter in the range is the 81A. It is actually too weak to make much difference, however, and an 81B is perhaps the most sensible one for general use. Moving through the range – 81C, 81D and 81EF – the warming effect becomes more pronounced. An 81D or 81EF is ideal for enhancing sunrise and sunset shots. It is worth buying 81B, C, D and EF. (See DVD 5.14.)

The pale blue 82 series removes excess warmth from the light. This is not something you would want to do too often though, because warm light generally looks beautiful. A more common use is to make pictures taken in dull or foggy weather even bluer. (See DVD 5.15.)

Colour conversion filters

These are stronger versions of correction filters and again they come in two groups – the blue 80 series and the orange 85 series. In each group there are three main strength – A, B and C, with A the strongest and C the weakest.

The blue 80 series is designed to remove the unwanted yellow/orange cast created when you take pictures on normal daylight-balanced film under tungsten lighting. For household tungsten bulbs you need a blue 80A, for tungsten studio photoflood lighting a blue 80B and for tungsten photopearl lighting a blue 80C. They can also be used to give your pictures an overall strong blue cast which looks very effective in mist, fog and rainy weather, or in moonlight. Setting your camera's white balance to Tungsten will have the same effect. (See DVD 5.16 and 5.17.)

The orange 85 series is used to balance any strong blue bias found in the light. An 85C will produce natural colours if you are shooting in really dull, overcast weather or in the shade in intense summer sunlight around midday. An 85A or 85B will convert tungsten-balanced film for use in daylight – without the filter your pictures would come out blue because tungsten film is much cooler than daylight-balanced film.

Colour compensation filters

These filters are used to balance colour casts created by other types of light source, such as fluorescent and sodium vapour, or colour deficiencies in daylight caused by the weather conditions. The most common types are Kodak Wratten gels, which come in many different colours and densities for accurate filtration.

Architectural and interior photographers use a special colour meter to measure the colour temperature of the light and to find out which CC filters are required to correct any deficiencies. These are unnecessary, however, for general use.

Soft focus filters

These handy filters create a gentle diffusion, so are great for adding atmosphere to portraits, still lifes, figure studies, woodland scenes, architecture and landscapes – any subject that will benefit from slight softening. (See DVD 5.19 and 5.20.)

You get the strongest effect on backlit subjects, and by shooting at wide lens apertures – the smaller the aperture, the less diffusion you get. Soft focus filters can also be used with any lens. Each brand gives a slightly different effect so examine a few before making your decision. Do not go for one that is too strong, however, as it will soften your pictures to a point where they appear out of focus.

Variations on the basic soft focus filter are worth checking out – such as sunsoft or softwarm filters, which have a warm-up filter built in, or soft spot filters that have a clear centre and soft edge. You can make your own by putting a tiny amount of Vaseline on a clear skylight or UV filter and change the effect by smearing it in different ways with your finger. (See DVD 5.18.)

Starburst filters

Even if you have never used one, chances are you will have seen the effect starburst filters create – they turn bright points of light, such as street lights or highlights on water into twinkling stars, with anything from two to 16 points depending upon the type you buy.

The effect is best shown on night scenes, but they can also be used in more creative ways – to create a star from the sun, or light reflecting on shiny surfaces. When shooting at night, try rotating the filter during a long exposure for a different effect. You could try making your own by etching fine lines onto a piece of clear plastic with a craft knife. The effect is rather clichéd now, but fun and every photographer has to take at least one starburst picture!

Using filters together

Although we have looked at individual filters and the effects they give, most can be used in combination with others. Polarizers, warm-ups and neutral density (ND) graduates are often used together by landscape photographers, for example, and warm-up and soft focus filters for portraits. Once you build up a reasonable collection of filters, the creative possibilities are endless. Just remember that the more filters you use together, the more you will degrade the sharpness and definition of the final picture. (See DVD 5.21.)

Caring for your filters

Filters, like lenses, need to be looked after if they're to give their best performance. Dust, dirt, scratches and fingerprints all reduce optical quality, so you should treat them with care and clean them at regular intervals.

- Always store unused filters in their boxes or a proper filter wallet to prevent damage or the build up of dirt.
- Handle round filters by the mount and square filters by the edges so you do not scratch or mark the important central area.
- Remove dust and dirt with a fine blower brush or a blast of compressed air.
- Clean greasy fingermarks using either a soft lens tissue or a micro-fibre lens cloth.
- Apply a few drops of lens cleaning fluid to a lens cloth and wipe in a circular motion, starting at the centre of the filter and working out.

Removing a jammed filter

Screw-on filters that are kept on the lens for long periods – such as skylights – or ones that have been over tightened have a habit of becoming stuck fast. The easiest way to remove a jammed filter is by applying even pressure around the mount so its shape does not distort while you try to unscrew it. There are three ways of doing this:

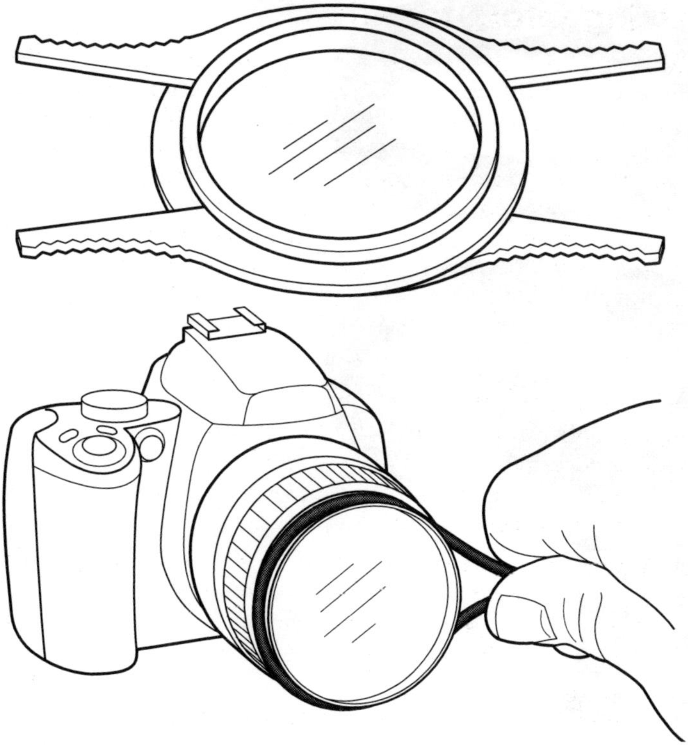

figure 5.1

1 Buy a purpose-made filter wrench which grips the filter mount evenly.
2 Wrap a piece of electrical flex or a cable release around the mount to grip the mount then gently turn the filter to unscrew it.
3 Push the filter against the bottom of a flat, rubber-soled shoe and twist.
4 Grip the filter mount very lightly with your fingertip and gently try to unscrew it.

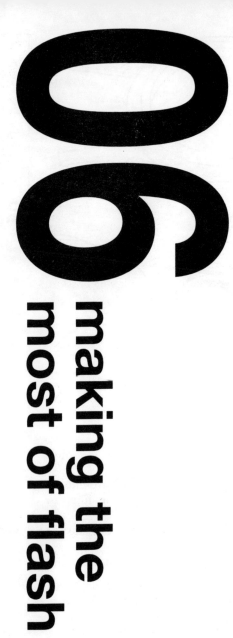

06

making the most of flash

In this chapter you will learn:
- how flashguns work
- the main features to look for on a flashgun
- how to master flash techniques.

A flashgun is one piece of equipment no photographer should be without. Not only does it mean you have got a portable and highly effective light source at hand at all times, but in some situations it can make the difference between taking a decent picture or no picture at all. Once you understand how your flashgun works you can also use it to create a range of stunning effects, from multiple exposures to freezing movement.

Unfortunately, most of us never get the full benefit from our flashgun. It spends months gathering dust at the bottom of our photo bag, only to be used for the occasional party snapshot or pictures of the kids opening their presents on Christmas morning.

The main reason for this is that flash has a reputation for being technical and over-complicated. These days, however, nothing could be further from the truth. Modern dedicated flashguns are sophisticated pieces of equipment that take all the guesswork out of taking perfect flash pictures every time, allowing you to concentrate on what matters most – the creative side of photography.

Flash synchronization

The powerful burst of light from a flashgun is created by an electrical current being passed through a gas-filled tube. The current is released when you trip the camera's shutter, so the light from the flash is generated at the exact moment the picture is taken – this is known as 'flash synchronization'.

When you are taking pictures in a continuous source of light, such as daylight, the camera's aperture and shutter speed are used together to give a correct exposure. However, because the duration of an electronic flash is so brief – often as little as 1/30 000 sec – only the lens aperture is used to control the amount of light reaching the film and determine correct flash exposure. The shutter speed is therefore almost irrelevant, but for one vitally important factor – flash synchronization.

The shutter in a digital SLR – and the vast majority of film SLRs – is known as a 'focal plane' shutter and consists of two 'curtains' made of either black cloth or a series of metal blades. When you press the camera's shutter release to take a picture, the first curtain opens to admit light to the film, then the second curtain closes behind it to end the exposure. When using high shutter speeds, such as 1/500 sec or 1/1000 sec, the second curtain begins its travel before the first curtain has completed its journey, so that in effect you have a slit moving across the shutter gate and exposing the image gradually rather than in a single 'hit'.

The maximum shutter speed you can use with flash – known as the 'flash sync speed' – is recommended because at shutter speeds higher than the flash sync speed, part of the picture will come out black because when the flash fires, the second shutter curtain is moving across the shutter gate and blocks out part of the image. By sticking to the correct sync speed, or a slower shutter speed, the gap between the two curtains is wide enough to evenly illuminate the whole image when the flash fires.

The flash sync speed on modern digital cameras tends to be 1/125 sec, 1/180 sec or 1/250 sec, although some professional SLRs have a faster flash sync speed up to 1/1000 sec in a few cases. Some types of film camera – mainly large-format and medium-format – can also be set to any shutter speed when used with electronic flash. This is because they use a different design of shutter, known as a 'leaf shutter', which is built into each lens, rather than a focal plane shutter in the camera body.

Leaf shutters comprise a series of blades like an aperture diaphragm that fan out to make an exposure, so you can obtain evenly-lit flash pictures at any shutter speed. This is one reason why, traditionally, portrait and wedding photographers tended to use medium-format cameras with leaf shutters – it meant they could use fill-in flash outdoors in bright sunlight, and not worry if fast shutter speeds were required to correctly expose the daylight.

Anatomy of a flashgun

Modern flashguns all tend to be very similar in the way they operate. The main difference, generally, is the power output of the flash, but other than that the features offered are very similar. Here is a list of the main features you need to look out for – and what they actually do.

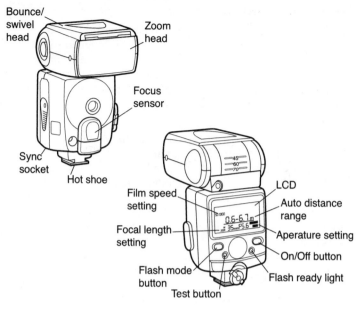

Bounce/swivel head

Zoom head

Focus sensor

Sync socket

Hot shoe

Film speed setting

Focal length setting

Flash mode button

Test button

LCD

Auto distance range

Aperature setting

On/Off button

Flash ready light

0.6-6.7 m
35 F5.6

figure 6.1

Power output

The power output of a flashgun is referred to as a 'guide number' (GN), which is expressed in metres at ISO 100 (m/ISO 100). The bigger the GN, the greater the range of coverage will be and, at any given flash-to-subject distance, the smaller the lens aperture you can use for increased depth of field. The more power you have, the more versatile the flashgun will be, so go for the best you can afford. A GN of 35–40 (m/ISO 100) is ideal for general use.

If you know the GN of a flashgun, you can calculate the lens aperture required to achieve correct exposure at certain flash-to-subject distances. All you do is divide the guide number into the flash-to-subject distance. For example, if your flashgun has a GN of 40, and your subject is five metres away, the aperture required at ISO 100 is 40/5 = f/8.

Alternatively, divide the GN into the aperture (f/number) to calculate the correct subject distance in metres at ISO 100. For example, if the GN of your flashgun is 32 and your lens is set to f/16, how far away should your subject be? Answer: 32/16 = two metres.

Dedicated control

The vast majority of modern flashguns are said to be 'dedicated'. This means that they have been designed to work in conjunction with the metering system and other controls of specific camera brands or camera models to make flash photography as convenient as possible and ensure perfectly exposed results are obtained in all situations.

The flashguns from marques such as Nikon or Canon are only designed for use with cameras bearing the same name – so a Canon flashgun will not be compatible with a Nikon camera, for example. In the case of independent brands such as Sigma and Metz, the same flashgun model can be used on different makes of camera but you have to specify which camera make you intend to use the flash on, or purchase the correct dedicated 'module' so the flash will give dedicated control when used on your camera.

TTL flash control

The main benefit offered by modern flashguns is dedicated TTL (through-the-lens) exposure control. In plain English this means that they link up with the metering system of the host camera so that all relevant camera settings, such as aperture and shutter speed, are set automatically and the output of the flash itself is carefully controlled so that perfectly exposed images are almost guaranteed. This makes flash photography with the latest digital cameras and dedicated flashguns a piece of cake, even for complete novice photographers.

Flash exposure compensation

This feature is very similar to your camera's exposure compensation facility in that it allows you to override the flash exposure and increase or reduce it to correct error or intentionally create an effect. For example, if you take a picture and the main flash-lit subject comes out too light you could dial in –1 stop of flash exposure compensation so the flash output is reduced and the subject is rendered darker. Similarly, if the flash-lit subject comes out too dark you could do the opposite and dial in, +1 stop so more flash is delivered and the subject comes out lighter.

When you use the flash exposure compensation, the main camera exposure governed by the aperture and shutter speed set is not affected.

Variable power output

With some flash techniques such as fill-in and slow-sync you will not always want your flashgun to fire on full power. This mode allows you to vary the output very precisely, by setting 1/1, 1/2, 1/4, 1/8, 1/16 and so on, often down to 1/64th power.

Slow-sync flash mode

If you use a flashgun in fully automatic mode it usually sets the camera to the correct flash sync speed, such as 1/125 sec. If you are shooting indoors or outdoors in low light, this often means that the flash-lit subject is correctly exposed, but the background comes out too dark because the camera exposure is too brief. By setting your camera or flashgun to slow-sync mode, the aperture required to correctly expose the flash part of the exposure will be set automatically, while a slower shutter speed is also set to record detail in the background by allowing the areas of the picture that are lit by ambient light to be exposed for longer.

This feature can be used for creative techniques such as slow-sync flash (see below). Setting your camera to aperture priority (AV) mode also tends to have the same effect.

Multiple flash/strobe mode

Some flashguns can be programmed to fire a rapid sequence of flash bursts automatically, allowing you to create multiple exposures of moving subjects – such as a golfer taking a swing.

Red-eye reduction mode

Many flashguns have a facility to help reduce the risk of red-eye, which causes a person's eyes to come out looking blood red. This usually works by firing a series of weak pre-flashes before the main flash exposure is made with the aim of making the pupils in your subject's eyes smaller so there is less chance of red-eye being caused. Some work better than others but none is foolproof so take other precautions (see below).

Hotshoe

This is the part of the flashgun which connects to the camera. It includes electrical contacts which ensure flash synchronization occurs and, in the case of dedicated flashguns, that correct exposure is achieved automatically.

Bounce/swivel head

This allows you to angle the head of the gun and bounce the light off a wall, ceiling or reflector to make the light more attractive and prevent red-eye (see page 82).

Diffuser

Some flashguns have a diffuser panel built in. This is basically a piece of translucent plastic that can be placed over the flash tube to soften and spread the light. Accessory diffusers are also available to do the same job.

Zoom head

This allows you to adjust the angle of coverage of the flash to give even illumination for lenses with different focal lengths – usually from 24 to 135 mm. With some of the more sophisticated guns you can dial in the required focal length and the zoom head adjusts automatically. Clip-on diffusers are also available to extend the coverage for lenses as wide as 17 mm, or to extend the range when you need to use a focal length that is longer than the maximum permitted using the built-in zoom head.

LCD (liquid crystal display)

This is the heart of a modern dedicated flashgun as it displays all the information you need – flash mode, ISO, aperture, focal length, flash exposure compensation and so on, allowing you to see at a glance all the flash settings and access them using a series of mode buttons.

Test button

This allows you to fire the flash without taking a picture, to ensure correct exposure will be obtained. This button is also handy when you want to fire the flash several times during a single exposure – when painting with light, for example, or to fire the flash at a specific point during a long exposure.

Flash ready light

This is a small light on the back of the flash that glows one colour when the flash is recycling after it has fired, then another colour to indicate it is charged and ready to fire again.

AF illuminator

Modern flashguns have an AF illuminator which shines a beam of light on your subject when you are shooting in low light so the lens can focus. This makes it possible to shoot in complete darkness.

Sync socket

This is where you plug a sync lead into the flash if you want to use it off the camera and still have full dedicated control.

Wireless sensor

Some flashguns have a special sensor that allows them to be used off-camera without the need for sync leads – when you press the camera's shutter release to take a picture the flashgun is triggered remotely. Several guns can be used together in this way, allowing you to create professional lighting effects.

First and second/rear curtain flash sync

Many modern flashguns can be used for both first curtain and second curtain sync, which relates to when during the exposure the flash is synchronized. If you use your flashgun in first-curtain mode it means that the flash will fire at the very start of the exposure. If you set second/rear curtain sync, the flash will fire at the end of the exposure.

If you are combining flash with a long exposure for slow-sync flash effects, second/rear curtain sync is generally preferred because it means that any blur will trail behind the flashlit subject rather than in front of it, and this will look more natural.

Getting the best from your flashgun

Now that you have invested in a brand new, state-of-the art dedicated flashgun, what next? Well, it's always worth sitting down and reading through the instruction manual to see just what your new toy is capable of, but chances are you will be too impatient for that and want to use it straight away.

The good news is that with a dedicated gun you can do just that – clip it onto your camera's hotshoe, switch both camera and flashgun on and away you go. Provided your camera is set to an auto exposure mode such as programme or aperture priority (AV) the flash will do everything else for you – set the correct flash sync speed, establish which aperture the lens will be set to and ensure that just enough flash is delivered to produce perfectly exposed results. No fiddling around with scales or dials – just point and shoot.

For parties and other special occasions, this level of automation is ideal because you can just fire away. However, using a flashgun on the camera's hotshoe, in fully automatic mode, is the least effective and least creative way to work, so if you want to make the most of it you will need to do better than that. The problem with direct, on-camera flash is that the light is very harsh and unflattering, casting ugly dark shadows, washing out highlights and fine detail and, in the case of people, often causing red-eye (see below). (See DVD 6.01.)

If you want to keep the flash on your camera but improve the light, one option is to buy a clip-on diffuser – usually a white plastic attachment that fits over the flash tube and diffuses the light so shadows are weaker. Another option is to use a bracket that allows you to position the flash higher over the lens. Neither is ideal, though, because the light is still quite harsh.

Bounced flash

The easiest way to improve the quality of light from your flashgun is by bouncing it off a wall, ceiling or reflector. Bouncing softens and spreads the light, thereby weakening shadows, eliminating red-eye and producing much more flattering results. (See DVD 6.02.)

Flashguns with an adjustable head are the most suitable for bouncing because you simply have to tilt or swivel the head. But any flashgun can be used – just take it off the hotshoe, connect it to your camera with a sync lead and point the whole thing towards the bouncing surface. White ceilings and walls are ideal for bouncing if the flash is attached to your camera's hotshoe. Alternatively, take the camera off your flashgun and bounce the light off a reflector which you can position anywhere in relation to your subject. Avoid bouncing the flash off coloured surfaces, though, otherwise the light will take on a colour cast. White is most suitable because it is neutral and highly reflective.

The only downside of bouncing is that you lose about two stops of light due to light being scattered and absorbed, although dedicated flashguns take this loss into account automatically to give you correct exposure. Also, if you find that your subject is a little underexposed, you can simply set the flash exposure compensation facility to +1 and that should solve the problem.

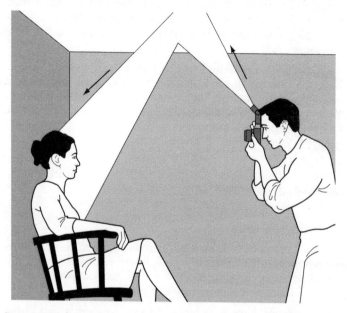

figure 6.2a–c Bouncing flash off a white ceiling will provide far more flattering results than using it direct.

If your flashgun has a twin tube, use it to fill in the weak shadows cast beneath your subject's nose and chin by light from the main bounced flash. Alternatively, place a reflector under your subject's chin to bounce light into the shadows.

You can create attractive side-lighting by bouncing the flash off a wall or reflector next to your subject. If you want to soften the shadows, place a reflector on the opposite side.

Using the flashgun off camera

By using your flashgun off the camera you will have far more control and will be able to produce studio-type lighting effects. All you need is a sync lead that connects the flash and camera together so that the flash fires when you trip the camera's shutter release to take a picture. If you have a dedicated gun, buy a dedicated sync lead so that you can still achieve TTL flash control and ensure perfectly exposed results.

For example, you could position the gun at 90° to your subject to create bold side-lighting. For more even lighting, place a white reflector on the opposite side of your subject so that it bounces light into the shadows. By introducing a second or third flashgun you can create more polished lighting effects, perhaps using one gun to light your subject's face and a second to light the background.

If one flashgun is attached to the camera via a sync lead and others are fitted with slave units, all of them will synchronize when you take the picture. Some of the more expensive dedicated guns even allow cordless TTL flash control so you won't even need slave units.

Portable softbox attachments are also available which fit over your flashgun and turn it into a mini studio-flash. It can then either be used on-camera, fitted to a flash bracket or attached to a remote flash stand and triggered remotely.

Avoiding red-eye

The most common flash problem is red-eye, which is caused by flash bouncing off the blood vessels in your subject's eyes. It is most likely to occur if you use the flashgun on your camera, although avoiding it is relatively straightforward.

Many flashguns have a red-eye reduction mode which either fires a pre-flash or a series of weak flashes before the main flash exposure is made. The idea is that the pre-flash makes the pupils in your subject's eyes much smaller so the risk of red-eye is reduced, although it doesn't always work.

If this is the case, here are some other suggestions:

- Ask your subject not to look straight into the lens.
- Use a flash diffuser to weaken the flash.
- Bounce the flash off a wall, ceiling or reflector.
- Take the flashgun off your camera's hotshoe and either hold it higher above the lens, or use a bracket to do this.

Creative flash techniques

Fill-in flash, slow-sync flash and flash for close-up photography are covered in the relevant subject chapters later on in this book. However, to whet your appetite, here are a couple of other techniques that are worth trying.

Painting with flash

Also known as 'open' flash because you fire the flashgun many times during a single, long exposure, this technique is ideal for illuminating the interior or exterior of a building, different parts of a scene in low light, a monument or tree, and so on.

Whatever the subject or scale of the picture, the best way to use open flash is by taking the flashgun off the camera and firing it manually with the test button, so you can control when it is fired and what it is fired at while the camera's shutter is locked open on B (bulb). This means that the sophisticated features of modern dedicated flashguns become obsolete, so do not worry if you only have a basic manual flashgun – it will be fine. If you do have an automatic or dedicated gun, set it to manual mode and full power so it delivers a consistent amount of light each time you fire the test button. Also, the more powerful the flashgun the better, as it will allow you to work at greater flash-to-subject distances, fire fewer bursts to achieve correct exposure and use a smaller lens aperture for greater depth of field.

To determine correct exposure with a manual gun, divide its guide number (GN) into the lens aperture you are using to find out how far away the flash needs to be from the area you are going to light with it. For example, if you have a flashgun with a GN of 45 and you are using an aperture of f/11, the correct flash-to-subject distance is 45/11 = 4.1 – or four metres when rounded down.

This is correct for ISO 100. If you are shooting at ISO 50 film, open up the lens aperture a stop to f/8 or reduce the flash-to-subject distance to three metres; if you are shooting at ISO 200 film, stop the lens down one f/stop to f/16 in this example or increase the flash-to-subject distance to six metres.

If the area you want to light with the flash is relatively small and accessible, say, a cross in front of a church, then you should be able to provide sufficient illumination in a single flash burst. With your camera on a tripod and the picture composed, all you do is trip the camera's shutter, lock it open on bulb (B) with a cable release, walk up to the area you need to illuminate so you are roughly the correct distance away to achieve an accurate exposure, and fire the flashgun with the test button.

If you cannot get close enough to light your subject with a single burst you will have to fire the flash more than once to build up the light on it. For example, if the correct flash-to-subject distance is two metres and you can only get within three metres, you will need to fire the flash twice. If you are four metres away you will need to fire it four times, and if you are five metres away you will need to fire it six times and so on. This is all to do with the inverse square law, which we needn't go into.

In situations where the area you want to light is too great for a single flash burst due to the flashgun's limited coverage, such as the front of a building or a dark interior, you have no choice but to use multiple flash bursts. You will also need to walk around your subject and fire the flash at different areas so you can gradually light the whole subject – or parts of it that need lighting.

This isn't as difficult as it sounds.

1 Mount your camera on a tripod and compose the picture, ideally using a wide-angle lens so you do not have to walk too far to reach the areas that will be lit by the flash.

2 Set your lens aperture to f/11 or f/16, the shutter to bulb (B) and your flashgun to manual and full power. Make sure you have a spare set of batteries for the flash in your pocket, and ideally use two flashguns so you can fire one while the other is re-charging in order to save time. Better still, take a friend along so you can both work on different areas and reduce the time it takes to illuminate your chosen subject.

3 Plan how you are going to light your subject – where to start, how many flash bursts you will need for certain areas that are further away, for example, a church tower, if you are going to use filters on the flash at any point to colour the light and so on.

4 Once levels have dropped sufficiently so you can lock the shutter open for a couple of minutes, trip the camera's shutter and lock it open on bulb with the cable release. Now head towards your subject and start firing the flash to illuminate it. This is where two guns will come in handy – especially if you need to use lots of flash bursts. Keep moving around and do not stand between the camera and the flashgun, otherwise your ghostly outline will record on the picture.

5 Once you feel that you have fired enough flash bursts to light your subject, go back to the camera and close the shutter to end the exposure. (See DVD 6.03 and 6.04.)

Multiple flash

Like open flash explained above, multiple flash involves firing your flashgun more than once during a single long exposure.

However, instead of doing this to illuminate a large area, you use the repeated flash bursts to capture several images of your subject on a single frame of film.

This technique can be used in a number of ways. If you have a flashgun with a strobe setting that can fire several times automatically, you can produce multiple exposures of fast-moving subjects, such as a hammer striking an egg or a person leaping through the air. Some flashguns can be programmed to fire up to 50 flashes over a set period of time so you can control the effect obtained and decide how many images you want to record.

Normal flashguns can also be combined with a long exposure and fired several times to record a repeated image of the same subject – such as a person walking towards the camera outdoors at night or in a darkened room. As with open flash, this is achieved by locking your camera's shutter open on bulb then firing the flashgun by pressing the test button each time your subject changes position. You also calculate correct exposure in the same way and use the flashgun set to manual mode.

It takes longer to complete a shot because you will have to wait for the gun to re-charge after each flash burst, but if you plan the picture carefully, great results are still possible.

Filtered flash

Placing coloured filters and gels over your flashgun is a great way to create unusual lighting effects and add a creative twist to pictures of everyday subjects. Using filters on a flashgun instead of over your lens is interesting because it means that only the areas lit by the flash will take on the colour of the filter, so you can colour the foreground or one element in a scene while leaving the rest unchanged – such as an orange filter used to light a tree in a picture taken at dusk, so it stands out against the cooler colours in the background. (See DVD 6.05.)

A development of this idea is to use one filter on your flashgun and another on the camera lens. If those filters are complementary colours, one will cancel the other out so the area lit by the flash looks normal while the rest of the scene takes on a colour cast. The best filters for this are the blue 80 series and orange 85 series, normally used to balance colour casts. If you place a blue 80B on your lens, the whole scene will look blue. However, if you then place an orange 85B on your flashgun, it will cancel out the blue cast so any areas lit by the flash will look natural against a blue background. By using the orange filter on the lens and the blue filter on the flash, the opposite happens and you get an orange background.

A variation of this is to use tungsten-balanced film in daylight with an orange 85B filter on the flashgun – a technique often used by fashion photographers. The result will be that all areas lit by daylight come out blue, because tungsten-balanced film is intended for use in warmer tungsten lighting, while the flash lit areas look natural because the flash has been warmed up by the orange filter.

You can achieve the same effect with a digital camera by adjusting the white balance (WB) setting. If you set WB to tungsten, for example, and shoot in daylight, the image will come out very blue – but if you then use flash with an orange filter over it, any areas lit by the flash will look natural. Try different WB settings with different colour filters and see what happens.

All three techniques can be very hit-and-miss, but if you are shooting digitally you can see how the first attempt turns out then re-shoot if necessary, using more or less flash bursts to get the effect just right.

One thing is certain – you will be amazed by the effects that are possible.

Flashgun tips

- Although flash can help you take pictures in tricky situations, and can be used to create eye-catching effects, do not be tempted to overuse it.
- Flash generally kills the mood of available light so in most situations you are better increasing the ISO setting on your camera or loading faster film if you need to shoot handheld, or mounting your camera on a tripod so you can safely use longer exposures.
- Remember that flash is banned in many places, such as inside stately homes, museums, art galleries and so on. If you see a 'No Flash' sign, do as it says.
- Flash can distract people, so take care if you are using it at sporting events where the consequences could be dangerous.
- Flash will draw attention to you, so if you are trying to shoot discretely, leave the flash in your backpack.

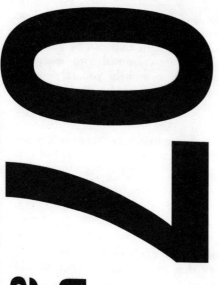

07 useful accessories

In this chapter you will learn:
- how to choose a tripod
- about alternative camera supports
- about bags and cases
- about cleaning a digital sensor.

Like it or not, photography is a gadget-driven hobby and no matter how much equipment you buy as an enthusiast, there will always be a long list of other items that can be added to your wish list. Whole catalogues are crammed with 'essential' gizmos and accessories that promise to help you take better pictures and tempt you to part with your hard-earned cash, and since digital photography took off the range of accessories available has exploded.

Of course, as with all hobbies, some items are more useful than others and many are downright unnecessary, so the aim of this chapter is to guide you through the essential accessories that every photographer needs.

Tripods

Although they may be a nuisance to carry around everywhere, tripods are a vital accessory that every photographer should own because they serve two important purposes.

First, they keep your camera rock-steady so you do not have to worry about slow shutter speeds causing shaky pictures. This means you can use slow film or low ISO settings for optimum image quality, stop your lenses down to small apertures to maximize depth of field and take pictures in low light, such as outdoors at night or inside dimly lit interiors. In other words, you do not have to compromise the quality of your pictures to ensure that they come out sharp.

Second, tripods slow down the whole picture-taking process. They force you to think more about each photograph you take and to spend more time perfecting the composition. They also make it easier to work with ND graduate filter and this results in better pictures.

The ideal is to find a model that is strong enough to keep your camera and longest lens steady, but compact and light enough to carry all day. If you only use 35 mm film or digital equipment and lenses up to, say, an 80–200 mm f/2.8 zoom, then a model weighing around 1.5 kg with a maximum load capability of 4–6 kg will be more than adequate. For medium- and large-format systems, panoramic rollfilm cameras and SLRs with longer lenses, you will need something more substantial, but there are tripods weighing in at around 2–2.5 kg with a load capacity of 6–8 kg that will do the job perfectly well.

The first step in achieving this is to stick with reputable professional brand names such as Manfrotto, Gitzo or Benbo.

You may pay more than buying a budget model from your local camera shop, but what you end up with will be a robust tripod that should last a lifetime and be reliable in all situations.

Here are a few important factors to consider when choosing a tripod:

- Make sure the leg locks are quick to operate, strong when locked, but easy to release. Quick-action locks are excellent, whereas screw-thread locks can stick with heavy use.
- The tripod should be able to extend to eye level without needing to use the centre column, which is one of the weakest parts of the tripod.
- Centre bracing for the legs increases stability but at the same time can be restrictive because on uneven ground you need to be able to adjust each leg independently.
- Check that you can adjust the angle of each leg independently.
- Check the low-level capability of the tripod – sometimes you may need to get close to the ground.
- Sealed feet are handy for use in wet and boggy ground – rubber feet are also the best in terms of grip.

The most important part of a tripod, but the one that tends to be given least thought, is the head. The world's strongest tripod will be worse than useless if you top it with an undersized and flimsy head. Do not automatically buy a complete tripod, because the head you get with it will not always be the best, and check out a variety of different models if you are unsure about which type to buy.

The two main types to choose from are traditional pan-and-tilt or ball and socket. The latter are more compact and lightweight because you do not have three control arms sticking out, plus they are quicker to use because the whole head is locked with a single action. Pan-and-tilt heads do allow more precise control, however, so it is down to what your priorities are.

A compromise between the two is a geared head that has the same controls as a pan-and-tilt head but uses geared knobs rather than arms, so it is compact like a ball head but offers the precision of a pan-and-tilt head.

Something else to consider is the material the tripod is made from. Traditionally, tripods have been fashioned from aluminium which is relatively light but also strong. However, in recent years, carbon fibre tripods have become popular because they claim to offer the same stability as alloy models for 25–40 per cent less weight.

There is no denying the benefits of carbon fibre – it is very strong and sturdy, yet light at the same time, plus it feels much nicer in cold weather – unlike alloy, which freezes your fingers (put fabric tape or pipe insulation around the legs to avoid this). But you pay a premium for this weight saving because they cost two, or even three times more than a comparable alloy model. Ultimately, the type you buy will be governed by how much you can afford to spend.

Other supports

Although a tripod provides the best form of support, there are other items available that can be used to keep your camera steady.

A **monopod** is ideal for supporting long lenses while still giving you the freedom to move around, or for preventing camera shake in low light. If you apply downward pressure to increase stability and use your body to provide extra support it is safe to use shutter speeds down to 1/4 or 1/2 sec. Sports photographers favour monopods because they help to support the weight of long and heavy telephoto lenses but offer freedom of movement to follow the action and use techniques such as panning.

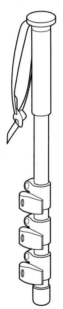

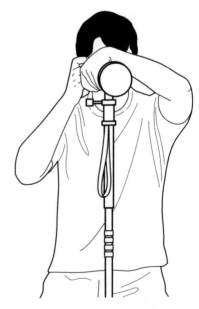

figure 7.1a Monopod   **7.1b** Monopod in use

Pocket or table-top tripods come in handy if you need to travel very light but know some kind of support will be required. Just look for a convenient wall, gate post, table, tree stump or any other flat surface it can be rested on to provide the necessary height. The majority of models fold down to just a few inches and can literally be carried in a pocket or handbag – though they are mainly designed to support small cameras such as digital compacts rather than heavy SLRs.

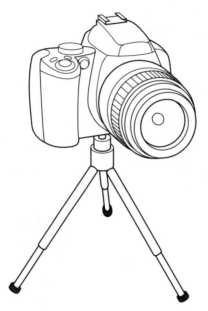

figure 7.2 Pocket tripod

If you are a keen nature photographer, a **beanbag** will prove invaluable for turning gateposts, window frames, car bonnets, walls and pillar boxes into makeshift supports by moulding to the shape of your camera to keep it perfectly still.

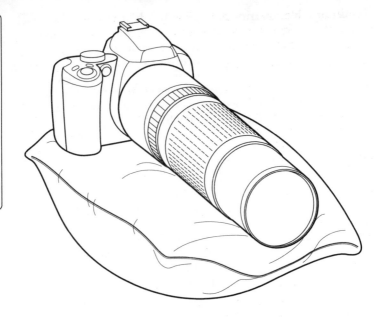

figure 7.3 Beanbag

Panoramic adaptors

Many digital camera users produce panoramic images by shooting a sequence of frames then 'stitching' them together digitally (see page 200). Modern software, such as the latest versions of Photoshop, is able to merge the images and produce perfect results with no sign of a join between frames. It is quick and easy – providing you set up your camera correctly before shooting commences. The key is to get the camera level and square so that as you progressively move the camera after each frame, it stays in line – even if you intend to create a full 360° stitch. If the camera is not set up properly then it may be difficult to merge the images and you will have to crop quite a lot off the top and bottom of the final stitch to level up the edges of the photograph.

With patience it is possible to level your camera using simple spirit levels either on the camera or on the tripod head. However, if you intend to do a lot of panoramic stitching a better option is a levelling base which fits between the tripod legs and head and allows you to level the head with precision even if the tripod itself is not perfectly level. By using this type of accessory, once the tripod head is level you can rotate it through 360° and it will stay in line.

The next accessory to consider is the **nodal point adaptor**.

If you mount your camera on a tripod in the usual way – using the tripod bush on the camera's base plate – as you rotate the camera between frames a phenomenon known as Parallax error occurs where the relationship between features that are close to the camera and others further away changes. Parallax error can make it tricky to stitch images accurately – though modern stitching software is very good at correcting any error.

If you want to eliminate parallax error at the taking stage, you need to position the camera on your tripod so that it rotates on its optical centre or 'nodal point'. There are numerous brackets available for this purpose, and they also help you to locate the nodal point for each lens as its position does differ from lens to lens.

To find the nodal point you need to adjust the position of the camera on the bracket until the relationship between near and far elements remains the same when you pan the camera between frames. Digital cameras make it easy to do this because you can shoot two frames that overlap by 30–40 per cent, check them on the preview screen, and if parallax error can be detected, adjust the camera again, shoot two more overlapping frames, and so on until parallax error is eliminated. You only need to run this test once because once you have established the position of the nodal point for each lens in your system, setting up the camera becomes much quicker.

Remote releases

If you are taking pictures with your camera on a tripod, it is a good idea to trip the shutter using a cable or remote release so you do not have to physically press the shutter button and risk camera shake. This is especially important when using long telephoto or zoom lenses as any vibration in the camera will be magnified, making the slightest camera shake obvious in the final image.

Basic electronic releases attach to your camera via a lead and have a button that fires the shutter and that can also be locked for time exposures so you do not have to hold it down for long periods. More expensive models also have timer settings so you can programme them to take shots at specific intervals – ideal for time-lapse photography – while infrared releases are cordless and fire the shutter using an infrared beam.

An alternative to using a remote release is to set the self-timer on your camera so there is a delay of several seconds between pressing the shutter release button and the shutter actually opening to make the exposure. This is usually long enough for the camera to settle down and any vibrations to cease before the exposure is made.

Spirit level

A small spirit level slotted onto your camera's hotshoe will show if the camera is perfectly level. This inexpensive accessory is ideal for architectural photography as it helps to avoid converging verticals, and ensures the horizon is truly horizontal in your landscapes so you do not end up having to crop the image. Many tripods also have a spirit level built into the head for this purpose.

Lens hoods

If you shoot into the sun or point your camera in the general direction of any bright light source, there is a high risk that flare will be caused by light glancing across the front element of the lens, any filters on the lens, and also stray light finding its way inside the lens. Flare usually appears as ghostly streaks or patches on the image. It can also add a haze across the whole image which reduces contrast and colour saturation.

To get rid of flare you need to shield the front of your lens to keep the light off it. This is best done using a purpose-made lens hood. Many lenses come supplied with a hood, though accessory hoods are also available. If you use a filter holder on your lens, you will need to buy a hood that clips to the front of the holder. These are usually of a concertina design so you can adapt them to suit different lenses – wide-angle lenses require a shallower hood otherwise it will encroach on the field of view and cause vignetting, whereas telephoto and telezoom lenses have a much narrower field of view so the hood can be much deeper.

An alternative to the traditional lens hood is to use some kind of shade to prevent stray light reaching the lens. Purpose-made shades are available, although a strategically placed hand or a piece of black card will work just as well.

Flare is usually obvious if you look through the viewfinder of an SLR camera, so you will know if the shade is doing its job and if it isn't you can adjust it until all signs of flare have gone. Digital camera users can also take a test shot and look at it on the preview screen just to be doubly sure.

Bags and cases

Photographic bags and cases are designed to serve three main functions: to make carrying your equipment as easy and comfortable as possible; to protect your equipment from damage and to provide easy access to the contents. When choosing one you will also need to consider the amount of equipment you need to carry and the type of conditions you expect to take pictures in.

Shoulder bags were traditionally the main choice among photographers, but in the last decade or so, photographic backpacks have become much more popular, for three main reasons:

1 They distribute the weight of the contents evenly across you back, which makes them more comfortable to carry for long periods or over long distances.

2 They are safer on uneven ground because both hands remain free and it is therefore much easier to keep your balance. Shoulder bags put all the weight on one side of your body, making you unbalanced. Prolonged use of heavy shoulder bags can also lead to back pain because there is a natural tendency to try to correct this imbalance by leaning to one side while walking.

3 They are much more versatile and capacious than shoulder bags so you can organize your equipment more sensibly and keep everything safe from impact and the elements.

The main manufacturers of photo backpacks are Lowepro, Tamrac and Kata – and they all produce a range of packs in different sizes and with different features to suit all subjects, needs and environment.

There are totally waterproof packs available that will float if dropped in water and keep the contents safe and dry – ideal if you often shoot from boats or work in wet environments. Some models have integral wheels so they can be pulled along the ground rather than carried, while others have a large pocket for a laptop computer – something many photographers need on location in this digital age.

In terms of size, go for a pack that is big enough to carry everything you generally need while on location, but has enough free space to accommodate an extra lens or two, just in case you expand your system. At the same time, do not go for one that is so big that you either fill it and then regret carrying all the weight, or you can't fill it and the contents tend to rattle around inside. Also, if you travel a lot, make sure the pack you buy does not exceed the maximum permitted size for hand luggage, otherwise you will encounter problems when checking-in for flights.

The only real downside of photo backpacks is that you need to remove the whole pack from your back and open it to access the contents. This is fine when shooting subjects such as landscapes where you tend to spend long periods in one place, but if you are shooting on the move, they are impractical. One alternative you could go for is a modular system that uses cases and pouches fitted to a belt or harness, so you can access everything you need – usually just lenses and film/memory cards while on the move and without having to put anything down. Another is to work with two small shoulder bags, placed over your head so the straps cross on your chest and you have one by each hip. That way you will be balanced, both hands will be free and you can access the contents of each bag with ease.

Finally, hard cases made from aluminium or high impact plastics come into their own when optimum protection is required, but they are unsuitable for carrying around. Travel and location photographers often use hard cases to hold their full system of equipment, so it is not damaged in transit, but then they transfer the required items to a backpack or shoulder bag when they arrive on location.

Cleaning kit

If you are out in the field it is worth carrying some basic items that will enable you to clean your cameras, lenses and filters.

Here are some suggestions of what to include.

- A stiff brush so you can remove sand, dust and dirt from camera bodies and lens barrels.

- One or two microfibre clothes that are reserved to wipe dirt, greasy marks and moisture from camera bodies and lens barrels.

- Additional microfibre cloth that is only used for optical surfaces – to wipe the front and rear elements of your lenses when necessary and also to clean filters. Make sure these cloths are stored in a plastic box or polythene bag to keep them clean as it only takes a few particles of grit to cause scratches when you wipe a lens or filter.

- A fine anti-static brush that you can use to remove dust and hairs from optical surfaces.

- A blower to remove dust and debris from lenses and filters. It can also be used to remove debris from the focusing screen and reflex mirror of non-digital cameras, but should never be used on the inside of a digital camera as it will blow dust straight onto the sensor.

- It is also a good ideal to carry a few large polythene bags so you can use them to cover your camera and lens if you are caught out in rain or snow. This will save time drying and cleaning everything later.

Sensor cleaning

One of the biggest problems with digital SLRs is that if any dust or debris gets inside the camera and onto the sensor, it will appear in every picture and you will have to spend time at the computer carefully removing every little black spec.

Changing lenses is usually the main culprit because when you remove a lens it leaves the sensor exposed. Some zoom lenses also 'suck in' dust when you use the push-pull action to adjust focal length, and no matter how hard you try, eventually black marks will appear on your pictures and the only solution is to remove them from the sensor.

There are professional sensor-cleaning services available – at a price – so if for some reason you end up with a lot of debris on your sensor this may be your best bet. However, on a day-to-day basis it is relatively straightforward to clean your own sensor and there is a whole range of products available to help you do that.

For dust, there are numerous different sensor brushes available that use ultra-fine bristles and a low static charge so that when you draw them across the sensor, dust is sucked into the brush. Spinning the brush for a few seconds prior to cleaning is usually all that is required to charge the bristles. The brush is then drawn once across the sensor to pick up the dust then spun again to remove that dust. This process can be repeated two or three times if necessary, though once is usually sufficient.

For marks and smears that cannot be removed with a brush, small swabs or wipes moistened with a weak solvent are required. Again, there are various brands available specifically for cleaning camera sensors. Never try to improvise and make your own as you could cause even greater problems and damage the sensor for good.

To aid sensor cleaning you could also invest in a sensor lupe, which is basically a magnifier that allows you to examine the sensor in detail and see exactly where the offending marks are.

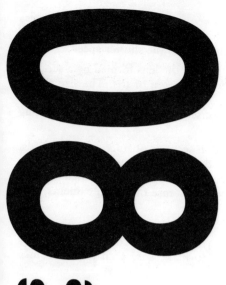

08

apertures and shutter speeds

In this chapter you will learn:
- about the relationship between lens apertures and f/numbers
- about depth of field
- about choosing the right shutter speed
- how to choose effective aperture and shutter speed combinations.

Whenever you take a photograph, two important camera controls are used to ensure that correct exposure is achieved. These variables are the aperture and the shutter speed.

The aperture is basically a hole in the lens formed by a series of metal blades, known as the diaphragm or iris. The size of this hole can be varied using a series of f/numbers or f/stops, allowing you to control precisely the amount of light passing through the lens.

The shutter speed, measured in seconds or fractions of seconds, indicates the period of time the camera's shutter stays open for so that light passing through the lens aperture can reach the film in the camera, or its sensor in the case of digital cameras, and make an exposure.

As well as helping you achieve correct exposure, apertures and shutter speeds also give you creative control over your photography and allow you to make sure each picture comes out exactly as you planned.

Making the most of the lens aperture

As we briefly discussed in Chapter 02, f/numbers follow a set sequence which is found on all lenses. A typical f/number or aperture scale on a 50 mm standard lens would be as follows: f/1.8, f/2, f/2.8, f/4, f/5.6, f/8, f/11 and f/16. The smaller the number is, the larger the aperture, and vice versa. The first f/number in the scale is known as the 'maximum' aperture, and the last is known as the 'minimum' aperture.

Not all lenses have the same maximum and minimum apertures. The scale on a typical 70–200 mm zoom lens starts at f/4.5 or f/5.6 and goes down to f/22 or even f/32, for example, while a 'fast' 70–200 mm zoom lens will have a maximum aperture of f/2.8. Other than that they are identical, so f/8 on a 50 mm lens will admit exactly the same amount of light to the film as f/8 on a 24–70 mm zoom or a 600 mm telephoto lens.

The main task apertures perform other than admitting light is to help determine how much of your picture comes out sharply focused and how much does not. This 'zone' of sharp focus is called the 'depth of field', and knowing how to control it is vital if you want to get the most from your photography.

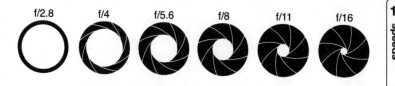

figure 8.1 The aperture range on a typical 50 mm standard lens is shown above. This range varies – on most zooms the maximum aperture is only f/4 or f/5.6, while on many lenses the minimum aperture is f/22 or even f/32.

Depth of field

Whenever you take a picture an area extending in front of and behind the point you focus on will also come out sharp. This area is the depth of field, and its size varies depending upon three things:

1 *The aperture set on the lens* – The smaller the aperture, the greater the depth of field. If you take a picture using an aperture of f/16, for example, much more of the scene will come out sharp than if you use a large aperture such as f/4 or f/2.8

2 *The focal length of the lens* – The shorter the focal length, the greater the depth of field is at any given aperture. For example, a 50 mm lens will give far more depth of field when set to f/8 than a 300 mm telephoto lens set to f/8, while a 24 mm wide-angle lens set to f/8 will give far more depth of field than a 50 mm lens.

3 *The distance between the camera and subject* – The further away you focus the lens, the greater the depth of field for any given focal length and aperture. For example, if you use a 50 mm lens set to f/8, depth of field will be greater if you focus that lens on ten metres than it will if you focused on one metre.

Taking these three points into account, if you want minimal depth of field so your main subject stands out and everything else if thrown out of focus, use a telephoto lens set to a wide aperture such as f/4 and keep your subject relatively close to the camera – this is usual practice in portraiture. (See DVD 8.01.) Conversely, if you want to keep everything sharply focused from the immediate foreground to infinity, as you would when shooting landscapes or architecture, use a wide-angle lens set to a small aperture such as f/16 or f/12. (See DVD 8.02.)

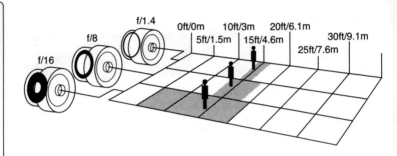

figure 8.2 This illustration shows how using different lens apertures determines how much of the scene either side of your main subject will come out sharp.

Assessing depth of field

Of course, it is no use just knowing how to make depth of field large or small. You also need to be able to gauge roughly what is going to be in and out of focus when you use a certain lens/aperture combination. There are two ways of doing this:

1 *Using the stopdown preview* – The stopdown preview, which is activated by a button on the camera or lens, closes the lens diaphragm down to the f/number set. By looking through the viewfinder you can then get a fair indication of what will and won't be in focus, although at small apertures such as f/16 and f/22 the viewfinder image goes quite dark and you need to keep your eye to the viewfinder for maybe 20 seconds until it adapts to the dark image. This is not a particularly effective way of assessing depth of field.

2 *Using the depth of field scale* – Some lenses – mainly fixed focal length or 'prime' lenses – have a depth-of-field scale on the lens barrel. To use it, focus on your subject, and find the f/number the lens is set to on either side of the depth-of-field scale and read off the distances opposite them – these are the nearest and furthest points of sharp focus at that aperture. In the illustration below, for example, you can see that with the lens focused on three metres, depth of field extends from around two metres to ten metres at f/16.

Unfortunately, the majority of photographers today tend to use zoom lenses and they lack useful depth-of-field scales making it difficult to assess depth of field in this way. Instead, you will need to reply on experience. (See DVD 8.03.)

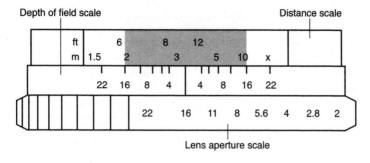

Depth of field scale   Distance scale

Lens aperture scale

figure 8.3

Maximizing depth of field

The next step is knowing how to achieve maximum depth of field at the aperture your lens is set to. This is necessary when photographing subjects such as landscapes and architecture if you want everything in the scene to come out sharp from foreground to infinity.

There is an old theory that depth of field extends roughly twice as far behind the point you focus on as it does in front, so if your lens is set to a small aperture, such as f/16, and you focus one-third of the way into the scene you should be okay. Similarly, with wide-angle lenses which give extensive depth of field, if you step the aperture down to f/22 and focus on infinity, the chances are everything in the scene will record in sharp focus. Unfortunately, neither method is foolproof so if you want to be sure of achieving front-to-back sharpness, a technique known as 'hyperfocal focusing' can be employed.

It works like this. Depth of field extends both in front of and behind the point you focus on, so if you focus on infinity some of it will be wasted because your lens cannot focus beyond infinity. To maximize depth of field you therefore need to focus it somewhere *between* the nearest point you want to record in sharp focus and infinity.

To find where this distance is, focus the lens on infinity then check the depth-of-field scale to find the nearest point of sharp focus at the aperture set. This distance is known as the 'hyperfocal distance'. By re-focusing the lens on the hyperfocal distance, depth of field will now extend from *half* the hyperfocal distance to infinity, as shown below.

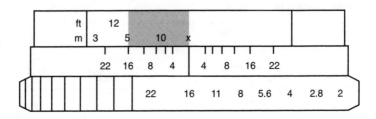

figure 8.4 With the lens focused on infinity, depth of field extends back to five metres at f/16, which is the hyperfocal distance.

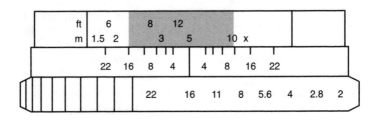

figure 8.5 By focusing the lens on five metres, the hyperfocal distance, depth of field now extends from two-and-a-half metres to infinity at the same aperture.

The downside of this technique is that it relies on your lens having a depth-of-field scale, but as we have already established, modern zoom lenses for digital SLRs tend not to have decent scales. Fortunately, all is not lost because the hyperfocal distance can be calculated using the following formula:

Hyperfocal distance = F (squared)/(fxc) where:

F = lens focal length in mm

f = f/number lens is set to

c = Circle of confusion (a constant value is used for Circle of confusion – 0.036 for 35 mm format and 35 mm-type digital SLR lenses)

For example, if you are using a 28 mm lens set to f/16, the hyperfocal distance is 28 × 28/(16 × 0.036)

$$= 784/0.576$$

$$= 1.361 \text{ m, rounded up to } 1.4 \text{ m}$$

By focusing the lens on roughly 1.4 m, depth of field will extend from half that distance (0.7 m) to infinity.

Making this calculation every time you take a photograph is impractical, so to save you the bother, here is a chart showing the hyperfocal distances for lenses from 17 mm to 200mm and apertures from f/11 to f/32.

Lens focal length (mm)

Aperture	17 mm	20 mm	24 mm	28 mm	35 mm	50 mm	70 mm	100 mm	200 mm
(f/stop) f/8	1.0 m	1.4 m	2.0 m	2.8 m	4.2 m	8.5 m	17 m	35 m	140 m
f/11	0.75 m	1.0 m	1.5 m	2.0 m	3.0 m	6.3 m	12.3 m	25 m	100 m
f/16	0.5 m	0.7 m	1.0 m	1.4 m	2.1 m	4.3 m	8.5 m	17.5 m	70 m
f/22	0.35 m	0.5 m	0.7 m	1.0 m	1.5 m	3.1 m	6.2 m	12.5 m	50 m
f/32	0.25 m	0.35 m	0.5 m	0.7 m	1.0 m	2.2 m	4.2 m	8.5 m	35 m

To use the chart, simply find the focal length you are using along the top, the aperture you want to use down the side, then read across to find the hyperfocal distance. For example, if you are using a 24 mm lens set to f/22, the hyperfocal distance is 0.7 m. By focusing the lens on 0.7 m, depth of field will extend from half the hyperfocal distance (0.35 m) to infinity. To check this is sufficient, focus on the nearest point you want to include in the picture then look at the distance scale on the lens barrel to see how far away that point is. If it is more than the nearest point of sharp focus you have just determined, you can fire away safe in the knowledge that you will get front-to-back sharpness. If it is less than the nearest point of sharp focus, there is a danger that the immediate foreground will not be sharp, so refer back to the table and stop your lens down to a smaller aperture.

These values apply for zoom lenses set to the relevant focal lengths, as well as prime (fixed focal length) lenses.

If you use a digital SLR that does not have a full-frame sensor, the focal length you need to refer to is the focal length after applying the magnification factor (mf). So, if the mf is 1.4 and you are using a zoom lens set to 20 mm, the focal length you need to refer to on the chart is 20 × 1.4 = 28 mm.

Why not copy the table onto a sheet of white card, or photocopy this page, then slip it into a clear plastic wallet so you can refer to it in the field? Achieving front-to-back sharpness will never be a problem again. (See DVD 8.04.)

Making the most of shutter speeds

As well as determining how long light passing through the lens aperture is admitted to the film or sensor inside your camera, the shutter speed also controls the amount of blur/sharpness recorded in every picture you take, because the longer the shutter is left open for the more likelihood there is of subject or camera movement recording.

The typical shutter speed range found on 35 mm and digital SLRs today is usually 30–l/4000 sec, which is more than adequate for all subjects. In addition, your camera will most likely have a 'B' setting (Bulb). This allows you to hold the shutter open for as long as you like so you can take pictures at exposure times longer than the automated shutter speed range is capable of – when shooting the sky at night, for example.

Choosing the right speed

For totally static subjects such as buildings, landscapes and still lifes it does not really matter what shutter speed you use, fast or slow. This frees you to concentrate on controlling depth of field by choosing the best aperture, then using whatever shutter speed is required to give a correct exposure.

For general use, 1/125 sec is a decent speed to aim for. Outdoors, in average weather conditions at ISO 100, 1/125 sec will give you an aperture around f/11 which will provide sufficient depth of field for most subjects, and if you are not using a heavy lens, camera shake won't be a problem. (See DVD 8.05.)

However, once you start photographing moving subjects your choice of shutter speed becomes very important because if you use one that is too slow you will end up with a blurred result. (See DVD 8.06.) One way to solve this dilemma is by using the fastest shutter speed your camera has, but this will not always be possible so you need to be aware of the minimum shutter speeds required to freeze different subjects. (See DVD 8.07.)

This will depend upon three factors:

1 The speed your subject is moving.
2 The direction it is travelling in relation to the camera.
3 How big it is in the viewfinder.

If your subject is travelling head on or diagonally, you can freeze it with a slower shutter speed than if your subject is travelling across your path. Similarly, a subject that is small in the frame can also be frozen using a slower shutter speed than if it fills the frame.

Below is a table of the minimum shutter speeds required to freeze various common subjects. If in doubt, use 1/1000 sec, which is fast enough to freeze most moving subjects.

	Full frame	Half frame	45° to camera	Head-on
Person walking (3 mph)	1/250 sec	1/125 sec	1/125 sec	1/60 sec
Person running (10 mph)	1/500 sec	1/250 sec	1/250 sec	1/125 sec
Cyclist (25 mph)	1/1000 sec	1/500 sec	1/500 sec	1/250 sec
Car or motorbike (40 mph)	1/2000 sec	1/1000 sec	1/1000 sec	1/500 sec
Car or motorbike (70 mph)	1/4000 sec	1/2000 sec	1/2000 sec	1/1000 sec

If you find yourself in a situation where the fastest shutter speed you can use is not fast enough, even with your lens set to its widest (maximum) aperture, all you need to do is increase the ISO setting on your digital camera (or load a faster roll of film). For example, if your camera sets 1/125 sec at ISO 100, increasing the ISO to 400 will allow you to shoot at 1/500 sec at the same aperture.

Slowly does it

Do not always be too eager to set fast shutter speeds – using a slower speed to intentionally blur moving subjects can lead to superb pictures. A common example of this is when photographing rivers and waterfalls. Instead of freezing it, most photographers prefer to mount their camera on a tripod and use a shutter speed of one second or more, so the flowing water records as a graceful, milky blur. This feeling of movement is emphasized even more because the rocks, trees and hills in the shot remain perfectly still, so they come out sharp. (See DVD 8.08.)

You can use a similar approach on all kinds of subjects: crowds of commuters rushing off a train, shoppers hurrying around town, runners at the start of a marathon, spinning fairground rides, a show jumper clearing a fence and so on. Using blur in this way adds a powerful sense of motion to your pictures that would be lost if you froze all signs of movement. Experiment with a variety of shutter speeds from about 1/30 sec down. The slower the speed, the more blur you will get. Techniques such as panning (see page 300) and slow-sync flash (see page 302) can also be used with slow shutter speeds when photographing moving subjects. (See DVD 8.09.)

If you cannot manage to set a shutter speed that is slow enough, even with your lens stopped down to its smallest aperture, there are two things you can do. Reducing the ISO or switching to a slower film may do the trick. If you are getting 1/15 sec at ISO 200 film, for example, changing to ISO 50 will give you 1/4 sec because it is three stops slower.

Alternatively, you can use a neutral density (ND) filter. ND filters work by reducing the amount of light passing through the lens without changing the colours in the scene. Various strengths are available, but a two-stop (0.6) or three-stop (0.9) version should be strong enough in most situations (see Chapter 06).

Controlling the shutter speed set

Once you have chosen which shutter speed you need to use there are various ways of making sure the camera sets it, depending upon the type of exposure modes featured (see pages 114–115 for more information on exposure modes). The easiest way is by switching to *shutter priority mode*, where you set the shutter speed and the camera automatically sets the aperture required to give correct exposure. The opposite happens in *aperture priority mode*, but you can obtain the shutter speed you want simply by adjusting the lens aperture.

In *program mode* both the aperture and shutter speed are set automatically by the camera then displayed in the viewfinder or LCD panel. If your camera has a *program shift* facility you can use it to adjust the aperture and shutter speed combination until you have the desired shutter speed.

If all else fails, revert back to *manual mode* and set both the aperture and shutter speed yourself.

Clever combinations

Throughout this chapter I have explained the significance of apertures and shutter speeds in isolation – apertures to control depth of field and shutter speeds to control sharpness/blur. Every time you take a picture, however, you will be using a combination of both, so the decision you have to make is which one should be given priority over the other.

With sport and action, where you are dealing with moving subjects, it is common practice to concentrate on choosing the right shutter speed and leaving the aperture to its own devices – fast shutter speeds and wide apertures tend to be the popular combination used. But with landscape, architecture, still life and, to a certain extent, people photography, the opposite applies – you concentrate on setting the right aperture to control depth of field and do not worry about the shutter speed.

In between these extremes are those situations where neither is particularly important – often you will find a shutter speed of 1/125 sec and an aperture of f/8 are perfectly adequate for your needs. But no matter what your subject is you should always think carefully about the aperture and shutter speed combination chosen, because creatively it puts all sorts of amazing effects at your fingertips, and it seems a great shame to have a complete range at your disposal if you only make use of the few in the middle. (See DVD 8.10.)

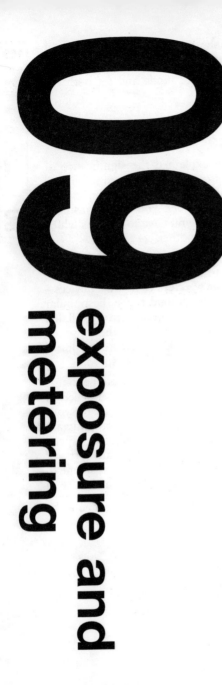

09

exposure and metering

In this chapter you will learn:
- how exposure works
- about exposure modes and metering patterns
- how to cope with tricky light
- how to assess exposure with a digital camera.

Exposure refers to the amount of light which is required by the film or digital sensor in your camera to record an acceptable image. Provide just enough light and you will produce a correctly exposed picture which faithfully records the scene before you. But give it too much or too little light and the picture will either be too light or too dark.

In what now seems like the dim and distant past, though in truth we are only looking at 30–40 years ago, determining the 'correct' exposure tended to be a rather time-consuming affair which demanded much knowledge – one reason why fewer people became interested in photography.

Today, however, the whole process is much simpler. Cameras have integral metering systems which use microchip technology to assess and measure the light with an amazing degree of accuracy, making it easier than ever before to take perfectly exposed photographs. Additionally, now that digital cameras are so widespread, even if the camera gets the exposure wrong, you can correct any error – within reason – once the image is downloaded onto your computer.

That is not to say you should not learn about exposure theory, of course. Being able to take correctly exposed photographs simply by pointing and shooting may be handy when you first become interested in photography, but as you progress and start experimenting with new subjects and techniques, an understanding of how your camera calculates correct exposure, and how you can override it or help it as and when required will prove necessary and invaluable.

The reason for this is because no matter how sophisticated modern cameras are, they will never be totally foolproof, so eventually you will encounter a situation that your camera finds difficult to assess and you will need to step in and make the decisions for it. Recognizing those situations is therefore an important skill.

Throughout this chapter we will look at the very basics of exposure and how camera meters work before going on to explore more in-depth areas of exposure and metering, and developing your knowledge step by step so that you can take successful pictures under the most testing circumstances.

Where it all begins

There are four factors that need to be taken into account when determining the correct exposure for a picture:

1 **The light levels in the scene** – If light levels are high, such as outdoors on a sunny day, a brief exposure will be required. If light levels are low, such as inside a dimly-lit room, you will need to use a longer exposure.

2 **The ISO you are shooting on** – The ISO setting of your camera, or the ISO of the film it is loaded with, indicates how sensitive it is to light. Low ISOs such as 50 or 1000 are not very sensitive so they need to be exposed for longer than higher ISOs such as 400 or 800, which are more sensitive.

   If you double the ISO, the exposure will halve and vice versa. For example, ISO 100 requires half the exposure of ISO 50, but double that of ISO 200. This applies whether you are shooting with film or digitally.

3 **The lens aperture** – As explained in Chapter 08, the lens aperture controls the size of the hole in the lens through which light passes on its way to the film or sensor. Each f/number admits half or twice as much light as its immediate neighbour. For example, f/8 admits half as much light as f/5.6, but twice as much as f/11.

4 **The shutter speed** – This controls the length of time light passing through the lens aperture is allowed to reach the film or sensor in your camera. Each shutter speed admits half or twice as much light as its immediate neighbour. For example, 1/60 sec admits half as much light as 1/30 sec, but twice as much as 1/125 sec.

Whenever you take a picture, the first step is to measure the light levels – the majority of modern cameras do this using their integral metering system. This information is then related to the ISO you are working at to determine the exposure required to produce a successful picture.

The lens aperture and shutter speed are the two things which produce this exposure, and you can use them in various combinations to achieve exactly the same exposure. Any of the combinations shown below would admit exactly the same amount of light and produce the same exposure.

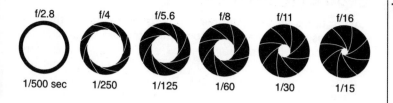

f/2.8   f/4   f/5.6   f/8   f/11   f/16

1/500 sec   1/250   1/125   1/60   1/30   1/15

figure 9.1 lens aperture and shutter speeds

ISO

Assuming the illustration above is based on ISO 100, for ISO 50 in the same situation you would need to double the exposure in each case. So the combinations would be 1/500 sec at f/2, 1/250 sec at f/2.8, 1/125 sec at f/4 and so on. Similarly, for ISO 200 you would need to halve the exposure. So the combinations would be 1/500 sec at f/4, 1/250 sec at f/5.6, 1/125 sec at f/8.

How cameras calculate correct exposure

Today, just about all modern cameras have a built-in metering system which measures the light passing through the lens to determine the exposure required. This is known as TTL (through-the-lens) metering.

Cameras with integral metering measure the light using a special photo-electric cell. This is usually a Cds (Cadmium Sulphide) cell which is powered by battery. Cds cells are favoured because they are very sensitive, so exposure readings can be taken in low light. They also react quickly and give accurate results.

An exposure reading is taken by pointing the camera towards your subject while looking through the viewfinder. The integral metering system then measures the light being reflected back toward the camera from your subject to determine the exposure required, and the aperture and shutter speed are set prior to the picture being taken.

Exposure modes

Having taken an exposure reading with your camera, the way that exposure is set depends upon the exposure mode you are using. Modern cameras come armed with a range of exposure modes – usually four – and although they all have the same end in mind, of getting enough light to the film or sensor to produce a correctly exposed photograph, the way they do it gives you varying levels of control over the aperture and shutter speed set.

Program mode

This is a fully automated exposure mode. When you take a meter reading, the camera sets both the aperture and the shutter speed automatically. The combination is usually chosen at random and is displayed in the camera's viewfinder and/or LCD panel on the top plate.

On most cameras you can adjust the aperture/shutter speed combination chosen to suit a particular subject – biasing it towards a small aperture (and slower shutter speed) for landscapes, say, or a faster shutter speed (and wider aperture) for sport and action.

Some SLRs have specialist program modes which do this for you, such as High Speed program which is biased towards selecting fast shutter speeds, or Depth program which selects small apertures for increased depth of field. Program mode is fast and convenient to use, so it is great for beginners, but it is too automated for experienced photographers.

Icons and pictograms

Many SLRs and compacts today have a series of symbols on a dial, such as mountains (landscape setting), a face (portrait setting), a flower (close-up setting) and so on. Set the dial to one of these icons and the camera functions are automatically biased towards that subject – in landscape mode you get a small aperture, in portrait mode you get a wide aperture and maybe automatic fill-in flash if the camera has an integral flash unit.

These modes are designed for beginners, the idea being that you can take successful pictures of different subjects with no prior knowledge. However, they give you no creative control, and are best avoided once you know what you are doing – which is basically when you have finished reading this book!

Aperture priority

With this semi-automatic mode you set the f/number on your lens to determine the aperture and the camera automatically selects a shutter speed to give correct exposure. The shutter speed is often displayed in the viewfinder and on the top plate LCD.

Aperture priority is the most versatile exposure mode for general use. It gives you control over depth of field because you choose which lens aperture you want to set and on many cameras apertures can be set in one-third stop increments, so it is ideal for landscapes and portraits. Aperture priority also links up with the camera's exposure compensation facility so you can override the metering system to avoid exposure error (see page 9).

Shutter priority

This is similar to aperture priority but, as you have probably guessed, you set the shutter speed and the camera automatically selects the aperture required to give correct exposure. Shutter speeds can often be set in one-third stop increments for greater accuracy and it is a handy mode for sport and action photography, where the choice of shutter speed is more important than controlling depth of field.

Metered manual

This is the most basic exposure mode of all. After taking a meter reading with your camera you set both the aperture and shutter speed yourself, using an indicator such as flashing LEDs in the viewfinder to show when correct exposure has been achieved.

This mode is ideal if you work with a handheld meter (see page 123), or if you like to feel that you are in total control. However, do not be misled into thinking it is any more accurate than any of the other modes above – all work with your camera's metering system and this one does not do anything different from the others. It is just slower to use because you set everything yourself.

Metering patterns

Although all cameras measure reflected light – the light bouncing back off the scene or subject you are photographing – the way they do it, and the accuracy of the reading you get, depends on the metering pattern the camera uses, or the one you have set it to. Modern SLRs usually offer two or three metering patterns. It is therefore important to know how each one works so you can use them in different situations to further reduce the risk of exposure error.

Centre-weighted average

This basic pattern is the one all SLRs used to use before more intelligent systems came along. It works by measuring the light from the whole image area, but preference is given to the central image circle because it is assumed that is where the main subject will be. In the 'average' situations mentioned above it can be relied upon to deliver accurate exposures (see DVD 9.01), but can also be fooled by non-average lighting (see page 117) and is best avoided in favour of...

Multi zone/multi pattern metering

These 'intelligent' metering systems – Nikon have 'Matrix', Canon 'Evaluative' – are considered the norm now and make taking perfectly exposed pictures easier than ever before. The reason for this is because they divide the scene into various zones and measure light/brightness levels in each. The number of zones varies from four to 16, depending on the camera model – the more zones, the more accurate the system is likely to be.

The zone readings are fed to a microchip computer in the camera and assessed. By doing so, the exposure reading you get is not overly influenced by a bright or dark area in the scene in the same way that centre-weighted systems are. They can also identify things like bright sky when shooting landscapes and make sure those brighter areas do not cause exposure error. (see DVD 9.02.)

These systems are not totally foolproof – if you point your camera at a snow scene it will still give an inaccurate reading because the reflectance of the scene is very high. However, they are much more reliable than centre-weighted and the best choice for general use.

Partial/selective metering

This pattern takes a reading from a small central area of the viewfinder, usually six to 15 per cent of the whole image area. This allows you to meter from a specific part of the scene and prevent really light or dark areas influencing the exposure obtained – such as when shooting into the light or your main subject is against a dark background.

Spot metering

This system is similar to selective, but measures light levels in a tiny central area of the viewfinder – anything from one to five per cent of the total image area. You can use it to take readings from small areas of a scene and in experienced hands it is the most accurate and useful system around as it means that accurate exposure can be achieved no matter how demanding the circumstances are. (see DVD 9.03.)

Multi-spot metering

Some SLRs allow you to take a series of individual spot readings, store each one in the camera's memory then average them out. This is ideal in situations where you are not sure where to meter from – by metering from the lightest and darkest areas then averaging them you will obtain an exposure that makes a good starting point, for example.

Dealing with tricky light

After reading the first part of this chapter you would not be blamed for thinking cameras are totally foolproof. If only life were so simple! All integral metering systems are designed to correctly expose scenes that reflect roughly 18 per cent of the light falling on them. These are referred to as 'average' scenes. Visually, this 18 per cent reflectance can be represented by a mid-grey colour known as 18 per cent grey.

Most of the scenes and subjects we photograph have this average reflectance, which is why most of the pictures we take come out correctly exposed. Modern metering systems are also much more sophisticated than they used to be so the chance of taking a badly exposed picture is slimmer now than ever before.

It can happen though, so you need to be aware of how your camera's TTL metering system 'reads' the things you point it at and be prepared to give it a helping hand whenever necessary. For example, a white surface reflects far more light than a black surface under the same lighting conditions, but your camera can't differentiate between the two and sets widely different exposures, even though they both require exactly the same.

The irony is that it is these tricky lighting situations which tend to produce the most exciting pictures, so unless you learn to recognize them you could miss out on many great photo opportunities. To help make sure this doesn't happen, here is a rundown of the most common situations and what you can do about them.

Bright background

Example: Person against a whitewashed wall, snow, shimmering water or sand.

Problem: The high reflectance of the background influences the exposure set and underexposure results.

Solution: Increase the exposure by a stop using your camera's exposure compensation facility.

(See DVD 9.04.)

Dark background

Example: Any subject in full sun against a dark, shady background, such as a person, flower or animal.

Problem: Dark things reflect less than 18 per cent of the light falling on them so your camera gives too much exposure and the picture comes out too light.

Solution: Reduce the exposure by one stop.

(See DVD 9.05.)

Bright subject

Example: A snow scene is the most extreme but wedding dresses and whitewashed buildings are common examples.

Problem: Your camera is fooled by the high reflectance and gross underexposure often results.

Solution: Increase the exposure by one or two stops.

(See DVD 9.06.)

Dark subject

Example: Any dark-toned subject filling a large area of the frame, such as portrait of a black cat, or a person in a dark suit.

Problem: Overexposure because your camera is fooled by the dark tones and tries to lighten them.

Solution: Reduce the exposure by at least one stop.

(See DVD 9.07.)

Including bright sky in the frame

Example: A landscape scene where one-third or more of the picture is occupied by sky.

Problem: The sky is brighter than the landscape and influences the exposure reading so you get perfectly exposed sky and underexposed landscape.

Solution: Tilt the camera down to exclude the sky and take a meter reading from the foreground. Set it in manual exposure mode or use AE lock to retain it.

(See DVD 9.08.)

Shooting into the sun

Example: Sunrise or sunset when the sun's orb is bright, or any situation where you are pointing your camera towards the sun.

Problem: It may only occupy a small part of the picture, but the sun's orb can fool your camera into giving too little exposure so the picture comes out dark. This is fine if you want to produce silhouettes, but not great if you don't.

Solution: Bracket exposures up to two stops over the metered exposure.

(See DVD 9.09.)

Assessing exposure with a digital camera

One of the great benefits of digital photography is that you can see a preview of each picture you take just seconds after tripping the shutter, and as the latest digital compacts and SLRs have a preview screen of $2^{1}/_{2}$–3 inches, the image you see is nice and big. (See DVD 9.10.)

Simply looking at the image on the screen will allow you to do an instant exposure appraisal – if it is obviously too dark then underexposure has occurred and if it is obviously too light, you have overexposed it. In either case, the shot can be re-taken with the exposure adjusted to compensate for an error.

The main problem with using the screen image to assess exposure is that the image itself is a small jpeg version of the main image – even if you shoot in RAW capture mode, the screen image will still be a jpeg – so it won't be a true representation of the full-size image and only major exposure error will be obvious – i.e. the image is *really* dark or *really* light.

A more accurate way of assessing exposure is to check the histogram of the image which shows the tonal range from shadows through mid-tones to highlights and how the pixels in your camera's sensor have been distributed across that range – a graph, in other words.

An ideal histogram will look different depending on the conditions you are shooting in, but generally there should be an even distribution of pixels across the tonal range, with detail recorded in the highlight and shadows and a greater concentration of pixels in the mid-tone region – which would show as a bump towards the middle of the graph.

Here are a few things to look out for:

- If the histogram does not extend all the way to the left it means that the shadows have been 'clipped' and no detail has recorded in the darker shadows areas. To solve this problem, increase the exposure by half to one stop then check the histogram again. Increase the exposure even more if necessary.

- If the histogram does not extend all the way to the right is means the highlights have been clipped and the lightest areas in the image will be white, with no detail recorded. There will also be a highlight warning flashing on the preview image. If this occurs, reduce the exposure by half to one stop and keep doing it until the highlight warning all but disappears.

- It is important to try to record at least some detail in the brightest highlights because if there is nothing there, you will not have any details to retrieve and reveal when you process the image. That said, in really contrasty conditions such as intense sunlight, you may not be able to record any detail in the brightest highlights because the brightness range is simply too high.

- Do not worry if very small areas are flashing a highlight warning – when you open the full-size image you may find that there is detail in those highlights, but the compressed preview image was not able to show that.

- If the histogram shows a high proportion of pixels in the lighter tones, the image is probably overexposed so reduce the exposure by half to one stop, re-shoot then re-check the histogram.

- If the histogram shows a high proportion of pixels in the darker tones, the image is probably underexposed. To rectify this, increase the exposure by half to one stop, re-shoot then check the histogram again.
- Remember that if you shoot in RAW capture mode it does not matter if the exposure is not absolutely perfect because you can make quite dramatic adjustments when the image is processed – in the same way that an over- or underexposed negative can be rescued at the printing stage and still yield a perfectly acceptable photograph.
- Also remember that in extreme situations the histogram may suggest that an image is under- or overexposed when in fact it is fine. If you shoot a snow scene, for example, there are going to be more light tones than dark so the histogram will seem to be showing overexposure when in fact it is fine. Similarly, if you shoot a silhouette, the histogram will show more dark tones which normally would indicate underexposure.
- Practice is the key – make a habit of assessing the histogram of images captured in different situations or of subjects with different tonal ranges so you get to know what they should – or shouldn't – look like.

(See DVD 9.11 and 9.12.)

Compensating the exposure

Whether you are shooting digitally or with film, overcoming exposure error involves overriding the exposure your camera sets, or would set. There are various ways of doing this, although the one you choose will depend upon the type of camera you own. Refer to your camera's instruction manual if you are not sure which facilities it offers.

1 **Using the exposure compensation facility** – This feature is found on the vast majority of SLRs and compacts and allows you to increase or reduce the exposure set by up to five stops, in half or third stop increments. It is a quick and easy way of adjusting the exposure in tricky light – though you need to remember to set the compensation back to zero when you have taken a shot, otherwise the amount of compensation dialled in will be applied to subsequent photographs whether you need it or not!

2 **Setting your camera to manual** – If it is possible to set your camera to manual mode both the aperture and shutter speed can be adjusted at will. So, after setting the exposure your camera suggests, you can then compensate it by adjusting either the aperture or the shutter speed or both.

3 **Using the backlight button** – This feature is found on many SLRs and compacts, and is usually a button positioned near the lens mount. When depressed, it increases the exposure automatically by about one-and-a-half stops so your main subject will not be underexposed when you shoot 'into the light'. Useful, but often the increase given is not enough in really bright conditions.

4 **Using the exposure memory lock** – This feature allows you to take an exposure reading from a specific part of the scene, then 'lock' it by partially depressing the camera's shutter release. For example, when shooting a landscape you could tilt the camera down to exclude the sky – which tends to cause underexposure – take an exposure reading from the foreground, then use the exposure lock to hold that reading when you raise the camera to recompose and shoot.

Bracketing exposures

The easiest way to avoid exposure error in tricky light is by taking a series of pictures of the same scene or subject, each at a different exposure, so you are guaranteed at least one perfectly exposed shot. This technique is known as bracketing. (See DVD 9.13–9.17.)

The best way to bracket is by setting your camera to aperture priority AE mode (or shutter priority AE if you prefer). All you do then is take a meter reading, fire off a shot, then using your camera's exposure compensation facility you can increase or reduce the exposure set by the metering system. Bracketing can be done in third, half or full stop increments, depending on the type of camera you have, and usually up to +/–5 stops.

Many SLRs also have an auto exposure bracketing (AEB) feature. With this you can dial in the increments of the bracket, say, +/– half a stop, then when you trip the camera's shutter it automatically exposes three frames of film – one at the metered exposure, one over it and one under it at the preset parameters.

More often than not, bracketing one stop over and one stop under the metered exposure would be sufficient, but in situations like those shown on this page, bracketing up to two stops over, under, or both over and under is recommended.

Spot metering

Another way of overcoming exposure error in tricky light is by spot metering – taking an exposure reading from a tiny area in the scene.

The main thing to remember if your camera has spot metering and you use it is that you are still measuring reflected light and the metering system is still calibrated for 18 per cent reflectance. So, if you meter from a really light or really dark area, you will still end up with a badly exposed image. In fact, the level of error is likely to be higher if you use spot metering badly than if you were using the camera set at a more general metering pattern.

The key with spot metering is to meter from a mid-tone – something that has roughly 18 per cent reflectance. When you are scouting a scene, look for something that you think has a similar density to a mid-grey colour. Green grass and foliage are ideal, along with weathered stone, roof tiles, tarmac, weathered timber, deep blue sky and so on.

If you can't find a mid-tone, meter from the lightest area, then the darkest, and find the average of the two. Use this exposure as your starting point and bracket.

For example, if your two readings are 1/60 sec at f/16 and 1/15 sec at f/16, the average is 1/30 sec at f/16. (See DVD 9.18.)

Using a handheld meter

As an alternative, you could use a handheld meter to take incident light readings. This type of meter measures the light falling onto a scene instead of that reflecting back, so the exposure reading you obtain will not be influenced by the reflectance of the subject or scene and a perfect exposure is almost guaranteed. However, what you have to remember is that you can only take incident readings when you are able to hold the meter in the same light that is falling on your subject. If you can't, you will get a false reading and exposure error will result. (See DVD 9.19.)

A grey card reading

An easy way to obtain correct exposure in tricky lighting is by using a grey card. This is a sheet of card which represents the 18 per cent reflectance light meters are calibrated for and can be purchased from good photo retailers for about £10. All you do is hold the card in the same light that is falling on your subject, move in close with your camera so the card fills the viewfinder, then take an exposure reading. Set this on your camera in manual exposure mode, or use the AE lock to hold it, then re-compose and take the picture.

Exposure and digital cameras

When I first wrote *Teach Yourself Photography* back in the early 1990s, digital cameras were a mere pipe dream and all photographers were committed to working with film. Today it's a different story. Some photographers, myself included, still work with film, but the majority have now switched to digital capture and many of you reading this book may never have taken a photograph on film.

This shift in technology is significant when it comes to the subject of exposure and metering because if you use a digital camera you have instant feedback and can immediately establish if an image is correctly exposed simply by looking at it on the preview screen and, more importantly, assessing the histogram.

If this tells you that the image has been over- or underexposed you can adjust camera settings and shoot again to make sure you get it just right. Not only that, if you shoot in RAW, a surprising amount of exposure error can be corrected once the image has been downloaded onto your computer so even if you get it wrong when the picture is taken you can always make it right later.

What this means in practice is that no matter how little experience you have as a photographer and no matter how demanding the situation, armed with a digital camera there is absolutely no reason on earth why you should end up with a badly exposed photograph. This is the first time since the birth of photography that technology has reached such levels of sophistication that you are almost guaranteed a perfectly exposed photograph.

Of course, there is far more to a successful image than getting the exposure right, but being able to rely on your camera to solve that problem for you means that you can concentrate on more creative aspects of the picture-taking process.

Exposing for effect

Finally, remember that exposure is very subjective. There is no such thing as the 'correct' exposure – only the exposure you think will record your subject in the most pleasing way for the type of picture you have in mind. So there is nothing wrong with totally ignoring what your meter says if you think better pictures will result by using your own judgement.

By varying the exposure you can radically change the mood of a picture. A landscape shot in dark, stormy weather can be made to look even more dramatic if you underexpose by half or even a full stop. This is known as a 'low-key' effect, because most of the tones in the picture are dark. Similarly, by using a controlled amount of overexposure to slightly burn out the highlights, you can create an atmospheric 'high-key' effect that is ideal for some portraits and still lifes.

Given the control that digital imaging technology now provides, this opens up a whole new world of creativity.

(See DVD 9.20 and 9.21.)

10 understanding light

In this chapter you will learn:
- how light changes through the day
- the effect of weather on light
- how to make the most of lighting direction
- to understand colour temperature.

The quality of light is one of the most important factors influencing the success of every picture you take. The way light falls on an object totally dictates its physical appearance: how much texture and detail is revealed, the strength and neutrality of its colour and whether it looks flat or three dimensional. This in turn influences the mood of your pictures and the way people respond to them emotionally. To get the most from your photography you therefore need to have a thorough understanding of light and how you can use it to your advantage.

The amazing thing about light – especially daylight – is that it never stays the same for very long. It can be hard or soft, strong or weak, warm or cold, and all these permutations can be put to good use because they change the way the world appears.

If you look down your garden on a cold, misty morning, for example, it will look totally different from how it will later in the day if the sun comes out, or in dull, overcast weather. What you need to do is study the way different forms of light work, so you can decide when a scene will look at its most attractive before committing it to film.

The colour of light also needs to be considered – especially when you are taking pictures under artificial lighting – because the film or sensor in your camera will not always see it the way your eyes do. If you are not aware of this, all sorts of problems can be encountered with colour casts.

Basically, light is what photography is all about. Without it you could not take a picture in the first place, but with it you can achieve amazing feats of artistic and technical excellence. (See DVD 10.01.)

Time of day

The greatest factor influencing the quality of daylight is the time of day. As the sun arcs its way across the sky between sunrise and sunset, the colour, harshness and intensity of the light undergo a myriad of changes, all of which can be used to your advantage.

Before sunrise there is a period known as pre-dawn (see DVD 10.02), during which any light present is reflected from the sky so it is very soft, shadows are weak and the world takes on a cool blue/grey hue. This is a good time to photograph coastal views and scenes containing water, especially in calm weather,

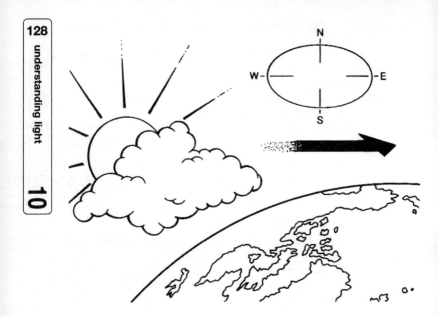

figure 10.1 time of day

when the surface of the water is unruffled so it reflects the scenery around you. As first light approaches, pastel colours begin to appear in the sky and the landscape looks very atmospheric. In clear weather in temperate regions, visible light may occur as early as 2 a.m. during mid-summer, but not until 6.30 a.m. during the depths of winter. In the tropics, twilight is very brief at either end of the day.

Once the sun peeps over the horizon it is all change. In a matter of minutes the sky becomes much warmer and any clouds present near the horizon reflect light and colour from the sun, though the landscape is still being lit by the sky overhead and often appears cool and subdued until the sun appears. (See DVD 10.03.)

When it does appear, warm sunlight rakes across the landscape, casting long shadows across the ground, revealing texture and picking out even the smallest rises and dips in the land. Shadows are weak when the sun is close to the horizon because they are partially 'filled-in' by light from the sky, and at sunrise often appear blue in colour because the sky is predominantly blue itself. This makes it possible to create beautifully evocative photographs at sunrise, with prominent features such as buildings or trees lit by the warming rays of the sun while the rest of the scene appears cool and subdued. (See DVD 10.04.)

Early morning is the most productive time to be out in the landscape. The light undergoes many changes in a short space of time, and you will often take more pictures during the first two hours of daylight than the rest of the day put together.

As the sun starts to climb into the sky the earth warms, the light becomes more intense and shadows grow shorter and denser. The warmth in the light also begins to fade back to neutral, and stays that way for much of the day. (See DVD 10.05.) This is known as 'mean noon daylight'. Once the sun climbs higher than $36°$ above the horizon the light reaches maximum intensity. During the summer this point is reached five hours after sunrise – usually around 9 a.m. and remains so until at least 4 p.m. In spring and autumn the period is shorter – usually between 10 a.m. and 2 p.m. – while in winter the intensity of the light and angle of the sun remains low enough to provide attractive light throughout day.

With the light at its most intense and the sun overhead, the landscape can easily look bland and flat. When photographing people you also need to take care because shadows are often cast in eye sockets and under noses, which is far from flattering. Use a reflector under the chin to bounce light into these areas, or step into the shade where the light will be much softer. (See DVD 10.06.)

This doesn't mean you should stop shooting altogether – smaller details can still make great pictures, and scenes that are full of strong colours such as flower meadows will look amazing – especially if you use a polarizer to increase colour saturation. This type of light is also ideal for abstract images and some architectural shots.

Summer is the worst season for harsh light as the sun continues to climb until it is almost overhead – up to $60°$ or more above the horizon at midday in temperate regions; as much as $90°$ at the equator – by which time little or no shadow detail is visible and contrast is often too high for colour film to fully record.

By mid-afternoon the sun will have begun its descent towards the horizon again and conditions improve. (See DVD 10.07.) As it falls ever lower in the sky the light warms up and shadows become longer and weaker, revealing texture and modelling to give your pictures a real three-dimensional feel.

The golden hour

Perhaps the most photogenic time of day is the hour or so before sunset, when the world is bathed in a beautiful golden light and even the most ordinary scene is brought to life. The light is often much warmer than at dawn because it is scattered and diffused by the thicker atmosphere – this is why the sun often looks bigger at sunset than it did at sunrise – and your pictures will come out warmer than you expected because film cannot adapt to changes in the colour temperature of the light like your eyes can. (See DVD 10.08.)

Long shadows also scythe across the landscape once more, revealing maximum texture and detail. Delicate undulations such as gentle ripples on a sandy beach are clearly defined by the raking light and the texture in surfaces that just a few hours earlier appeared smooth. And then, of course, there is the sunset itself. There are few sights more magical than the sun's golden orb slowly dropping toward the horizon, and in the right conditions it is pretty much impossible not to take great pictures. (See DVD 10.09.)

At sunset, contrast is high if you are including the sun's orb in your picture so you have to decide how you want to expose the scene. The usual approach is to create silhouettes of key foreground details such as buildings, trees and people with the fiery sky behind. This is done by exposing for the sky and sun, which your camera will naturally do if you leave the exposure to its metering system. All you have to do then is bracket a series of exposures, up to around two stops over the metered exposure, and you are guaranteed several successful frames.

Where you want to record detail in the foreground without burning out the sky, use a strong neutral density grad filter – 0.9 is usually the best choice – to reduce the brightness between the sky and landscape. You can then expose for the landscape and the glorious colours in the sky will record as well.

If you need to enhance the light at sunrise or sunset, use an 81-series warm-up filter – an 81C or stronger is ideal.

Once the sun has disappeared twilight transforms the sky into beautiful shades of blue, purple and pink, providing you with yet more opportunities to take successful pictures. (See DVD 10.10.) If you are shooting scenes containing water, so the sky is reflected, you can continue shooting until it is almost too dark to see. (See DVD 10.11.)

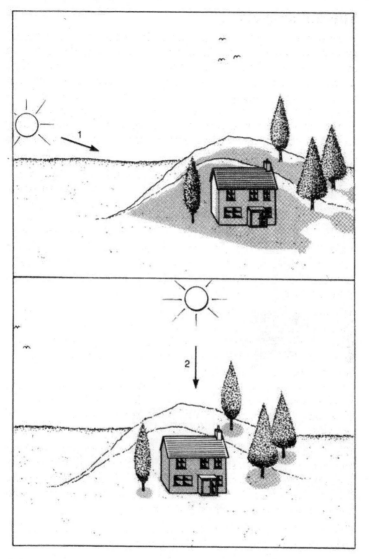

figure 10.2 The quality of light changes dramatically at different times of the day, and in doing so can totally transform the mood and appearance of a scene.

Weather or not

If every day was clear and sunny, the light would be predictable and photography very easy because you could plan your pictures down to the last detail. (See DVD 10.12.) For most of us, however, unpredictable and constantly changing weather adds a whole new dimension to the quality of light.

Clouds are the biggest culprit. They come in many shapes, sizes and densities, with each type having a different effect. If a fluffy white cloud decides to drift in front of the sun then you will notice an immediate change. Suddenly the light levels drop a good stop or two, shadows become much weaker, and the light itself is much softer. This is because the cloud acts like a diffuser, spreading the light and reducing its harshness.

As the cloud cover increases, so the effect becomes more noticeable. In overcast weather the blanket of cloud effectively turns the sky into one enormous softbox, killing shadows almost completely and creating a very gentle form of illumination. A similar effect can be produced in the studio by placing a large softbox over a studio flash.

Most photographers dismiss dull weather as boring and uninspiring, but it is perfect for portraiture, fashion, glamour, still-life and close-up photography. Admittedly, the soft light does tend to make colours look flat and subdued, but for the subjects mentioned above this is often a bonus. (See DVD 10.13.) Alternatively, you could load up with black and white film and exploit the wonderful range of tones produced – dull days produce perfect conditions for producing moody black and white photographs. (See DVD 10.16.)

Colour landscape photography is less suited to dull weather if you are shooting sweeping views, but some types of scene and subjects can benefit from it such as woodland, waterfalls and small details in the landscape.

Mist and fog are more interesting, reducing the landscape to two dimensions. Fog is less photogenic because it reduces visibility, weakens colours and makes everything appear rather flat, but a light mist at dawn can be incredibly photogenic. (See DVD 10.17.)

Dull, rainy weather is less inviting, but you can produce successful pictures in heavy downpours. Try using a slow shutter speed to blur the rain so it records like mist, or shoot against a dark background so the raindrops are clearly visible.

Stormy weather offers even more scope. (See DVD 10.14.) The prospect of being soaked to the skin may not fill you with excitement, but bad weather has a habit of breaking unexpectedly, and when it does you will be handsomely rewarded with shafts of radiant sunlight illuminating the landscape against a bank of black clouds, or a colourful rainbow arching across the sky. (See DVD 10.15.)

Lighting direction

The late, great fashion photographer Norman Parkinson once said, 'Kodak has been telling amateur photographers for years to keep the sun over their shoulder when taking a picture, but that's the worst thing you can do.'

He had a point. Back in the good old days it was necessary to adopt this approach in order to ensure you got a correctly exposed picture. But cameras are far more sophisticated now and can cope well in all kinds of lighting conditions, so you need not restrict yourself. The way light strikes your subject is important because it can make a profound difference to the quality of your pictures.

Frontal lighting is created when you do keep the sun behind you so your subject is evenly lit and contrast is easily manageable. This approach can work well early or late in the day, when your subject is bathed in lovely golden light, but because the shadows fall away from the camera and out of view the results tend to look rather flat. If you are taking portraits your subject will also be looking directly at the sun and this may cause them to squint due to the excessive brightness. (See DVD 10.18.)

Side-lighting is a far better option. Keep the sun to one side of the camera and shadows rake across the scene, highlighting texture in all but the flattest surfaces, emphasizing form and adding a strong sense of depth to your shots – particularly when the sun is low in the sky and shadows are long. (See DVD 10.19.)

You need to be careful when shooting landscapes and buildings, though, because you can easily end up with large areas obscured by shadows. The same applies with portraiture – one half of your subject's face will be in shadow, so unless you want that effect, use a reflector to bounce light into the shadows and reveal detail.

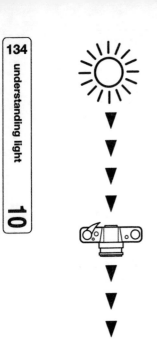

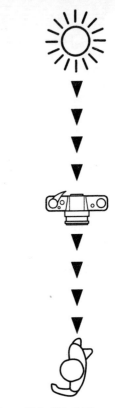

figure 10.3 Frontal lighting   **figure 10.4** Side lighting

Backlighting can be used to create stunning results, although you need to expose very carefully to avoid problems. If you fire away with your camera on automatic, anything between you and the bright background will record as a striking silhouette because it is in shadow – statues, trees, buildings, people and all sorts of other subjects make great silhouettes.

The other option is to correctly expose for your main subject in the foreground, so the background burns out to create an atmospheric high-key effect. If you are shooting outdoor portraits, for example, you can use the sun to create a halo of light around your subject's hair, and throw some light into their face with a reflector or a burst of fill-in flash (see Chapter 17).

Flare can be a problem when you are shooting into the sun, so make sure your lenses are spotlessly clean and use lens hoods to keep stray light away from the front element. (See DVD 10.20 and 10.21.)

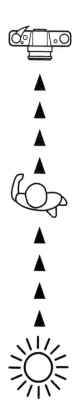

figure 10.5 Back lighting

Hard or soft – which is best?

It may sound contradictory, but light can be both strong and soft at the same time, or weak and hard. A studio flash unit fired into a large softbox attachment will produce an intense but very diffuse form of light, whereas the light from a tungsten bulb hanging over your dining room table is very weak, but at the same time very harsh.

Hard (harsh) light is generally created by a single and small source. The sun is a good example. On a clear summer's day it casts dense black shadows that create contrasty, vibrant images. This is ideal for adding punch to your pictures – colours seem intense, although colour saturation is actually greater in slightly overcast weather – and shadows add depth.

Soft light comes into its own when you want to add atmosphere to your portraits, landscapes or still lifes. The absence of strong shadows allows you to capture every detail, and the results are far more soothing to look at. (See DVD 10.23.)

Hard light can be made much softer by placing some kind of 'diffusing screen' between the source and your subject so it is spread over a wider area. Clouds serve that purpose outdoors. Indoors you have many options. Softboxes and brollies will do the job if you are using electronic flash. Alternatively, you could fire your flashgun through a frame covered in tracing paper, or bounce the light off a white wall or ceiling. Window light is also ideal for portraiture and still life photography. If it is too harsh just tape a sheet of tracing paper or muslin over the glass, or use net curtains to diffuse the light coming in.

Differentiating between hard and soft light is important because it can have a profound effect on the pictures you take. So think carefully about the type of mood you would like to convey before tripping the shutter, and if the light is not quite right wait until it is, or modify it to suit your needs.

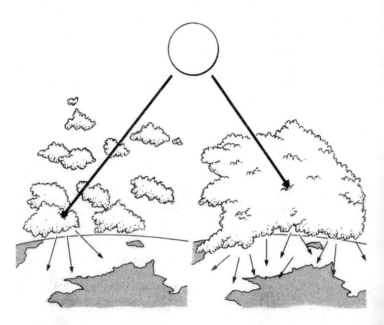

figure 10.6 Changes in the weather have a profound effect upon the harshness and intensity of the light. Bright sunlight (left) is very hard and casts dense shadows, but if the sun is obscured by cloud (right) the light becomes much softer and shadows are noticeably weaker.

Coping with contrast

The harshness of the light is also important because it dictates the contrast level in a scene – the difference in brightness between the highlights and the shadows. In sunny weather contrast is high because you have bright highlights and deep shadows mixed together, whereas on a dull, overcast day the brightness range is far smaller so contrast is lower. (See DVD 10.22.)

Colour film and digital sensors can record a brightness range of about five stops, but if you shoot around midday in bright sunlight, or include a light source such as the sun in your pictures, that range will be far greater so something has to give. If you expose for the highlights, the shadows will block up, but if you expose for the shadows, the highlights will burn out.

Your only option is to decide which part of the scene is more important – the highlights or the shadows – and expose for them. Alternatively, you could compromise by taking a meter reading from both and finding the average. With subjects such as portraiture and still life you can control contrast by using reflectors to bounce the light around. This is not possible with landscapes and architecture, so you either have to make the best of what you have or return when the light is less contrasty.

The colour temperature of light

It is not only the harshness and intensity of light that changes – its colour is constantly changing, too. Sometimes it is cold, sometimes it is warm and sometimes it is neutral. As a means of measuring and quantifying these changes, photographers use a system known as the Kelvin scale, which refers to light in terms of its colour temperature.

Temperature is used as a form of measurement simply because the way the colour of daylight changes is exactly the same as if you heat a substance. Heat an iron bar, for instance, and it will eventually glow red, then orange to yellow until it is white hot. Beyond that, the bar would melt, but if it didn't, and its temperature continued to rise, it would eventually appear blue. The cooler the light is, therefore, the higher its colour temperature, and the warmer it is the lower its colour temperature.

Do not be confused into thinking colour temperature actually has anything to do with heat though – it only refers to the actual colour of the light.

Our eyes can adapt to changes in the colour temperature of light automatically, so it always looks more or less white – this is known as 'chromatic adaptation' or 'colour constancy'. Unfortunately, photographic film and digital sensors cannot, and they record light as it really is – warm or cold.

Normal photographic colour film and the CCD array in your digital camera are balanced to record colours naturally in light with a colour temperature around 5500K. Such conditions are assumed to be found on an average sunny day around midday under blue sky containing a proportion of white clouds. (See DVD 10.24.)

Providing the colour temperature of the light does not vary by a large degree – above 6000K or below 5000K – then it is unlikely you will notice any obvious colour casts on your pictures. Beyond those limits, however, colour casts will begin to rear their ugly head and you have to decide whether or not to combat them. When colour temperature is lower than 5500K, warm casts are produced, and when it is higher than 5500K, cool casts are produced.

Where daylight is concerned, the colour temperature can be influenced by a number of factors. Dull, drab weather tends to produce cooler light, and therefore a blue colour cast, because cloud cover filters out wavelengths at the warmer end of the spectrum and scatters those at the cooler end so they predominate in the light reflected from the sky. The same applies in the shade under clear blue sky where the colour temperature of the light can be as high as 10 000K, or at high altitudes where there is a greater concentration of ultraviolet light and bluer wavelengths. (See DVD 10.26.)

At the other extreme, the colour temperature of daylight is much warmer at sunrise and sunset, gradually increasing during the morning until it reaches the 'neutral' 5500K, then decreasing through the afternoon as the sun drops in the sky. So, if you photograph a scene just after sunrise or just before sunset, it will record far warmer than you actually remembered it because the colour temperature of the light is very low – down to perhaps 2000–2500K. Those pictures will also appear far warmer than pictures of the same scene taken several hours later in the morning or earlier in the afternoon, when the sun is higher in the sky and the light is more neutral. (See DVD 10.25.)

The time of day at which the daylight becomes neutral depends enormously on the time of year. In western Europe and the northern USA in summer the sun rises very early and sets late, so in sunny weather the colour temperature of the light may reach

5500K as early as 6 a.m. and hover around that until 6 p.m. In spring and autumn the period is shorter – around 8 a.m. to 4 p.m. – while during winter the sun does not climb very high in the sky and the colour temperature of the light often never gets beyond 4500K, so the light is always slightly warm, even at midday.

With artificial light sources the difference in colour temperature compared to 'average noon daylight' is generally huge. (See DVD 10.27.)

One notable exception is electronic flash, which is specifically made to have a colour temperature of 5500K, like average daylight. Tungsten, the most common form of artificial lighting, has a colour temperature around 3000–3400K, while the light from a fire is below 3000K and that of a candle flame or oil lamp as low as 2000K.

The table below shows the recommended filters to combat colour casts in common lighting situations. If you shoot digitally then you can adjust the white balance on your camera according to the conditions or lighting you are in – Cloudy, Tungsten and so on. Colour balance can also be adjusted on the computer, so if you do not get it quite right when the picture is taken, you can always balance any visible colour casts later.

That said, do not always be too eager to correct them because sometimes colour casts can be a benefit. Only a fool would want to filter out the warmth in the light at sunset, for example.

Light source	Colour temp (°K)	Filtration
Clear blue sky	10 000K	Orange 85B
Shade under blue sky	7500K	81D warm
Dull, overcast weather	7000K	81A warm
Average noon daylight	5500K	None
Electronic flash	5500K	None
Early morn/eve sunlight	3500K	Blue 80C
Tungsten photofloods	3400K	Blue 80B
Sunrise/sunset	3000K	Blue 80A
Domestic tungsten bulbs	2800K	Blue 80A + 80C
Torch bulb	2500K	Blue 80A + 80C
Candle flame	2000K	Blue 80A + 80B

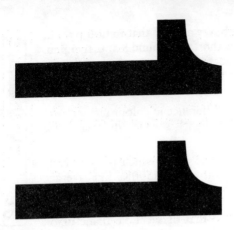

composing a picture

In this chapter you will learn:
- about the importance of composition
- about focal points and the rule of thirds
- how to exploit perspective and scale
- about using foreground interest and lines.

Equally as important as the quality of light is the way your pictures are composed or 'put together'. A successful composition is visually balanced and stimulating to look at. It leads the viewer's eye around the frame, so it takes in all the important elements without any great effort. An untidy composition does the opposite. It leaves the eye wondering exactly where to go, and fails to hold the attention of the viewer for more than a few seconds.

Every time you raise a camera to your eye to take a picture you are 'composing', but the mistake most photographers make is failing to spend enough time deciding if what they have got in the viewfinder is actually interesting before pressing the shutter.

There is no magic formula for composing a picture. With subjects such as landscape and architecture it is a case of looking at what lies before you, then deciding how you can best capture it by choosing a suitable viewpoint and controlling exactly what appears in the final picture by using the right lens. (See DVD 11.01.)

Painters have a distinct advantage over photographers because they start off with an empty canvas then set about filling it, so if the natural composition of a scene is not particularly inspiring they can move things around a little, or add things that do not exist in reality. Unfortunately, you do not have that privilege. Your canvas is already full, so you have to decide which bit is the most interesting then make the most of it.

Let's have a look at exactly how you can do that...

Step by step

Often you will find the composition of a picture can be improved not by switching to another lens, but simply by using your feet. The majority of enthusiast photographers seem to be afraid to get close to their subject, but it is vitally important that you fill the frame, and often you will find a picture can be improved immensely by taking a few paces forward.

Admittedly, images can be cropped in the darkroom or on the computer to improve the composition, but you should always strive to get it right at the point the exposure is made because if you get into the habit of thinking pictures can always be improved later – which is one of the dangers of this digital age – then sloppy practice may result which filters down into other areas of your photography.

Legwork is equally important when it comes to finding the best viewpoint. It is easy to fire away as soon as you see something interesting, but nine times out of ten you will get a far better picture if you spend a few minutes wandering around, looking at your subject from different angles before deciding which one to use.

Do not automatically assume you have to take pictures with the camera at eye-level either. Try shooting from a slightly higher position every now and then, by standing on a wall or climbing up a step-ladder. Many professionals carry a step-ladder in the boot of their car for this very purpose, because you can see far more from an elevated position.

Alternatively, bend down, or stretch out on your stomach so you get a worm's eye view of the world. By doing this you can create stunning pictures of the most mundane subjects, simply because we are not used to seeing things from such an odd position.

Remember, composition begins with your feet. Only when you have discovered the best viewpoint can you start making other important decisions. (See DVD 11.02 and 11.03.)

The focal point

Most photographs will have or should have a main point of interest. This is known as the focal point, and it serves two important purposes. First, it is the element in the shot that the viewer's eye is naturally drawn to, and second, it adds a sense of scale to your pictures. (See DVD 11.04.)

For example, if you photograph a farming scene and there is a tractor chugging away in the distance, that tractor automatically becomes the focal point. The same applies if you photograph a hillside and there is a hiker halfway up it, or a seascape with a fishing boat bobbing on the waves.

Including a focal point is not enough to create an interesting composition though – the way you position it in the frame is equally important. Most photographers place the focal point in the middle of the picture, but this is often the worse thing you can do because the results tend to look very static. A far better place is a third of the way into the shot, which is where the rule of thirds comes in...

The rule of thirds

This age-old compositional device was developed by painters to help them achieve visual harmony, but it can be used just as well by photographers.

All you do is divide your camera's viewfinder into nine equal-sized sections using two horizontal and vertical lines, so an imaginary grid is formed. You then compose the scene so the focal point is placed on one of the four intersection points created (see below).

The rule of thirds is also useful for positioning the horizon. Instead of putting it across the middle of the frame, where it splits the scene in half and creates static, lifeless pictures, you should place it one third from the top or bottom of the scene, so you are emphasizing the landscape or sky rather than giving equal weight to both. The only exception to this is if you are capturing the reflections in a lake, say, and the symmetry created will work in your favour.

Just one word of warning: do not *force* your pictures to comply with the rule of thirds. In the right situation it works well, but if you overuse it your pictures will become very predictable. It is only a guide, and should be used as such. (See DVD 11.05.)

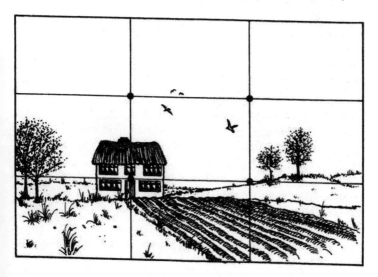

figure 11.1 By using the rule of thirds to help you position the focal point in your pictures the composition will be visually balanced. Any of the four intersection points indicated is suitable.

Foreground interest

Another way of making your pictures more visually arresting is by emphasizing the foreground. This not only provides an obvious entry point into the picture – the bottom is an obvious place for the eye to start – but also adds depth and scale, which are important considerations when you are capturing a three-dimensional scene on a two-dimensional piece of film.

All sorts of natural features can be used as foreground interest: rocks on a lake shore, a chunk of driftwood on the beach, a road, wall, fence, trees and so on. Or if you cannot find anything you can create it by asking someone to pose in the foreground.

Wide-angle lenses are ideal for emphasizing foreground interest, simply because they exaggerate distance and scale. By moving in close to a boulder with a 28 mm lens, for example, you can make it loom large in the frame so it dominates the shot and creates a powerful composition.

The vast depth of field wide-angle lenses offer at small aperture such as f/16 also means you will not have any problems keeping everything sharp, from the immediate foreground to the distant background.

Using lines

Lines are one of the most powerful compositional 'tools' at your disposal, simply because we cannot resist following them wherever they go. If you keep a lookout when you are wandering around you will find lines cropping up everywhere. A road, river, wall, fence, avenue of trees, row of telegraph poles, road markings, shadows, furrows in a ploughed field and many other things create lines that can be included in your pictures.

The best results tend to be produced when you use lines to lead the eye into the scene and towards the focal point. You could stand on the banks of a river, for instance, and use a wide-angle lens so the river fills part of the foreground before snaking off into the distance.

The direction the line is travelling is important because it affects the strength of the composition. Horizontal lines are restful and easy to look at because they echo the horizon itself, and suggest repose. Vertical lines, on the other hand, are more active so they give a picture tension and make it more challenging to look at.

Diagonal lines are more effective because they carry the eye across the scene so more of it is taken in. Ideally the line should travel from bottom left to top right because that is the way we naturally 'read' a photograph.

Finally, do not forget about converging lines, which create a powerful feeling of distance and scale due to the way they taper off into the distance. The furrows in a ploughed field are a good example, as are the sides of a long, straight road or railway tracks. Again, for the best results use a wide-angle lens and include the vanishing point – the point where the lines appear to meet – in the background of your shot.

Perspective and scale

Photography is a two-dimensional medium simply because a flat image can only record height and width. However, because we are able to tell which parts of the scene are closest to the camera and which are further away, we can visualize the third dimension – depth – and thus gain a sense of reality. This is an important consideration when composing photographs.

The impression of depth is made possible due to the spatial relationship between objects, more commonly referred to as perspective, and when harnessed creatively this can make an enormous difference to the success and impact of a photograph.

The most common feeling of depth is created by overlapping planes or forms in the landscape – if one plane in a scene partly obscures another, such as in a hilly location, there must obviously be distance between them. However, there are other forms of perspective that can be even more powerful.

Diminishing perspective relies on the fact that the further away an object is from us, the smaller it appears. If you stand next to a building, for example, it will dwarf you, but walk 50 m down the street and it will appear much smaller. This is why including foreground interest in a wide-angle landscape photograph gives a strong feeling of distance and depth – the old wooden gate you use to fill the foreground appears far bigger than the hills in the distance, so there must be distance between them because we know the hills are bigger than the gate.

Another way to exploit diminishing perspective is by photographing a series of similar-sized objects, such as an avenue of trees. The tree closest to the camera will appear to be the tallest and the one furthest away the smallest, with each tree appearing smaller than the one before.

Aerial perspective is based on the fact that colour and tone diminishes with distance due to atmospheric haze, mist and fog. If you gaze across a mountainous scene at sunrise, for example, the mountains closest to the camera will appear darker in colour or tone than those further away. The same applies with trees in mist, or the undulations of a rolling landscape. To emphasize the effect, use a telephoto lens and home in on the more distant parts of the scene where the haze or mist is stronger, or shoot into the sun so that the more distant parts of the scene are much brighter than those closest to the camera.

Scale and size recognition

Another way of implying distance and depth in a landscape photograph is by including objects which help us to quantify the scale of a scene.

People are the most obvious choice here, as the human body is relatively consistent in size. So, if you capture a person dwarfed against a waterfall, it immediately becomes clear that the waterfall is huge, whereas without the people we would not have anything to compare it to. The same applies with buildings and other common forms such as trees and animals.

Using frames

One way of tightening up the overall composition of a shot, focusing attention on your main subject and hiding unwanted details is by using a frame around the edges of the picture.

All sorts of features make interesting frames, both natural and man-made. The overhanging branches of a tree can be used to fill out large areas of empty sky when shooting landscapes, for example. Doorways, window openings, archways, a hole in a wall or a gap in a fence are also suitable.

Failing that you can create your own frames using black masks with a heart, oval, circle, keyhole, star or binocular shape cut out of the middle. Filter manufacturers such as Cokin make sets of masks to slot into their filter holders.

If the frame itself is in shadow it will record as a silhouette to give striking results. You should take a meter reading out in the open, though, otherwise the darkness will fool your camera into overexposing. Also, set your lens to a small aperture – f/11 or f/16 is ideal – if you want the frame and everything else to come out sharp.

Make the most of your lenses

We have already looked at how to use lenses back in Chapter 02, but it is worth recapping on a few points that can help you when it comes to composing your pictures.

- Zoom lenses allow you to compose your pictures precisely by making slight adjustments to focal length. Take advantage of this by cropping out unwanted details and wasted space so your shots are tightly composed – there is nothing worse than a windy composition.
- Use your telephoto lenses to isolate the most interesting areas of a scene, throw the background out of focus so all attention is concentrated on your main subject, and to compress perspective so distant features appear crowded together.
- You can create dynamic, sweeping compositions with wide-angle lenses. Move in close to features near the camera so they dominate the foreground and add a dramatic sense of scale, emphasize the effects of lines in a scene by exaggerating perspective, and use the extensive depth of field to obtain front-to-back sharpness.

Picture format

The majority of photographers automatically use the camera horizontally, mainly because it is designed to be held that way and is easier to use. However, turning the camera on its side can make a vast difference to the composition of a picture, so you should consider both options.

The beauty of the horizontal or 'landscape' format is that it is restful and soothing to look at because it emphasizes horizontal direction and echoes the horizon. You can also include more of what is on either side of the camera.

By using your camera in the vertical or 'portrait' format you can include far more foreground or sky, and because the eye has further to travel from top to bottom a stronger sense of vertical direction is created. This leads to more active, dynamic compositions.

So the next time you are out taking pictures, photograph the same scene using both formats then compare the results – you will be surprised by the difference.

How a tripod can help

It may sound rather dubious, but your compositional skills can be improved immensely simply by using a tripod. The reason for this is because with your camera mounted on a stable support you can take as long as you like composing each shot. If you are not quite sure what to do you can stand back and have a think, or move a few metres to your left or right to check the view, and when you return the shot you have already composed will be exactly the same.

Using a tripod also gives you more control. For example, you can stop your lens down to small apertures to obtain maximum depth of field without worrying about a long shutter speed causing camera shake. If you are handholding this may not be possible, so you will be forced to compromise and accept second best.

In other words, a tripod slows down the whole photographic process, makes you think more and gives you more control, so this should result in better pictures.

Developing an eye for a picture

The best way to improve your compositional skills is undoubtedly by practising, learning from your mistakes and studying the work of other photographers to see why they approach their subject in a particular way.

We all have our own way of looking at the world, and as your experience grows you will find that you tend to compose pictures in a particular style because it works for you. Often you won't even be aware that you are doing it. But that is the essence of good compositional skills. Once you know what works and what doesn't it should be committed to your subconscious, so that when you come across a scene you intuitively know how you want to compose it. If you think about it for too long, your work will lack individuality and originality.

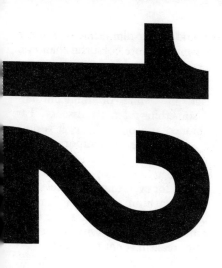

12

black and white photography

In this chapter you will learn:
- to see in black and white
- about using filters for black and white
- about converting digital images to black and white
- about metering and exposure for black and white.

In an age when digital cameras and colour film technology are at their peak, and the world we live in is more colourful than ever before, the idea of taking pictures in black and white may seem a little strange.

In recent years, however, black and white, or 'monochrome' photography has experienced something of a renaissance. Far from being considered old-fashioned and out of date, it is now seen as quite the opposite – creative, contemporary and expressive. Black and white images are regularly used for lavish advertising campaigns, and if you open any glossy magazine you will see black and white images used for everything from celebrity portraits to reportage to high fashion. As photographic technology advances, many image-makers are taking a step back and realizing that while colour may be realistic, it isn't necessarily expressive or emotive – sometimes realism is not the answer.

The main attraction of black and white is the fact that by stripping the colour from an image you divorce it from reality so the photographs you produce become a more effective means of self-expression. Instead of relying on realism and familiarity they become abstracts that use patterns, textures and the play of light and shade to gain appeal.

Photographs take on a different meaning, and we can see into them much more with the distraction of colour taken away. This applies to all subjects, be it portraiture, landscape, figure studies, abstract, still life or architecture. (See DVD 12.01.)

Before the advent of digital imaging, it was common for enthusiast photographers to have home darkrooms where they developed film and enlarged negatives to make high quality prints. Many still do; the art of hand-printing is very much alive, and if you would like to discover the magic of black and white printing yourself, the next chapter will lead you through the equipment and techniques required to get you started.

Today, however, you no longer need a darkroom to create stunning black and white photographs because negatives can be scanned and colour images, whether they started life as film or a digital file, can be converted to mono and manipulated on the computer with far greater precision than the traditional darkroom could ever offer, before being printed using an inkjet printer (see Chapter 13).

Learning to see in black and white

The biggest hurdle you have to overcome when working in black and white for the first time is to understand how a glorious colour scene will translate to black, white and the numerous grey tones in between. (See DVD 12.02.) A good way to learn initially is by photographing the same scenes or subjects in both black and white and colour so you can compare the two images and note how certain colours record as grey tones – or by making copies of digital colour images, converting one version to black and white by desaturating it, and noting how different colours respond.

Ideally, set up a shot or look for a scene that contains a wide range of different colours – reds, yellows, oranges, greens and blues. What you find when you do this will prove invaluable in the future as it will help you visualize if a scene will work well in black and white, and also what you may need to do at both the taking stage and the printing stage to ensure a successful image is produced.

For example, if you photograph red and green objects in close proximity in colour their relative difference in colour creates a contrast that makes each item stand out clearly. In black and white, however, red and green record as similar grey tones so that contrast is reduced and the impact of the photograph with it.

When shooting landscapes you need to remember that the sky will almost certainly overexpose if you expose for the foreground, and think about how the many different shades of green in the scene will translate. With still life shots, you need to visualize how the different objects will relate to each other when they are converted to grey tones so they do not merge and spoil the composition. Of course, while this practical knowledge will be of use, you should not live and die by it.

One of the great joys of black and white photography is that it allows you to express your own creative vision far more clearly than colour can, so detailed technical accuracy may be far less important to you than the overall mood and feel of the image. Also, while what you capture on the original negative or digital file is important, 99 per cent of the time it is what you do with the image in the darkroom or computer that counts, because it is only in the printing stage that a black and white photograph really comes to life, and you are able to make visual your thoughts and feelings.

You can adjust contrast to control the way highlights, shadows and mid-tones relate to each other, for instance. You can lighten or darken selective areas of the print to change its tonal balance. You can also crop the image to alter the composition, tone it with different colours and so on. (See DVD 12.03.)

Using filters

If you are shooting with black and white film, coloured filters can be used to control the way different colours record as grey tones and therefore alter the tonal relationship in a scene to a small or large extent.

The main colours used to achieve this are yellow, green, orange and red. Each will cause its own colour to record as a lighter grey tone in black and white and its complementary colour to record as a darker grey tone. So, red will lighten red and darken green while green will lighten green but darken red.

Here is a summary of the effects achieved by each filter.

Colour	Effect
Yellow	Ideal for general use as it gives a subtle effect, slightly darkening blue sky and emphasizing clouds. It is mainly used for landscape photography as a standard filter, but also lightens skin tones and helps to hide skin blemishes.
Yellow/green	Handy for landscape and garden photography because it lightens foliage in the scene and also help to separate green tones. Also darkens blue sky a little.
Orange	Gives a more dramatic effect by noticeably darkening blue sky so clouds stand out, therefore it is ideal on sunny days. It also emphasizes clouds in stormy weather and darkens greens so the contrast between the landscape and sky is increased. Finally, it helps to reduce haze. It is the best choice for dramatic landscapes and architecture.
Red	This is the most dramatic filter of all for black and white. Blue sky goes almost black so clouds stand out starkly and greens are darkened considerably. It can give a dark, sombre effect but needs to be used with care – especially in bright, sunny weather.
Blue	Though less common than the others, a blue filter increases the effects of haze, brings out details in the face and strengthens skin tones so it is useful for male portraiture.

One other type of filter worth using for black and white film photography is the polarizer. As well as improving clarity by reducing haze and glare – just as it does in a colour photograph – it also darkens blue sky so it records as a darker grey tone and emphasizes clouds. In sunny weather the effect produced can be as dramatic as a red filter, but one benefit of the polarizer is that it doesn't darken greens in the scene. For a really dramatic effect, try combining a red filter with a polarizer – blue sky will go black and you will get a significant increase in contrast. (See DVD 12.04–12.10.)

Digital black and white

If you shoot digitally rather than exposing film, it is still possible to produce stunning black and white photographs. In fact, many black and white photographers who have made the switch from film to digital capture feel that their images are even better because the digital darkroom, or 'lightroom', offers a much greater degree of control when it comes to localized exposure, contrast and tonal balance because mistakes can be rectified on screen before anything is committed to print. Creative techniques such as lith printing, toning, soft focus and grain are also easier to apply.

The key to success with digital black and white photography is converting the original colour image to black and white. This may sound simple – a growing number of digital cameras even boast a black and white capture mode now so you can see the image on the preview screen in black and white – but to do it properly requires patience and skill.

First and foremost, if you are using a digital camera to take the photograph – rather than scanning a colour slide or negative – you should capture the image in colour as that colour information will be useful later. It is also a good idea to shoot in RAW capture mode rather than jpeg as you will have more control when it comes to converting the image to magical monochrome. The RAW file also contains all the information recorded by the camera's sensor – think of it as a negative – it has the same level of exposure latitude as a negative and no data is lost, whereas the jpeg format is a glossy format that compresses the image file.

Once the image is in your computer, either as a download from a memory card or a scan from a colour film original, there are various ways to convert it to black and white. Adobe Photoshop is the most common and versatile software for image manipulation and the techniques outlined below all require Photoshop. Other software packages such as Adobe Lightroom, can also be used to convert colour images to black and white.

1 Convert to Greyscale

The easiest way to change a colour image to black and white is by converting it from RGB mode to Greyscale – Image>Mode>Greyscale. Doing this removes all colour information from the image so the file size is reduced, but the end result often appears rather flat and lifeless unless you then adjust contrast using Levels and Curves, so it is best avoided.

2 Desaturate

Just as quick is simply to open the image file then use Image>Adjustments>Desaturate to remove all the colour. The difference with this technique is that is it non-destructive and all colour information is retained so you can use it as the basis for digital toning (see page 206). However, basic desaturation often results in a poor black and white image and you will need to make adjustments to Levels and Curves to put some life back into it. (See DVD 12.11–12.13.)

3 Using Lab Mode

This tends to be the most effective 'quick and dirty' way of converting to black and white as the end result often looks strong without additional work. To use it, go to Image>Mode>Lab Mode then select Windows>Layers to open the layers palette and click on Channels. Next, get rid of either the 'a' channel or 'b' channel – it doesn't matter which – by clicking one and dragging it to the trash icon. (See DVD 12.14–12.17.)

4 Using Channel Mixer

A more versatile technique is to use Channel Mixer so you can alter the tonal balance of the image by adjusting each colour channel individually. This is rather like using coloured filters on your lens when shooting black and white film (see page 206).

To use this method, open your image file in Photoshop then make an adjustment layer – Image>Layer>New Adjustment Layer>Channel Mixer and tick the Monochrome window in the

Channel Mixer dialogue box. By using an adjustment layer you won't affect the original colour image so you can always change your mind.

In its default mode, the Red channel is always set to 100 per cent and the other colour channel at 0 per cent. This gives an effect similar to using a red filter on the lens when taking a black and white photograph – anything red in the original colour photograph will appear as a light grey tone while blues and greens will be dark. If you reduce the red channel to 0 per cent and then increase green or blue to 100 per cent the effect will be similar to using a green or blue filter on the lens and the grey tones will change dramatically.

To get the best results from Channel Mixer, adjust the sliders for each colour channel until you are happy with the effect. Only small adjustments are required and the + and – amounts applied should ideally total 100 per cent – so you could set red to 50 per cent, blue to 50 per cent and green to 0 per cent, for example. (See DVD 12.18–12.21.)

5 Increasing colour saturation

Before you make adjustments in Channel Mixer, try increasing the colour saturation of certain colours in the original colour image so they produce a bolder grey tone. To do this, open the image then use Image>Adjustments>Hue/Saturation. In the Hue/Saturation dialogue box, go to the Edit window and select the colour you wish to adjust. For example, if you want to make blue sky darker in an architectural shot, choose Blue then adjust the Saturation slider to make the blue more intense. It will probably look way over the top in colour but when you convert to mono in Channel Mixer this will result in a darker grey tone. (See DVD 12.22–12.25.)

6 The film and filter method

A more complicated technique – but also more powerful and versatile – involves creating two hue/saturation adjustment layers. One is desaturated and acts like black and white film while the second acts as a filter and can be adjusted to change the tonality of the image.

- First make an adjustment layer. Go to Windows>Layers then click and hold the New Adjustment Layer icon and select Hue/Saturation. Click OK to get rid of the Hue/Saturation dialogue box then change the Blending Mode of this layer to Colour. Next, double-click the layer icon and rename it 'Filter'.

- Create a second adjustment layer as above then, in the Hue/Saturation dialogue box, move the Saturation slide to –100 per cent so all colour is removed from the image, then click OK. Now double-click the icon and rename the layer 'Film'. Also, check that the Film layer is positioned above the Filter layer in the layers palette otherwise the technique will not work.

- Click on the filter layer then double-click to open the Hue/Saturation dialogue box. Now adjust the Hue and Saturation sliders and note how the tones in the black and white image change. Make adjustments until you are happy with the effect.

- For even more control, you can adjust Hue and Saturation for each colour individually. To do this, double-click the Filter icon in the layers palette to open the Hue/Saturation dialogue box, click the Edit window where it says Master, then choose each colour in turn and adjust its hue and saturation.

This technique takes a little getting used to, but with practice you will soon be producing dramatic black and white images with bold tones.

Instead of using Photoshop techniques to convert colour images to black and white, you could use different software packages such as Adobe Lightroom – which many photographers consider to be more user-friendly and intuitive than Photoshop.

There are also numerous 'plug-ins' for Photoshop such as Convert To Black and White Pro that make the job easier and give you more control – allowing you to mimic the characteristics of specific black and white films and the effects of using coloured filters to control contrast. (See DVD 12.26–12.30.)

Black and white technique

Learning to visualize how colours translate to grey tones is the first step in honing your black and white technique because it will help you to understand what the final image may look like when printed – and guide you towards making certain decisions to influence that final image. However, there are other factors to consider when taking pictures in black and white.

Metering and exposure

Perhaps the most important is how you expose a black and white photograph, because that will govern how much detail is recorded in the negative and, consequently, how easy that negative is to print.

The old adage is when shooting in colour expose for the highlights and when shooting in black and white expose for the shadows. This is not a bad technique to adopt, but unless you understand how camera meters work it is likely to cause more harm than good.

A much simpler approach in normal lighting conditions is to expose for a mid-tone and then let everything else fall into place around it. This should produce a negative that contains a full range of detail and tone from white through to black, which you can print on a normal grade of paper – grade 2. Digitally, the main priority is not to let the highlights 'blow-out' otherwise no detail will be recorded in those areas and no amount of image manipulation can change that. So, if you can see highlight warnings flashing after recording an image, reduce the exposure by half to one stop and re-shoot.

Most modern camera meters will naturally set a mid-tone exposure in average lighting as that is what they are designed to do, so you could simply go along with what your camera sets. The other option is to take a spot reading from a specific part of the scene that represents a mid-tone.

Where the lighting is not 'average' you need to make a decision about how you wish to interpret the scene and expose accordingly. If you are photographing a tree against bright sky, for example, you need to decide if the mid-tones and shadow areas are more important than the highlights. If you expose for a mid-tone, for example, the bright sky will be overexposed and on a normal print this would produce a high-key backlit effect, whereas if you expose for the sky itself, the mid-tones and shadows will be underexposed and on a straight print the tree would come out as a silhouette or near silhouette.

If in doubt in situations like this you can always make a series of exposures then decide later which interpretation you prefer and choose the best negative for printing. You also have a large degree of creative licence in the darkroom, so if you change your mind it is usually possible to achieve the effect you want by using different contrast grades of paper, varying the print exposure and giving more or less exposure to certain parts of the image.

If you are shooting digitally, in RAW, then the image file you produce will be rather like a negative and offer a good degree of exposure latitude. That said, in high-contrast situations it is worth shooting the scene at the metered exposure then one stop over it and one stop under it, so you have three files to choose from.

Composition

Although you can change the composition of a black and white photograph by cropping it during printing, do not let this fact lull you into a false sense of security as it could lead to sloppy technique.

Instead, aim to compose each picture in camera exactly as you want it to be printed, so that you have to think carefully about the way the lines, shapes, patterns and textures are arranged so they relate expressively to one another. Some photographers even print their black and white pictures with the film rebate showing – evidence that the image has not been cropped.

There is no need to go to such measures (although the technique can look very effective) and there is nothing wrong with cropping an image if it improves the end result, but being disciplined about composition when you take the picture in the first place will not only produce better compositions, it will also make you a more considered photographer over all.

Make the most of light

Light has different meaning in black and white photography compared to colour. When you take a colour photograph, the light can actually have a colour of its own – warm, as at sunrise and sunset, or cold as on a cloudy or foggy day. Colour film and digital sensors record these variations in the colour of light even if the eye cannot see them, but black and white film is clearly incapable of doing this, which can be both good and bad.

From a positive point of view there is no colour to influence the mood of your pictures, so you can shoot portraits or candids indoors in artificial lighting and produce striking images without worrying about a sickly orange cast spoiling them. The type of lighting that would normally produce rather drab, boring, colour photographs on a dreary overcast day, for example, can also produce wonderfully evocative black and white photographs, so you can exploit conditions that would leave colour photographers heading for home. Also, if you set out with the intention of shooting colour, only to find that the weather turns dull, you can either switch to black and white or, in the case of digital, shoot with the aim of converting your images to black and white later.

The downside is that you have to work harder with light when shooting in black and white because the colour of the light cannot contribute to the mood of the final picture – a black and white sunset simply cannot compete with one shot in colour because without the golden glow its emotional impact will be lost.

Fortunately, this factor can also work in your favour, because in using light to define shape, texture, pattern and form – the elements on which black and white photographs rely – your eye for a picture can only get better.

The power of black and white

One factor you must never overlook is the sheer emotive power of black and white. By removing the colour from an image it becomes far easier to convey a message and allow the viewer to get straight to the point of what you are trying to say. As the late, great Ansel Adams once said – 'Forget what it looks like. How does it feel?'

This can work on many levels and with different subjects, from landscapes to abstracts, but black and white is never more powerful than when it is used to depict people, whether in a posed, formal situation or one of conflict and bloodshed – which is why black and white is the chosen medium of so many photo journalists. (See DVD 12.31–12.40.)

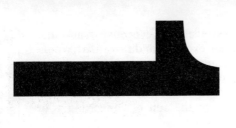

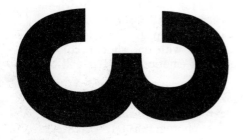

13 developing and printing

In this chapter you will learn:
- how to set up a darkroom
- about developing film and making prints
- about dodging and burning
- about spotting and toning prints.

When I first became interested in photography back in the early 1980s, developing and printing your own black and white (and in some cases colour) film was popular among enthusiasts. Bathrooms, under-stairs cupboards, spare bedrooms and lofts were often pressed into service as darkrooms and hours were spent watching images appear as if by magic on blank sheets of paper – all it took was a few smelly chemicals and lots of patience!

Today I still have a permanent darkroom and continue to make prints in the tried and tested fashion. However, the art of developing and printing has been replaced to a large extent by digital imaging technology and instead of 'darkrooms' photographers now spend their time in 'lightrooms' manipulating images with the aid of a computer and sophisticated software and producing prints using inkjet printers.

There is nothing wrong with this modern alternative, of course. Ultimately, it is the quality of the end result that counts, not how you created it, and no one can deny that working with a computer and inkjet printer is far more convenient than locking yourself away in a darkened room.

At the same time, however, nothing can beat the magic of watching an image appear on a blank sheet of paper, and it is well worth attempting to make your own prints if only to experience that magic first hand. Thanks to digital technology, traditional darkroom equipment can also be purchased cheaply now, so setting up a darkroom has never been easier. (See DVD 13.01.)

Developing a film

Developing black and white film is actually very easy if you think about what you're doing. The process involves just three chemicals, and once the film has been loaded into a suitable tank in complete darkness, everything else can be carried out in daylight.

Here's a shopping list of the items you'll need.

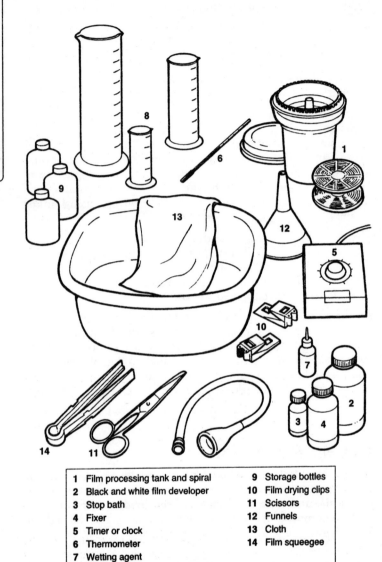

1	Film processing tank and spiral	**9**	Storage bottles
2	Black and white film developer	**10**	Film drying clips
3	Stop bath	**11**	Scissors
4	Fixer	**12**	Funnels
5	Timer or clock	**13**	Cloth
6	Thermometer	**14**	Film squeegee
7	Wetting agent		
8	Measuring graduates and jugs		

figure 13.1 Equipment needed for developing film

Developing tanks

Tanks come in a range of sizes and designs to hold anything from one to half a dozen or more films. The film itself must be loaded in complete darkness to avoid fogging, which you can do either with a light-tight changing bag or by blacking out a room in your home.

Before venturing into the dark, practise loading an old roll of film onto the spiral in daylight, so you get used to the task. Modern spirals are simple to use – once the end of the film has been fed into the grooves you just rack each side back and forth and the film is drawn onto the grooves automatically.

To make loading the film easier, cut off the film leader with a pair of scissors so the end curves outwards. You can then feed the end of the film onto the spiral in daylight so you don't have to fumble in the dark. Avoid pulling more than about three inches of film out of the cassette though – any more and you'll risk fogging the first couple of frames. You should also make sure the spiral is completely dry, as any moisture will prevent the film being loaded properly.

Once the film is loaded onto the spiral just pop it into the tank and secure the lid. You can now emerge into daylight again because the tank is light-tight.

Chemicals

Purchase film developer and fixer in small quantities initially – 250 ml bottles of liquid concentrate are fine. Once you open a bottle of developer or fixer it starts to oxidize due to exposure to the air and eventually becomes exhausted, so larger quantities are only worth buying if you process a lot of film.

Liquid chemicals are the easiest to use – you just measure out the right amount and dilute it with water. Others come in powder form which you have to mix to produce stock. Quantities of stock are then measured off and diluted further to give you a working solution.

Mix the chemicals with clean water, according to the manufacturer's instructions, using measuring graduates to get the quantities right. Write 'Dev', 'Stop' and 'Fix on them in waterproof marker pen so they don't get mixed up and cause cross-contamination.

Most developers are known as 'one-shot' because they have to be discarded after use, so only prepare the amount you need – usually 300 ml per film. Fixer and stop bath can be re-used many times if it is stored in tightly-capped bottles, so mix enough to fill your storage bottles.

With all three chemicals prepared you're almost ready for action, but first you need to check their temperature using a thermometer. The standard temperature for processing black and white film is 20°C (68°F). The instructions supplied with the developer will give you the processing time at 20°C.

If the chemicals are too warm, place the graduates in a basin cold water for a minute or two; if they're too cold, use warm water to raise the temperature a little. Check the temperature every few minutes until they reach that all-important 20°C.

The processing routine

1 Pour the developer briskly into the tank and start the timer. Once all the chemical has settled in the tank, tap the base to dislodge any air bubbles that have gathered on the film.

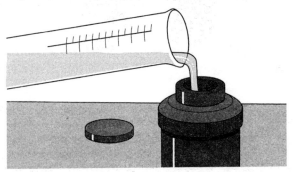

figure 13.2a

2 Agitate the film for 15 seconds by inverting it three or four times. This helps to ensure even development and should be repeated for 10 seconds every minute, or according to the manufacturer's instructions.

3 Keep an eye on your clock or timer and 10 seconds before the development time ends, start pouring the solution out of the tank into a jug.

4 Pour in the stop bath. This is a weak acetic acid that arrests the developer by neutralizing any alkaline in the tank and lengthens the life of the fixer. After about a minute pour it back into the storage bottle as it can be re-used.

5 Pour in the fixer, which clears the milkiness on the developed film and makes the image permanent. This usually takes a couple of minutes, after which the fixer can be returned to its storage bottle for re-use. Each time you fix a film, put a mark on a label on the bottle so you know how many times the fixer has been used.

6 Wash the film under running water for about 30 minutes to get rid of any chemicals before examining it. For the best results use a forced film washer to ensure even, thorough cleaning.

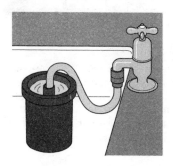

figure 13.2b

7 Before removing the film, place a couple of drops of wetting agent in the final rinse to break down surface tension so excess water slides off and the film dries evenly.

8 Remove a few inches of film from the spiral and attach a film clip to it, then draw out the rest of the film and fix a weighted clip to the other end.

9 Remove excess water with a squeegee – make sure it is clean, otherwise grit may scratch your film. Alternatively, run the film between your fingers.

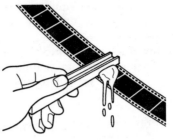

figure 13.2c

10 Hang the film up to dry in a clean, dust-free room for at least 12 hours. Once dry, cut the film into strips of 5 or 6 negatives and place them in storage sheets. (See DVD 13.02.)

Making black and white enlargements

Once you've processed a roll of film, the next stage is to make prints from the negatives. To do this you'll need the following items:

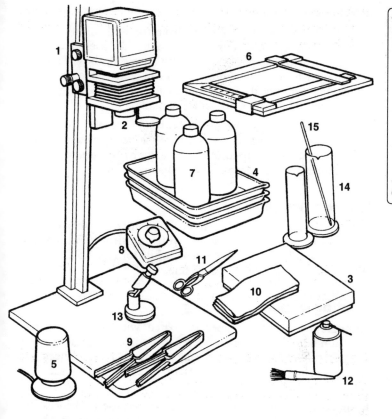

1	Enlarger	**9**	Print tongs
2	Enlarger lens	**10**	Cloth
3	Photographic printing paper	**11**	Scissors
4	Print developing dishes	**12**	Blower brush/canned air
5	Safelight	**13**	Focus finder
6	Masking frame	**14**	Graduates
7	Chemicals	**15**	Thermometer
8	Exposure timer or clock		

figure 13.3 Equipment needed for making black and white enlargements

Enlargers

An enlarger works like a slide projector and allows you to project an image from your negative onto the baseboard where the light-sensitive paper is placed. By adjusting the position of the enlarger head on the column you can control the size of the image. Most standard 35 mm and medium-format enlargers will allow prints up to 50 × 40 cm to be made.

If you intend using variable-contrast (VC) black and white printing paper (see below), make sure the enlarger you buy has a colour head as you need to dial-in colour filtration to achieve different contrast grades with VC paper.

Enlarger lenses

The lens you use on the enlarger determines the sharpness of your prints, so buy the best one you can afford. For 35 mm negatives you'll need a 50 mm lens, while for 6 × 4.5 cm, 6 × 6 cm and 6 × 7 cm 80 mm works fine.

Printing paper

Photographic printing paper is coated with a light-sensitive emulsion like film; the only difference is you can handle it under a weak safelight – usually orange, copper or red. Check the packet or box the paper comes in to check which safelight colour you need.

Resin-coated paper is the easiest to use because it absorbs less chemistry, doesn't need to be developed for so long and has a plastic base which dries completely flat. Traditional fibre-based paper is favoured by experienced printers for its superb quality, but it curls while drying so you need to flatten it afterwards.

A wide range of paper sizes are available, from 14 × 9 cm (5 × 3 in) to 60 × 50 cm (24 × 20 in). For general use 25 × 20 cm (l0 × 8 in) is favoured, while 40 × 30 cm (16 × 12 in) or 50 × 40 cm (20 × 16 in) is better for framing, portfolio prints and exhibitions.

In terms of surface finish, glossy is by far the most popular because it gives very clean, crisp prints with a bright sheen; especially glossy RC paper. Matte, semi-matte, lustre or silk prints are easier to look at though because the surface is less reflective.

Finally, paper used to come in various contrast grades so you could produce the best prints from negatives with different contrast levels. Today, however, these graded papers have been all but replaced by variable-contrast paper which allows you to obtain any contrast grade, from 0 (soft) to 5 (hard) in half-grade steps, from the same box of paper. This is achieved by using filters which are fitted above or below the enlarging lens, or dialing-in the necessary filtration on your enlarger's colour head.

Choosing the right paper grade for a particular negative can be tricky at first but comes with practise. Negatives with a normal contrast range tend to print best on grade 2 or 3, while contrasty negatives may require a softer grade such as 0.5 or 1 to capture the optimum tonal range, and negatives with a flat tonal range may require a harder grade such as 4 or 5 to add punch. You can also vary the grade used to obtain specific effects. A high contrast negative can be printed on grade 4 or 5 paper, for example, to produce a stark, dramatic image. (See DVD 13.09.)

Chemicals

Again, you need developer, fixer and stop bath. Mix up enough to cover the print in the tray – 1 litre of each is ideal – and store them in tightly-capped bottles. This time the developer can be re-used as well as the fixer and stop bath. Keep a note of the number of prints processed and discard the chemicals once they are exhausted.

Enlarger timer

Although you can count down the print exposure time in your head, or use a watch, an in-line timer is far more accurate. This is wired to the enlarger and can be programmed to give the required exposure automatically.

Developing trays

You'll need four – one each for the developer, stop bath and fixer and a fourth for water. Buy trays that are the next size up from the paper used – 30 × 25 cm (12 × l0 in) for 25 × 20 cm (10 × 8 in) paper, say – so you can handle the print easily.

Safelight

This is a lamp with a coloured plastic dome that allows you to see what you are doing in the darkroom without fogging the printing paper. Red or orange used to be the standard colour, but a pale brown or copper is better for variable-contrast paper.

Masking frames

This device holds the paper flat on the enlarger baseboard and allows you to mask off the edges to create a neat white border. It can be adjusted to accept different sizes of paper, so buy one to take the biggest size you're likely to use – 40 × 30 cm (16 × 12 in) or 50 × 40 cm (20 × 16 in).

Other items that will come in handy are plastic tongs, so you can handle the print in the chemicals without contaminating your skin; a focus finder, which allows you to focus the negative accurately on the enlarger baseboard; a can of compressed air and blower brush for cleaning your negatives prior to printing; a sheet of card for making a test strip; and a cloth for wiping-up any spillages.

The darkroom

Serious printers usually have a room that is permanently set aside for use as a darkroom. The window will be blacked-out with a blind or board, and the equipment will be set up on a carefully devised system of work benches and shelves. There may even be running water and a sink for optimum convenience.

However, the majority of photographers manage by commandeering the bathroom for an evening. A sheet of plywood placed over the bath tub makes an ideal surface for the developing trays, while a small table or cabinet can be used to support the enlarger.

You'll have running water from the wash basin, and the window can be blacked-out using board or a second pair of curtains – the latter is usually enough if you print at night. It is also a good idea to hang something over the door on the inside to prevent light leaks if someone decides to switch on the landing light. To check the room is completely light-tight, stand in it with the lights turned off for a minute or two so your eyes adjust, then look around – you will be able to clearly see any small leaks.

Another method is to place a sheet of printing paper on the enlarger baseboard, place a coin on the paper, leave it for a few minutes then develop and fix the print. If you can see a circle on the developed print where the coin was, it means the paper has been fogged slightly because your darkroom is leaking light.

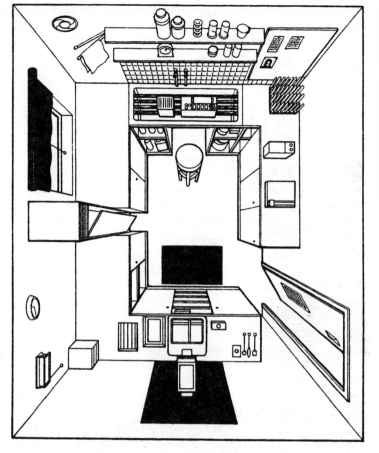

figure 13.4 The darkroom

Making a contact sheet

Deciding which shots to print is difficult to judge just by looking at the negatives, so your first job after processing a new roll of film is to produce a contact sheet or proof print.

To do this, place a 25 × 20 cm (10 × 8 in) sheet of glossy resin-coated printing paper on your enlarger's baseboard then lay the strips of negatives on it, emulsion downwards – there's enough room for a whole roll of 35 mm or 120 film. To hold the negatives flat so they come into contact with the paper, place a sheet of clean glass on top of them.

All you do then is set your enlarger lens to an aperture of f/8, make sure the enlarger head is high enough for the light from it to cover the sheet of negatives, and expose the paper.

Try an exposure of 10 seconds then process the print, or do a test strip first (see below) to determine the best exposure for that particular roll of film – it varies depending upon the film type and density of the negatives and you may need to make more than one contact sheet using different exposures to get a decent image from each negative. (See DVD 13.03.)

Making a test strip

Once you've decided which negative you would like to enlarge, the next stage involves producing a test strip so you can establish the exposure required to give a successful print.

To do this, place your negative in the enlarger, adjust the head to give the correct image size on the masking frame, then set the enlarger lens to f/8. Now cut a strip from a sheet of the same type of printing paper you will use for the final enlargement – a quarter of a 25 × 20 cm sheet is big enough. Position it on the masking frame so it covers an area of the image giving both highlight and shadow detail.

Switch on the enlarger and expose the whole strip for two seconds. Next, cover a quarter of the strip horizontally by holding a sheet of black card a couple of inches above it and expose for another two seconds. Now cover half the strip and expose for two seconds, then cover three-quarters and expose for two seconds. This gives you a test strip with bands exposed for two, four, six and eight seconds, from which there should be one that is correctly exposed.

Process the test strip as for a normal print (see below), then examine it under room or window lighting. Ideally, the correct exposure should fall in the middle of the strip, so you can then see from the lighter or darker bands if areas of the print will need dodging or burning-in (see below for details). If the whole of the test strip is too light, make a second one but increase the increments used during exposure. If it is too dark, reduce the increments. (See DVD 13.04.)

Making the final print

You have processed the film, made a contact print and test strip, and determined the exposure required. Now all that remains is to make an enlargement.

Here's a step-by-step guide to the procedure involved.

1 Remove the negative strip from its sleeve, remove any dust with a blower brush then place it in the enlarger's negative carrier.

2 Switch the room light off, turn the enlarger on, then with the enlarger lens set to maximum (widest) aperture, check the image is sharply focused on the baseboard using a focus finder. Stop the lens down to f/8 and set your timer to the exposure required.

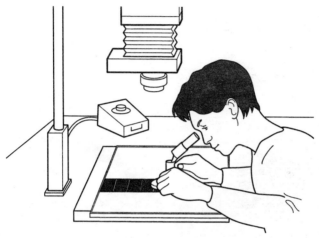

figure 13.5a

3 Place a sheet of printing paper under the masking frame with the shiny side upwards. Expose the print for the required time either by counting it down in your head or using an in-line timer.

4 Slide the print into the tray of developer, which should be roughly 20°C for the best results. Agitate the tray by rocking it up and down at one end so the print is evenly developed. Develop for the recommended period – usually one and a half minutes.

5 Remove the print from the developer using tongs 10 seconds before the period ends, and allow excess developer to drain off before placing it in the stop bath. Rock the tray for 30 seconds, drain again then transfer the print to the fixer. After the recommended fixing time you can switch on the room lights to assess your handiwork.

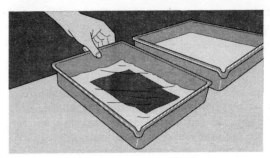

figure 13.5b

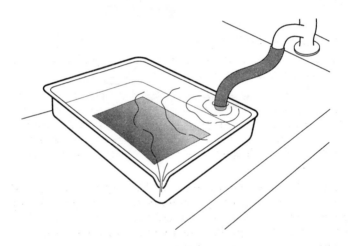

figure 13.5c

6 Wash the print under running water – 10 minutes for resin-coated paper and 40 minutes for fibre-based. To do this, place a processing tray in your bath tub and trail a pipe into it from the tap, so fresh water is constantly washing over the print and removing excess chemicals.

7 Drain-off surplus water from the print using a print squeegee or your hand, taking care not to scratch the surface. Lay the print out on a flat, dry surface or, especially with fibre-based

paper, hang it on a line to dry overnight and weigh the bottom corners down with clothes pegs to reduce curling. Fibre-based prints can be flattened afterwards beneath a pile of books.

Assessing the print

Once the print has been fixed and washed, take a close look at it to see if you're satisfied with the end result. Is it too light or too dark? Would it look better if selected areas were lighter or darker? Could printing on a different paper grade improve it?

If you start out with a perfect negative it is possible to produce a successful print on your first attempt. However, more often than not you'll need to work on it a little to get the best possible result. (See DVD 13.05–13.07.)

Dodging and burning-in

The most likely scenario is that parts of the initial print are perfect while others are too light or too dark.

If you enlarge a landscape, for example, chances are the foreground will be well exposed, but the sky is too light because the brightness range of the negative is too high for the print to record in a single exposure. Similarly, if you take a picture by exposing for the highlights, important areas on the print may be lost in shadow.

To rectify this, techniques known as 'dodging' and 'burning-in' are used. Dodging involves shading areas of the print during exposure so they receive less light and come out lighter. Burning-in does exactly the opposite in that you expose areas of the print for longer while shading the rest of it, so they go darker.

If large areas need burning-in, such as the sky, you can use a sheet of card or your hand to cover the rest of the image. For smaller areas, cut a hole in a piece of black card so you can 'paint' them with light. Similarly, small areas can be dodged by cutting a piece of card in the shape of the area to be dodged then taping it to a length of fine, stiff wire. (See DVD 13.08.)

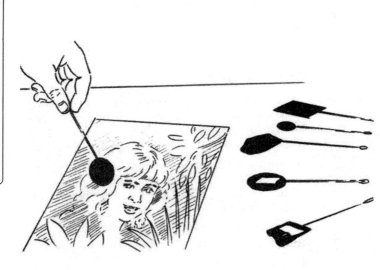

figure 13.6 Small areas can be dodged using discs of card taped to the end of stiff wire. Make a range of 'dodgers' so they are at hand when required.

To prevent the mask used for dodging or burning appearing on the final print, move it gently throughout the exposure. The actual increase or decrease in exposure required for the areas to be treated can be determined by examining your test strip. Failing that, make another test strip that concentrates on the problem areas.

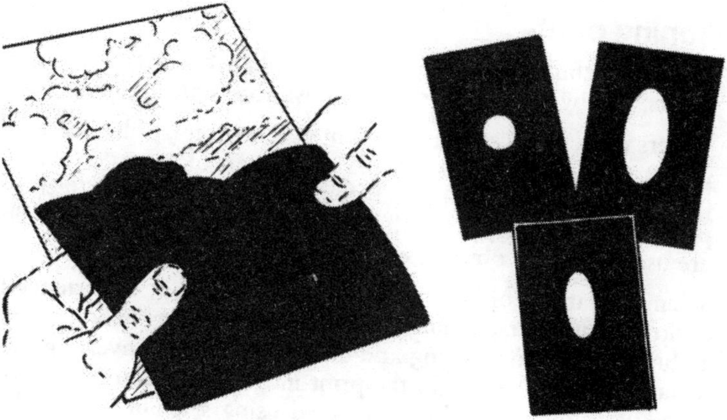

figure 13.7 To burn-in large areas like the sky, make a mask from black card or cup your hands to form the desired shape.

Spotting prints

If you clean your negatives carefully prior to enlargement, the final print should be perfectly clean. However, it is inevitable that tiny dust spots will find their way into the enlarger, causing small white spots and blemishes to appear on the print surface.

These marks can easily be removed using special photographic dyes such as Spotone and a fine sable brush – 00 and 0 sizes are ideal for spotting. All you need to do is dilute a tiny amount of dye with water until the shade matches the tone of the area to be spotted, then cover the blemish by carefully applying spots of dye and building-up the density gradually until the blemish is gone.

Spotting is best carried out on a flat surface in a well-lit area, so you can see exactly what you're doing. The dyes are available from good photo dealers, while brushes can be purchased from art and graphic suppliers.

Toning prints

Various techniques can be used to enhance black and white prints, but by far the easiest and most accessible is toning.

Toners come in a range if different colours: sepia, blue, copper, green, gold and selenium. Sepia creates an olde-worlde warm brown colour and is perfect for adding a nostalgic feel to portraits, landscapes and still lifes, while blue, copper and green are used for more obvious effects.

Selenium and gold toners are favoured by experienced darkroom workers, mainly because they help to make prints archivally safe from fading and discoloration by converting the remaining silver halides in the print into a stable compound. A range of colours can also be created using selenium and gold toners, depending upon the type of printing paper used.

Toning kits are available in all colours, and the whole process can be carried out in daylight using existing prints. (See DVD 13.10.)

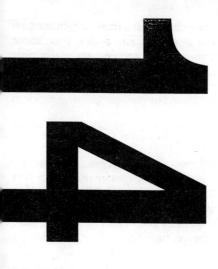

14

digital image processing

In this chapter you will learn:
- whether to use RAW or jpeg format
- how to scan negatives and slides
- how to work with Photoshop
- how to manage your image collection.

Whether you take pictures with a digital camera or shoot film and then scan your favourite negatives and slides, once those images are downloaded on to a computer you are really only part-way through the imaging process rather than at the end, because before those images are ready for printing or presentation, they will all be in need of post-production work to get them just right.

More often than not you will need to adjust exposure, contrast, colour balance and colour saturation to bring the image to life – especially with RAW files from a digital camera. If there are spots or blemishes on the camera's sensor, or if there was dust on the film when you scanned it, the offending black marks left on the image will also need to be retouched, while distracting elements such as telegraph wires in the sky or discarded litter that you didn't see when the picture was taken can also be removed.

Wonky horizons are a common problem that can easily be rectified and in some cases cropping will be necessary to improve composition. Finally, your images may benefit from a degree of digital sharpening, especially if you intend to make big enlargements.

This 'digital processing' may seem rather involved, but once you establish a sensible workflow it is surprising how quickly you can work through a batch of images.

RAW versus jpeg

The biggest decision you need to make when working with a digital SLR is whether to shoot in jpeg format or RAW.

Many novice photographers choose jpeg partly because the file size for each image is smaller, so more images can be stored on a memory card and also because certain image parameters are set by the camera which means less post-production work later. Colour balance, white balance, sharpening and colour saturation are all applied in-camera and if you want to change them later you need to be experienced in the use of imaging editing software such as Adobe Photoshop (see below). If you shoot in RAW, these same parameters are recorded but they are not applied to the image. Instead, when you open a RAW file you can access and change them using specialist RAW conversion software that is very intuitive and easy to use.

RAW files take up more memory than jpegs, so you get less images on a memory card, but as the name implies, they are 'raw' and uncorrected – rather like a film negative compared to a machine-made print – so for serious photographers they are much more versatile.

Processing RAW files

Okay, so you have decided to shoot in RAW format with your digital camera, you have filled a memory card with RAW files and those files have been downloaded to your computer. Now what?

The first step is to open the files, and to do that you will need suitable RAW conversion software. Camera manufacturers supply their own proprietary RAW converters with each camera, usually for free, but there is also a growing number of third-party programs from manufacturers such as Apple, Adobe, Phase One, Microsoft and even Google. Adobe Photoshop CS3 also includes Adobe Capture Raw so if you already use CS3 you will not necessarily need anything else.

The benefit of most third-party packages is that they not only allow you to open the files and make adjustments to exposure, colour, contrast, crop, rotate and even convert to black and white, but also to keyword images, arrange them into groups, create slide shows, catalogue collections and even output prints. Any changes made are seen immediately on a preview screen and often you can compare the corrected image with the original to see how different it looks.

Best of all, with some of the latest software such as Adobe Lightroom and Apple Aperture, any changes made are saved as a series of actions rather than being applied to the image, so they are non-destructive and take up far less memory than if you made a copy of the image then applied changes to it. In fact, some packages offer all the correction tools you are likely to need and to an extent make editing software such as Adobe Photoshop unnecessary.

The amount of work an image requires will depend partly on how well it recorded in the first place and also what you want the final image to look like. If you got the exposure nigh-on perfect, as you will in most situations thanks to the wonders of modern metering, and shot in good light the RAW image should look fine. The key is not to see RAW conversion software as a panacea of all ills. Yes, you can rescue a badly-exposed image, within reason, you can adjust colour and white-balance to remove unwanted colour casts and boost saturation to increase impact. What you cannot do is turn a dull, grey day into a sunny one or conjure up an amazing sunset, so you should always try to get everything right in-camera, to minimize the amount of time you spend at the computer later, and also aim to make the final image a true representation of the scene as you remembered it – not as you would have liked it to appear. (See DVD 14.01.)

Adjusting exposure

This is perhaps the easiest adjustment to make – if an image is too dark, adjust the slider to make it lighter and if it is too light, adjust the slider the other way to make it darker. That said, there are limits as to how far you can take this before you introduce other problems. If the image is underexposed and you need to brighten it, doing so will make any noise in the shadow areas more obvious. Overexposure is trickier to correct, especially if there are highlight areas burned out – you can retrieve detail where none was recorded. When it comes to exposure, then, try to get it perfect in-camera and if in doubt, bracket (see page 122). (See DVD 14.02 and 14.03.)

Correcting white balance

More often than not you will shoot with your camera set to Auto White Balance (AWB) and find that it works perfectly well. However, if you find that a set of images come out with an unwanted colour cast you will need to correct it using one of the tools in your RAW converter.

You may have a list of white balance presets similar to those in your camera – Tungsten, Fluorescent, Cloudy etc. – and by selecting one the cast is corrected. If you shoot in tungsten light with the camera set to AWB, for example, the images will come out with a yellow/orange cast that can be balanced using the Tungsten preset.

An alternative option is a colour temperature slider that allows you to increase or reduce the colour temperature (expressed in Kelvin). This is more flexible than presets because you can make smaller incremental changes to suit the look of the image. (See DVD 14.04 and 14.05.)

Correcting contrast

Contrast is the difference between the darkest and brightest parts of an image. If you take a picture in dull weather, for example, that difference will be small so contrast is low, whereas if you shoot into the light at sunrise or sunset the difference will be enormous and contrast very high. Subtle adjustments to contrast can make a big difference to an image but at the same time, if you overdo it you can ruin everything!

Most RAW converters use simple contrast sliders that are easy and quick to use because you see the effect immediately. Use the Highlight slider to pull back overexposed skies (using an ND grad when you take the picture is preferable) but be aware that if the sky is completely blown out it will simply turn grey when you adjust the slider because there is no detail to reveal. The highlights in the rest of the image will also be affected so you may be better off making small adjustments and then working on selective areas in Photoshop.

Use the Shadow slider to darken the shadows a little so contrast is increased and the image has more impact. Be careful to make only small adjustments otherwise the effect will be over the top. If you try to lighten the shadows using this control the results are often disappointing as the shadows merely turn grey and noise is highlighted. (See DVD 14.06.)

Adjusting curves

Once your experience grows, a more sophisticated way of adjusting contrast is by using the Curves controls. Done well, this can make a huge difference to the whole look of an image. You can also make adjustments to one part of the image without affecting anything else, and reverse any changes that do not have the desired effect.

One quick adjustment to try is moving the mid-tone curve. To do this, click on the centre of the curve and carefully drag it down towards the corner of the Curves window to darken the image or upwards towards the top corner to lighten it. Any changes made to the image when you do this are mainly applied to the mid-tones while the shadows and highlights are affected only marginally.

Another option is to create and S-shaped curve where the highlights and shadows are enhanced. To do this, click on the curve about three-quarters of the way down the line and again three-quarters of the way up it. This creates two fixed points on the curve and anything between those points will not be affected by any adjustments you make. Now carefully adjust the two points so the curve represents a shallow S-shape.

Many RAW converters also have preset curve adjustments that you can try such as Linear or Medium-contrast. Try these first to see if they give you the desired effect, especially if you are a beginner to RAW conversion.

Scanning film

If you do not already shoot with a digital camera, the alternative way to create digital images is by scanning film originals – negatives and slides. As discussed in Chapter 04, there are two types of scanner available – flatbed and dedicated film scanner. Both types do the same job in that they use sensors to analyse and sample a piece of film and convert the image to pixels so you can then open it in Photoshop and work on it like you would an image from a digital camera.

Scanning is a relatively straightforward process, but needs to be done with care if you want to achieve optimum quality. The slide or negative you are about to scan should always be cleaned with an anti-static brush or cloth to remove all traces of dust, dirt and finger marks as the scanner will record every imperfection and you will then need to spend time removing them (see page 191). Many film scanners have special software which automatically removes dust and scratches, but do not rely on it completely.

All scanners and scanning software work in slightly different ways so it would be impossible to give you an accurate step-by-step guide to scanning. That said, certain factors should be considered no matter what combination of scanner and software you are using.

1 Open the image and ask the scanner to produce a pre-scan so you can look at it on the scanner preview screen, crop the image as required and make any necessary adjustments. Factors such as contrast, brightness and colour balance can be changed at this stage, but if your scanner is working properly and the film image is correctly exposed the pre-scan should bear a pretty good resemblance to the original. Adjustments are also better made in Photoshop or on other software such as Adobe Lightroom – think of this as being

similar to shooting with a digital camera in RAW capture mode. Make sure Unsharp Mask or any other form of sharpening is also turned off – sharpening should be one of the last things you do to an image, not the first.

2 If you are scanning black and white negatives you can choose to scan in monochrome or greyscale mode at 16bit output. However, colour originals should always be scanned in colour mode (RGB) even if you intend to convert to black and white later. If your scanner has a maximum output of 48bit, choose this – it effectively means that each of the three colour channels will be scanned at 16bit. You can convert the scan to 8bit later if you like, to make the file size smaller.

3 The resolution you scan at will influence the quality of the final image and how big you can print it. The standard resolution used for printing and publishing is 300 ppi, so you can either set the scanner resolution to 300 ppi and choose a maximum output size such as 16 × 12 inch or set the scanner to maximum resolution – this may be 4000 ppi or higher and scan the film original at 100 per cent. The latter approach is theoretically the most sensible one because it means you are using your scanner to its full potential. If you scan a 35 mm negative or slides to 4000 ppi, its maximum output size at a print resolution of 300 dpi will be 18 inch, which is about the limit of how big you could print a 35 mm image. However, when scanning medium- or large-format film the file sizes can be 300MB or more. Such large files are unnecessary for normal usage, use a lot of your computer's RAM when open and take up a lot of disk space to store. A more practical option therefore is to scan to the biggest output size you expect to ever need at 300 ppi, remembering that even though you only have an A4 printer now, you may one day upgrade to A3+ or even A2. It is better to produce scans that are bigger than you need right now rather than have to rescan in the future.

4 When the image is ready for scanning and you click on Scan or OK, you will usually be asked to give the file a name and choose a file format. Make sure the format you choose is TIFF or PSD (Photoshop format). Do not choose jpeg as it is a 'lossy' format so every time you copy the file, data will be lost and eventually the image quality will suffer.

5 If the settings you used for the scan produce a good result, save them so you can use the same presets on subsequent scans.

6 With scanning complete you can open the image file in Photoshop and start working on it, adjusting Levels and Curves, removing any dust spots, getting rid of scratches, correcting colour balance and so on. See below for advice on how to do this.

Working with Adobe Photoshop

The world's number one image editing software is, and has been for many years, Adobe Photoshop, and although the latest RAW converters such as Adobe Lightroom share many of Photoshop's adjustment features, when it comes to complex image manipulation, selective correction and the application of creative techniques (see Chapter 15), there is no equal.

At the time of writing the latest version of Photoshop is CS3 (Creative Suite 3). It is more sophisticated than ever and includes other useful applications such as Adobe Capture Raw for RAW file processing and Adobe In Design. However, it is also expensive and includes many features you will never use, at least in the beginning, so a better alternative initially is probably Adobe Elements which is a fraction of the price of CS3. (See DVD 14.07.)

Photoshop Toolbox

Perhaps the most confusing thing about Photoshop when you first start using it is knowing what all the symbols in the toolbox stand for and what those tools actually do. To help you get started, here is a brief explanation of the main tools. The number of tools you have at your disposal will depend on which version of Photoshop you are using. (See DVD 14.08.)

- **Marquee** – This tool allows you to select an area of the image and isolate it so you can apply changes without affecting the image outside the pattern of dashed lines that indicates the boundary of the selection. The shape of the selection depends on the marquee chosen – you can choose from Rectangular, Elliptical and Single Row.
- **Move** – Use this tool to move a selected area of an image or a whole image – handy if you want to create a montage by placing several images on an enlarged canvas or if you want to take part of one image and place it on a different image.
- **Lasso** – This allows you to draw around a specific part of an image so you can work on it selectively – when lightening or

darkening parts of an image such as the sky, for example. There are three options: *Freeform* where you select as if drawing by hand; *Polygonal* which links the points between mouse clicks so you can select an area using a series of straight lines and *Magnetic* which follows the edge of an object.

- **Magic wand** – This allows you to select neighbouring pixels of a similar colour or add dissimilar pixels.

- **Crop** – This allows you to select and enclose an area of the image, and then remove everything outside the selection to crop the image to a new shape.

- **Slice** – This is mainly used for website design and allows you to slide an image into smaller sections.

- **Healing brush** – Similar use as the Rubber Stamp but this tool automatically attempts to match the pixels it pastes over a selected area. You can vary the size and style of the brush and also its opacity.

- **Airbrush** – Works like an airbrush with spray paint and lets you spray diffused strokes of colour or tone using a pattern and hardness of spray that can be preset from available menus.

- **Paintbrush** – Paints colours and effects onto an image. You can vary the size, shape, hardness and opacity of the brush and it is more precise than the Airbrush tool.

- **Pencil** – Same idea as the Paintbrush but works like a pencil rather than a brush. Again, its size, shapes, hardness and opacity can be changed to suit different applications.

- **Rubber stamp/Clone stamp** – This tool is mainly used when removing unwanted blemishes in an image such as dust and scratches. It works by allowing you to copy or 'clone' pixels from one area and paste them over another. There are many options available in terms of brush size and type. Opacity can also be varied.

- **Erase** – This tool can be used to erase pixels or layers. For example, if you combine two copies of the same image, one with a darker sky than the other, you can erase the lighter sky from one layer so the darker sky shows through. The Background Eraser paints in the background colour while the Magic Eraser changes areas of the image back to how they appeared before the last changes were made.

- **Gradient tool** – Fills the selected area with a gradual transition of colour or tone, usually from foreground to background, although you can create customized gradients. It is handy for darkening the sky in landscapes, for example.

- **Blur** – Reduces contrast between neighbouring pixels.
- **Dodge** – Use this tool to lighten areas of an image – like dodging a print under the enlarger.
- **Burn** – Opposite to the Dodge tool – it allows you to darken an area of an image, like burning in a print under the enlarger.
- **Text tool** – Allows you to add type to an image and vary the size and style of type as well as the typeface.
- **Pen** – Lets you draw a path outline, either as a point-to-point (pen tool) or freehand (Freeform pen tool). You can then convert this to a selection or stroke with colour/tone.
- **Sharpen** – Increases contrast between neighbouring pixels to make the image appear sharper – though more precise sharpening methods are recommended.
- **Smudge** – Smears the colours of an image.
- **Notes tool** – Allows you to apply notes to an image; perhaps to remind you what still needs to be done to complete work on it.
- **Eyedropper** – If you select this tool and then click on a point on the image it will select the colour of that point as the foreground colour. To make the selected colour the background colour instead, Alt/Click the point.
- **Hand** – If you enlarge an image so it is bigger than the screen you can use the hand tool to scroll to a different part of the image.
- **Zoom** – The Zoom tool allows you to enlarge an image on screen so you can examine it in more detail, for example, to check that an adjustment made or effect added has been successful.
- **Paint bucket** – Select this tool when you want to fill a selected area with the foreground colour that is in use or a predefined pattern.
- **Sponge** – Decreases colour saturation in the areas it is applied to.

Basic adjustments in Photoshop

If you are shooting in RAW format, the following advice may not apply because more often than not you will open and process those files using a separate RAW converter, as explained above. However, if you choose to use Adobe Capture Raw to convert your RAW files, you shoot in jpeg format instead of

RAW or you import scanned images into Photoshop, the following steps will help you achieve ultimate quality.

1 Open the image in Photoshop

Do this either by dragging and dropping the image icon over the Photoshop icon on your computer's desktop, double-clicking the image icon if Photoshop is already open or by using the File>Open>Browse option in Photoshop and then selecting the image you want to work on. (See DVD 14.09.)

2 Make a copy

Once the image is open, make a copy of it so you can keep the original safe – File>Save As – give it a name and make sure it is saved as a PSD (Photoshop) file or a Tiff file. Alternatively, the method used by more experienced photographers is to make a duplicate layer of the image – Layer>Duplicate Layer. Any changes and adjustments are applied to the Duplicate Layer, leaving the original image (the background layer) unaffected. If something goes disastrously wrong you can then delete the Duplicate Layer and the original image will be intact. (See DVD 14.10.)

3 Adjust levels

Go to Image>Adjustments>Levels and the Levels dialogue box will open. Levels will allow you to adjust the brightness and contrast of the image. The easiest way to do this initially is by moving the three sliders that represent the Shadows, Mid-tones and Highlights. Move the Shadow slider (the small black triangle) to the right and the shadows will go darker. Move the Highlight slider (the small white triangle) to the left and the highlights go brighter. These two controls allow you to increase contrast.

If you move the Mid-tone slider (the small grey triangle) instead, you can lighten or darken the image mainly in the mid-tones, although the shadows will also go darker if you adjust to the right and the highlights will become brighter if you adjust to the left.

Levels alone can often give you enough control to improve contrast and brightness, though it usually takes only small adjustments to achieve the desired effects. As your experience grows there are more complex ways of using Levels, but this basic technique will get you started and show what is possible. (See DVD 14.11.)

4 Adjust curves

Instead of using Levels to adjust contrast and brightness you can use Curves instead. This is a little more complicated for beginners, but as your experience grows you will find it to be a much more powerful tool so it is well worth acquainting yourself with it at an early stage.

To open the Curves dialogue box, go to Image>Adjustments> Curves. In the Channel window towards the top of the box you will see RGB. This is the basic setting and the best one to use initially as any changes you make will be applied to all three colour channels in the image – red, green and blue. Once you are more used to working with Curves you can select individual colour channels.

Drag the cursor to the centre of the RGB Curve and click to a point on the graph. If you pull the curve up or down from that point you will see that the image becomes lighter or darker, mainly in the mid-tones. Similarly, if you click on the bottom point on the curve and move it up or to the right, the shadows will become lighter or darker, and the same with the highlights if you click on the top point on the curve and drag it to the left or downwards.

As the effects of any adjustment of the curve shows instantly on the image you can experiment until you are happy with the overall look of the image. Big adjustments can create some weird and wonderful effects such as solarization (see page 202) so do not be afraid to experiment and see what happens. (See DVD 14.12.)

5 Use brightness/contrast

If you go to Image>Adjustments, one of the options in the pull-down menu is Brightness/Contrast. This does the same thing as both Levels and Curves but in a much more simplified way. By all means try it but do not see it as a quick fix – when it comes to digital imaging, there aren't any if you want full control over the end result. (See DVD 14.13.)

6 Selective exposure control

Levels and Curves (or any other Photoshop tool for that matter) do not have to be applied to the whole image – by using the Marquee or Lasso tools you can select smaller areas and adjust brightness and contrast independently, leaving the rest of the image unchanged. For example, if the sky in a landscape image is too bright, you can select the sky area and make it darker. This combination of tools can also be used to control brightness and contrast in black and white images in the same way that you would dodge and burn in the darkroom (they are more versatile than the actual Dodge and Burn tools in Photoshop). (See DVD 14.14.)

7 Work on the colours

If the colours in an image are not quite as you would like them you can make changes quickly and easily using Image>Adjustments>Colour Balance to make subtle or obvious changes to the individual colour channels. Image>Adjustments> Selective Colour can also be used to make certain colours such as red, blue, green, white or black lighter, darker, more or less saturated, or to change the hue. Again, there is no right or wrong here – the changes you make will be down to personal taste and the look you have in mind. (See DVD 14.15.)

8 Increase colour saturation

Images from a digital camera often lack colour vibrancy, especially if you shoot in RAW. To overcome this and make the colours closer to how they appeared in reality, use Image>Adjustments>Hue/Saturation and increase Saturation by 15 to 20 per cent. This tool can also be used to make the colours intentionally more vivid than they were, either to overcome the effects of shooting in dull weather, which naturally reduces colour saturation, or for creative effect.

As always, try not to go over the top. Over-saturation is one of the biggest mistakes made by photographers new to digital imaging, simply because it is so easy to do and so hard to resist. However, you can always tell when this has been done, so no one will be fooled! (See DVD 14.16.)

9 Remove dust and blemishes

Dust and dirt on your camera's sensor will show up as black marks on the images – as will dust, hairs and scratches on negatives and slides that are scanned. Fortunately, getting rid of them in Photoshop is easy. All you do is enlarge the image on screen so the offending mark is clearly visible, and then click on the Rubber Stamp tool. Next, go to the Brush menu and select a brush that is big enough to cover the blemish. If it is too big or too small you can change its size. Opacity can also be changed. Both hard and soft brushes can be selected. Hard brushes are better for dust spots, whereas soft brushes are more suited to less obvious blemishes.

Once you have chosen your brush, move it to an area close to the blemish where you can clone pixels of the same colour and tone you want to work on, hold down the Alt key and click the mouse to copy the pixels. Next release the Alt key, move the brush over the blemish and click the mouse to paste the copied pixels over the blemish so it disappears.

Cloning out small blemishes such as dust spots is quick and easy. Bigger areas such as hairs or scratches require more work. It is tempting to simply increase the brush size to speed things up, but if you are too hasty you will leave evidence of your actions on the image – so stick with a small brush and take your time.

The same technique can be used to get rid of unwanted elements such as telegraph wires or litter and, with experience, you will be able to clone out obvious features without anyone knowing they were ever there! Instead of the Rubber Stamp, try using the Healing Brush to remove small blemishes. (See DVD 14.17.)

10 Rotate the image

If the image you open is the wrong way round you can correct this using Image>Rotate Canvas. Select one of the set values such as 90°CW to rotate the image 90° clockwise, or 90°CCW to rotate it 90° counter-clockwise. Sometimes an image will also work better if you flip it horizontally, so it is effectively back-to-front. The only time this looks odd is if there is text in the scene that will appear back-to-front and give the game away.

The Arbitrary option in Image>Rotate Canvas can be used to correct a wonky horizon. Just enter a value you think is sufficient then hit OK. The image will be rotated by the amount entered which can be in fractions of degrees as well as whole numbers. Then all you have to do is crop the image edges to complete the process (see below). (See DVD 14.18.)

11 Cropping

Although it is sound photographic practice to try to compose an image in-camera as you want it to appear, no photographer gets it right every time and on occasions you may feel that the composition can be improved if you crop the image on the computer, either in a small way or to radically transform the picture – maybe cropping an image composed in landscape format to upright format or even to a panorama. The creative options are yours – you could create several different versions of the same image if you like.

To crop in Photoshop all you need to do is click on the Crop Tool icon in the toolbox, click on to your image and drag the crop tool over it. Do not worry about getting it just right at this stage – you can then fine-tune the position of each side of the crop and by enlarging the image on-screen you can make very small adjustments to the position of each side of the crop box.

When you are happy with the crop, hit the Return key and the image will be cropped. If you decide not to bother, click on the Crop Tool icon then click on Do Not Crop.

If you are planning to do a radical crop, make sure you copy the image first or work on a duplicate layer so you can delete the layer later if you change your mind. (See DVD 14.19.)

12 Sharpening

Images straight from a digital camera are rarely as sharp as they could be due to the way data is recorded – especially if you shoot in RAW format. Similarly, if you scan a slide or negative it could usually benefit from a little digital sharpening to maximize image quality. There are numerous pieces of software available that have been written specifically for image sharpening and various in-depth sharpening techniques you can try as your experience and knowledge grows. Initially, however, the Unsharp Mask tool in Photoshop is fine.

To use it, open your image then go to Filter>Sharpen>Unsharp Mask. Next, position the cursor over an area of the image where there is plenty of contrast so that area is highlighted.

You have three sliders in the Unsharp Mask dialogue box – Amount, Radius and Threshold.

- Amount controls the strength of the effect.
- Radius controls the spread of the sharpening effect; the greater the radius the sharper the result.
- Threshold sets a contrast value below which no sharpening occurs. This helps to prevent large areas of even tone such as the sky looking grainy.

The levels you input depend on the type of image you are working on. However, it is important to note that you can very easily over-sharpen an image and spoil it because the effect will be unnatural. It is equally important to realize that sharpening will not make an out-of-focus or blurred image look sharp – it can only make a sharp image appear sharper.

Experimentation is the key – try different values and note how they affect the appearance of the image. To get you stated try these:

- For general: Amount 75–150 per cent; Radius 1 or 2 pixels; Threshold 0 levels.
- For detailed images: Amount 175–225 per cent; Radius 2 pixels; Threshold 0 levels.
- For areas of tone: Amount 55 per cent; Radius 20 pixels; Threshold 11 levels.

(See DVD 14.20.)

13 Managing your image collection

The more digital images you produce, either through digital capture or scanning, the more difficult you will find it to locate specific images in the future – or even remember you ever created them – if you do not formulate some kind of cataloguing system so you can organize your growing collection. Doing this when you only have a few dozen images may seem unnecessary but as time passes and your enthusiasm grows, a few dozen will quickly become a few thousand, by which point organizing them will be a very time-consuming process.

Initially you could simply create a set of folders that are titled by subject – Landscapes, Still life, Abstracts, Travel etc. – and as new images are added to the collection they can be filed in the appropriate folder. Alternatively, if you tend to specialize in a certain subject, such as landscape photography, you could file by location – specific counties or regions within counties.

Long term, of course, any simple system like this will be limiting because you may have lots of images scattered around different folders that are linked by a specific theme – such as Sunsets, Water, or a particular colour – and trying to locate them all will be nigh-on impossible.

This is where purpose-made cataloguing software comes into its own, or the latest RAW converters such as Adobe Lightroom. They used cross-reference systems based on key-wording which means that as you process a new batch of images you can give them keywords relating to the subject, location and anything else you feel is relevant. Then, if you ever need to call up images that fall into a certain category you simply input suitable keywords and any images that have been tagged with any of those words will be found.

Picture libraries have been using systems like this for decades and it allows them to effectively manage collections that often include millions of images. Now you can have access to the very same technology and get yourself organized sooner rather than later.

14 Saving and backing-up

Make sure all these changes have been saved – File>Save and if necessary, make a copy of the image using File>Save As.

Finally, though you may trust your computer's hard drive as a safe place to store your images, eventually it will begin to fill up and, more importantly, there is always a danger that it will suffer a catastrophic breakdown which results in all data being lost.

To ensure that such an occurrence will never have disastrous implications, it makes sense regularly to copy all new work to an external source – either an external hard drive or by copying images to DVD. Better still, do both and keep one copy at a different location so that in the event of fire, flood, theft or anything else that could result in images being lost for ever, at least you have a safe copy somewhere else!

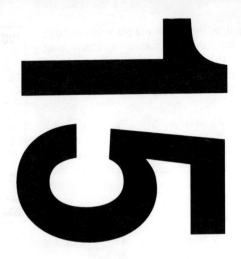

15 creative digital techniques

In this chapter you will learn:
- about using adjustment layers
- creative digital techniques
- about stitching panoramas
- how to restore old photographs.

Although the majority of digital images you download to your computer will require only basic adjustment and enhancement before you feel that they are ready for printing, projection or whatever end use you have in mind, your work does not have to end there because there is an endless range of creative techniques that can be applied to them using software such as Adobe Photoshop.

Many of these techniques are designed to mimic the effects of certain filters, specialist films and printing processes. However, one factor that unites them all is that they are quicker and easier to apply and infinitely more controllable than the traditional methods because you can carry out all the steps in broad daylight, correct any mistakes you make along the way and keep experimenting until the final image is exactly how you want it.

They can also be practised by novice photographers, without the need for specialist equipment beyond a computer and suitable software, or years of experience.

This chapter looks at just ten different techniques, but there are dozens more worth experimenting with so see image manipulation as the beginning of your creative journey rather than the end and you will never run short of ideas or inspiration.

Adjustment and duplicate layers

Before looking at specific techniques, it is worth mentioning first that whenever you want to add effects to a digital image, it makes sense to create an adjustment or duplicate layer first and work on that so the main image remains unaffected. Not only does this mean that mistakes can easily be rectified, but if you do not like the effect or something goes horribly wrong, you can simply discard the layer and start again.

An additional benefit of working on an adjustment layer is that you can then choose different blending modes and opacity levels to control the way the effect you have created actually works on the main image. If you set opacity to 100 per cent, for example, the full effect will be seen but if you reduce it to 50 per cent, it will be less obvious.

To create an adjustment layer, open your main image in Photoshop then go to Layer>Adjustment Layer> and choose the type of layer you want from the options. Alternatively, if you simply want to make a duplicate layer go to Layer>Duplicate Layer and give it a name.

You can view your layers using Window>Layers. Always make sure the duplicate or adjustment layer is at the top of the layers palette, and when you have completed the effect on the layer, try different blending modes and opacity levels to see which gives the best effect.

At the end of all this you can go to Layer>Flatten Image to combine the layers and make the effect permanent. However, by leaving the layers as they are you always have the option to make changes at a later date or delete the layers altogether.

Adding grain

Grain in photographic film is formed by clumps of silver halides in the light sensitive emulsion – the faster the film, the bigger these clumps and therefore the coarser the grain. In creative hands it can produce amazing results, adding a stark, gritty feel to black and white images and a soft, pointillistic effect to colour photographs.

Digital images have pixels instead of grain and no matter how high you set the ISO, the effect is never the same as shooting film – so if you want grain, you will need to add it digitally. Here are four easy methods. All can be used on both colour and black and white images but the effects seem to suit black and white best.

1 Using noise

Open an image in Photoshop then select Filter>Noise>Add Noise. You can control the effect using the amount slider and it is seen instantly on the main image. Levels and Curves may need adjustment as well to boost contrast.

2 Using the grain filter

Open your image then go to Image>Filter>Texture>Grain and a dialogue box will appear. A pull-down menu next to the grain type gives you various options. Regular and Soft are the most effective while Intensity and Contrast sliders allow you to vary the strength of the grain.

3 Reticulation

This Photoshop tool was mainly intended to mimic the effects of reticulation in film emulsion, which is a pattern of tiny cracks created when the emulsion is subjected to extreme temperature changes during processing thus causing it to expand and contract. However, it is also an effective way of adding grain. To use it, go to Filter>Sketch>Reticulation and then adjust the three sliders until you like the effect. The image is likely to go dark once reticulation is applied but you can adjust the tones using Levels and Curves or by going to Channel Mixer, clicking the Monochrome box and adjusting the sliders for the different colour channels.

4 Using the film grain filter

This is perhaps the closest you will get to the look of real grain, although you need to use it with care as the effect can easily look over the top.

Open your image and then select Filter>Artistic>Film Grain. A large dialogue box appears showing a preview of the image and you can adjust this to show the whole image or part of it. Next, adjust the Grain slider to increase or reduce grain size, then the Highlight Area and Intensity sliders. Finally, adjust Levels and Curves or use Channel Mixer to improve the tones of the image. (See DVD 15.01 and 15.02.)

Creating movement

Panning is a great technique to use if you want to add a sense of motion to action shots (see page 300) but it is quite a tricky technique to master. If you are struggling, why not consider adding motion to your pictures digitally using the Motion Blur filter in Photoshop? The great thing about this technique is that it even works if your main subject is static. Here is how it is done. (See DVD 15.07 and 15.08.)

- Open an image of a suitable subject such as a car in Photoshop.
- Add a small amount of motion blur to the whole image. Use Filter>Blur>Motion Blur. In the Distance window set a small amount such as 2 or 3 pixels. (See DVD 15.03.)
- Use the Lasso tool to make a selection around the car using a feathering of between 5 and 10 pixels. Select the car and wheels then use Select>Inverse so you can work on the

background while the car is left unaffected. (See DVD 15.04.)

- Select Filter>Blur>Motion Blur then move the Distance slider to the right and watch how the background blurs. Go to 60 or 70 pixels. You can also change the angle of the blurring – try a value of 4 or 5. (See DVD 15.05.)

- If you want to add even more blur to the top and bottom of the image, make selections with the Marquee or Lasso tools, set feathering to 50 pixels and apply more Motion blur.

- The wheels on the car will appear static when in fact they should be spinning. To mimic this, use the Lasso tool to make a selection around one wheel then go to Filter>Blur>Radial Blur, click on the Spin option, set Quality to Best and move the Amount slider to the right until you feel the effect is right. Repeat this for the other wheel. (See DVD 15.06.)

Stitching panoramas

There are specialist panoramic cameras available that allow you to produce stunning panoramic images on film with a single exposure. However, they are all limited by a small lens range, and a much more versatile way is to shoot a series of individual digital images then use software to 'stitch' them together because you can use any lens and cover any angle of view up to 360°.

- Choose a suitable scene, scan across it and decide what you would like to include in the final stitch. Panoramas are 'read' from left to right so make sure there are elements in the scene that will carry the viewer's eye from one area to the next, and try to avoid large areas of empty space.

- Select a lens that will give you the right angle of view, bearing in mind that you may need to crop a little off the top and bottom of the final panorama. It is therefore better to include a little extra foreground and sky. Lenses from 28 to 200 mm are generally the most suitable.

- Set up your tripod then attach the camera in portrait format. This is not essential but digital cameras have more pixels along the longer edge, so if you use the camera on its side you will increase the pixel count on the depth of your panorama.

- Use a spirit level or a levelling base to ensure that the camera is level and remains so as you pan horizontally. A Nodal Point bracket can also be used to rotate the camera on its Nodal Point and avoid parallax error.

- Take a meter reading from a part of the scene that represents an average area of tone – so not the lightest area or the darkest but somewhere in between. Set your camera to manual mode so the exposure is locked and does not change as you move the camera. This ensures that all the images are captured using the same exposure so they have the same density and can be stitched together seamlessly.
- Position your camera, focus and make the first exposure.
- Move the camera a little to the right so that it overlaps the first image by 30–40 per cent and make the second exposure.
- Repeat this process until you reach the far side of the scene, making sure that the images always overlap by 30–40 per cent. This aids seamless stitching. (See DVD 15.09.)
- Download the images to your computer and batch process the RAW files so that if any changes are made to contrast, colour balance or exposure the same changes are made to all the images.
- Put the images in a folder and give it a name.
- In Photoshop go to File>Automate>Photo Merge, find the folder containing the images using Browse and then Click OK and let the software get to work.

What should happen is that Photo Merge creates a perfect panorama. You may have to crop the top and bottom a little if the camera was not set up perfectly square, but other than that, the final image should require little or no extra work. (See DVD 15.10 and 15.12.)

Other software packages are available for stitching software – PTGui, Realviz Stitcher and PanaVue Image Assembler are among the most popular.

Soft focus

Gaussian Blur is the most popular tool used to create soft focus in Photoshop, although if you add Gaussian Blur direct to the main image it will simply appear to be out of focus, so for the best results you need to create an adjustment layer and add the blur to that.

- Open your image in Photoshop and make a duplicate layer by selecting Layer>Duplicate Layer. Name it Soft Focus or whatever you like.
- Open the layers palette – Window>Layers – making sure the duplicate layer is above the background layer (the main image) and click on it to make it live.

- Go to Filter>Blur>Gaussian Blur. In the dialogue box that appears you will see a small preview window and a Radius slider. The further to the right you drag the slider, the more blur is applied. Try a value of 4.0 or 5.0 initially. (See DVD 15.13.)
- In the Layers palette, click on the window where it reads Normal and choose Darken or Luminosity mode. Next, slowly adjust the Opacity slider from 100 per cent down and you will see the sharpness of the background layer begin to become more obvious. When you are happy with the effect, stop. (See DVD 15.14–15.16.)

Solarization

Also known as the 'Sabatier effect', solarization was traditionally created by briefly exposing photographic film or paper to light during development so it became partially fogged, resulting in a strange positive/negative effect. The effect can be striking, although trying to do it the old-fashioned way was always unpredictable and prone to failure. Doing it digitally is a breeze in comparison.

Using the solarize filter

All you do is open your image in Photoshop – it can be colour or black and white – then use Filter>Stylize>Solarize. There are no sliders or controls – the image is automatically solarized. Sometimes this step alone works fine, but if it does not try adjusting Levels and Curves – and Hue/Saturation in the case of colour images. (See DVD 15.17–15.20.)

Using curves

This technique is more involved but does give you more control over the final image. Ideally work on quite bold images that contain strong shapes and tones – statues, monuments and buildings are ideal.

- Open your selected image then go to Image>Adjustments>Curves to open the Curves dialogue box.
- Using your mouse, click on the bottom left point on the RGB curve and drag it to the top of the box so the image goes white.

- Click on the centre of what is now a horizontal line and drag the curve down so the tones in the image are reversed.
- Drag the curve down to the left and right of the centre point and then pull the centre point back up so the curve resembles a letter 'W'. This will create a solarized effect. Adjust the curve some more if necessary, and adjust Levels until you are happy with the effect.
- On some images you will achieve a more interesting effect if as a final stage you invert the image – Image>Adjustments> Invert.

Restoring old photographs

Photography has been around for over 150 years, so there are few families who do not have at least a few old black and white or sepia-toned prints of their ancestors. More often than not these have suffered the ravages of time and suffer from creases, tears, stains, scratches and fading.

Restoring old photographs by hand is a time consuming and skilful process that usually requires the expensive services of a professional with the necessary tools, skills and experience. Thanks to digital imaging, however, it is now possible to do the job yourself to a very high standard in a matter of minutes.

- The first step is to make a scan of the original photograph using a flatbed scanner. Many old photographs are quite small, but you can scan them to a much larger output size – 10 × 8 inch at 300 dpi is fine.
- If the image is toned, you can always remove the colour using Image>Adjustments>Desaturate then add a tone later (see below) when all retouching work is complete.
- If the image has faded over time you may also need to boost the tones using Levels and Curves.
- Once you are happy with the general appearance of the image, enlarge it using View>Zoom in or the Option>+ shortcut so you can highlight an area that needs working on.
- Problems such as scratches, creases, small holes and dust spots can be dealt with using the Clone Stamp tool and the Healing Brush tool (see page 187) which allow you to paste pixels from one area of the image over blemishes so they disappear.
- The Healing Brush tool does this automatically and tries to find pixels that are a good match, although it sometimes

leaves a 'smudged' mark. The Clone Stamp tool gives you more control because you can decide which area of the image you copy to paste over the blemish.

- To use the Healing Brush tool, click on the correct icon in the Photoshop toolbox (see page 187) then click on the Brush control at the top of the screen where you can change the diameter of the brush in pixels, the hardness (100 per cent is the default setting) and Spacing (25 per cent is the default setting). Use a small diameter brush and take your time, rather than using a large brush that speeds things up but is more likely to leave a mark.

- To use the Clone Stamp tool do the same as above and select the brush type you require – usually a soft-edged brush with opacity set to 60–70 per cent is the most suitable as you can work on an area gradually. Pixels are copied by placing the brush cursor over a suitable area and then holding down the Alt button while clicking the mouse. You can then paste those pixels by moving the cursor over the area you need to repair and clicking the mouse once more.

- Once you get used to working with these tools you will find that blemishes can be corrected quickly and easily. In both cases, however, the phrase 'more haste, less speed' certainly rings true and to do a convincing job you need to blow up the image so it is nice and big on screen and then work carefully on small areas using a small brush.

- If you have big repairs to do, such as creases, it is worth using View>Zoom out or the Option>– shortcut to reduce the size of the screen image so you can check progress.

- If a person depicted in the picture has a damaged eye, try copying the other eye and then paste it over the damaged one. To do this, enlarge the image so it is nice and big on screen, make a selection around the intact eye with the Lasso tool, copy it – Edit>Copy – make a new selection around the damaged eye, and then paste in the replacement eye using Edit>Paste. If the eye is small, as it would be in a group shot, this simple method may work perfectly well. If it is an individual portrait and the subject's eyes are bigger you may need to work more carefully, and also 'flip' the copied eye before you paste it over the damaged one, otherwise it will look unnatural.

- Once all damage has been corrected and any rough print edges have been cropped out you may want to sharpen the image prior to printing. Do this using Filter>Sharpen> Unsharp Mask but be careful when you set the sliders not to over-sharpen as the effect will look odd and may spoil your hard work (see page 191).

- Finally, if the original print was toned you may wish to re-tone your restored photograph. There are various ways to do this – see Toning prints below. (See DVD 15.21.)

Lith printing

In the darkroom lith printing can be a frustrating technique to practise. It takes time, is very hit-and-miss, and when you achieve a great result, repeating it with any degree of accuracy is almost impossible. In the lightroom, however, it is a different story – convincing lith effects are quick and easy to achieve and infinitely repeatable, as most digital techniques are.

- Select your black and white image and open it in Photoshop. You can start with a colour original but it must be converted to black and white before proceeding (see page 193).
- Go to Window>Layers, double-click the background layer and rename it 'Shadows'.
- Go to Layer>Duplicate Layer, double-click the layer icon and name it 'Highlights'. (See DVD 15.22.)
- To recreate the light highlights and mid-tones that are characteristic of lith prints, click on the Highlights layer then go to Image>Adjustments>Curves. In the Curves dialogue box, drag the bottom left marker upwards until the output level reads around 90. (See DVD 15.23.)
- Lith prints also exhibit dark, dense shadows. To mimic this, click on the Shadows layer then go to Image>Adjustments>Curves and drag the top right marker on the curve line to the left until the output level again reads around 90. (See DVD 15.24.)
- The shadow areas of lith prints exhibit coarse grain. To recreate this, click on the Shadows layer then select Filter>Artistic>Film Grain and experiment with different levels of grain (see above). (See DVD 15.25.)
- Lith prints have a colour in the lighter tones. To recreate this, click on the Highlight layer and then select Image>Adjustments>Hue/Saturation. When the dialogue box opens, click the Colorize window then set different Hue and Saturation values until you are happy with the effect. Try a Hue level of around 20 and a Saturation level of around 25. (See DVD 15.26.)

- Finally, click on the Highlight layer and change its blending mode to Multiply in the Layers palette. This reveals the grain in the shadows and gives you a clearer idea of how the final image is going to look. (See DVD 15.27 and 15.28.)

Toning images

Photographers have been toning black and white prints ever since the birth of photography. We have all seen old photographs with their characteristic sepia-brown tint, although in modern times different colours such as blue, copper and green have been added to the options available, while toners such as selenium and gold are preferred for their archival characteristics rather than the colour change they impart – which can be minimal, depending on the printing paper used.

Digital toning, in comparison, offers endless scope for experimentation because you can use any colour, combine colours, tone very specific areas of an image and leave the rest as black and white – the options are limited only by your imagination. And none of the techniques involved requires smelly chemicals! (See DVD 15.29.)

Using hue/saturation

The quickest and easiest way to tone a black and white image in Photoshop is by using Image>Adjustments>Hue/Saturation. When the dialogue box appears, click on the Colorize window, then simply adjust the Hue and Saturation sliders to create a myriad of different tone colours. The Hue slider governs the colour, while Saturation varies its strength.

With care you can create convincing tones in traditional colours such as sepia, selenium, blue, copper and gold, as well as inventing your own.

Using colour balance

An alternative to Hue/Saturation is the Colour Balance control found under Image>Adjustments>Colour Balance. As well as allowing you to create a range of attractive tone colours by adjusting the sliders towards red, green and blue or cyan, magenta and yellow – the more you push a slider in any direction, the stronger the colour – you also have the option to tone either the shadows, mid-tones or highlights by clicking on one of the options under Tone Balance.

This means that split-toned effects can be created with ease. For example, if you click on Shadows under Tone Balance then adjust the yellow/blue slider towards blue, the shadows will take on a subtle blue tone. If you then click on Highlights and move the cyan/red slider to the right a little, the shadows will take on a gentle sepia tone that replicates the effects of sepia and blue toning.

Digital zooming

It is relatively easy and lots of fun to create zoomed images using a zoom lens. However, as always, creating the effect digitally gives you much more control over the final result and also allows you to apply it to images in your archive, rather than going out in search of a suitable subject.

- Go to Filter>Blur>Radial Blur. In the dialogue box that opens you will see two options under Blur Method – Spin and Zoom. Select Zoom.

- There is also a slider that allows you to control the degree of blur applied. Start off with a low level of maybe 10 and see what happens – you can always increase or reduce it. This will apply a zoom effect to the whole image, but at this stage you do not want it to be too heavy.

- The effects of zooming with a lens tends to be more obvious towards the edges of the picture so to mimic this, make a selection in the centre of your image using the Lasso tool and set Feathering to around 100 pixels. Next, go to Select>Inverse.

- Now go to Filter>Blur>Radial Blur again, make sure Zoom is selected and apply an amount of 20–25. Because the central area has been selected then inversed, this command will affect only the areas of the image outside the selected area, so the central part of the image will remain unchanged. (See DVD 15.30–15.32.)

Photoshop filters

Numerous Photoshop filters have been mentioned in this chapter but so far they have all been used to create relatively subtle effects. Now it is time to get really creative and experiment with some of the more unusual options – all of which can create stunning results when used with care and on the right kind of image.

Diffuse glow

Use this filter to add a glow to backlit images – portraits, woodland scenes – anything will do. If applied to black and white photographs it can also mimic the effects of infrared film. Use Filter>Distort>Diffuse Glow to open a dialogue box then play with the three sliders to vary the effect. With colour images it might also be worth adjusting the Hue/Saturation sliders to make the end result even more unusual. (See DVD 15.33.)

Distort

If you select Filter>Distort you will find a range of filters such as Pinch, Shear, Spherize, Twirl and Liquify. They are all extreme filters and need to be used on images where the main subject will still be identifiable once the effect has been added. That said, you can have a lot of fun trying them out – especially on portraits! (See DVD 15.34 and 15.35.)

Artistic filter

Go to Filter>Artistic and you will see a drop-down list of different filters that allow you to add different graphic and painterly effects to photographs, often making the original image look more like a piece of graphic art than a photograph. Some work better than others. Poster Edges is one of the best. Try them on simple, bold images that rely on strong shapes and colours for their appeal rather than fine detail. (See DVD 15.36 and 15.37.)

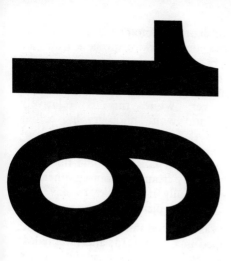

16

digital printing

In this chapter you will learn:
- how to choose the best printer and ink
- to master print colour management
- to use different printing papers
- how to make exhibition-quality prints.

One of the many benefits of digital technology is that it allows you to stay involved in the image-making process from the moment you press the camera's shutter release to producing the final print. The same applies with film photography, of course, and if you so wish you can set up a darkroom to process and print your work. However, while this is relatively straightforward with black and white photography, colour processing and printing is more complicated and the risk of failure is much higher. Consequently, colour photographers have tended to reply on commercial labs to handle this task, which not only takes control away from the photographer but can also be very costly – especially if you like to have big enlargements made of your favourite pictures.

Today, this is no longer the case. Digital images are 'processed' using a computer as explained in Chapter 13, and lab-quality prints can now be produced at home using a modern inkjet printer for a fraction of the price a commercial lab would charge. As a result, printing your work is no longer an expensive luxury but an integral part of the photographic process. You can make prints for portfolios, to frame and hang on the wall, to give to family and friends as presents and, if you are ambitions, to exhibit and sell. In addition to making prints you can also present your work in others ways – by uploading them to photographic websites, by creating your own website, self-publishing books and so on. (See DVD 16.01.)

Printers and inks

The most common type of printer used by photographers is known as an inkjet printer – so named because it uses a series of nozzles or jets to apply tiny dots of ink on the printing paper. The more nozzles a printer has (1440 is quite common now) the finer the print quality. Inkjet prints are often referred to as 'giclee' prints which is the French way of saying 'to squirt' – exactly what inkjet printers do.

There are many models of inkjet printer available now from manufacturers such as Epson, Canon and Hewlett Packard, in sizes to suit all needs and with price tags to suit all budgets. All are capable of amazing results thanks to advances in printer technology and ink and paper manufacture and even the most basic budget models will allow you to produce lab-quality prints.

The smallest size worth considering for photographic work is A4 – this will allow you to make prints up to 8.3 × 11.7 in (210 × 297 mm). This is perfectly fine for general use, but if you want to make bigger prints then it is worth considering an A3+ printer which has a maximum print size of 13 × 19 in (329 × 483 mm). Some models of A3+ printer can also be loaded with 13-inch (329-mm) wide inkjet paper rolls so you can also produce panoramic prints up to that width and as long as you like.

Once you go beyond A3+, print price and size jumps dramatically as you enter the realm of the 'wide-format' printer. A2 is the smallest size in this category, capable of generating prints up to 16.5 × 23.3 in (420 × 594 mm) and also handling 17-inch (431-mm) paper rolls. There are also 24-inch (609-mm), 44-inch (1117-mm) and 64-inch (1625-mm) printers available for professional studios and commercial printers.

The main area where inkjet printers have improved is in the inks that they use as this not only leads to better image quality but also improved archival performance (how long the print will last without the image deteriorating).

Ten years ago, inkjet printers generally used just four inks – cyan, magenta, yellow and black (CMYK). They were capable of high quality, but the images had a habit of fading or changing colour after a short period of time because the inks were dye-based and not particularly permanent or stable. Black and white prints also tended to exhibit a colour cast; a problem that was exacerbated by a phenomenon known as metamarism where the colour of the print changes when viewed in different types of light.

Today, it is common for printers to use eight or more different inks; still based on the same CMYK make-up but with lighter versions of each colour and also one or two 'grey' inks as well as black. Not only does this lead to finer print quality, but you can also produce neutral black and white prints with a broad tonal range – instead of having to set up a second printer with a black and white inkset. The inks are also pigment-based so they are much more stable and inkjet prints now offer the same archival qualities as traditional silver-based prints.

When you come to buy a printer, make sure it uses individual ink cartridges for each colour. These printers are much more economical to use because when one colour runs out you only replace that colour. Printers that use a single colour cartridge containing all the colours waste ink because when one colour runs out the whole cartridge has to be replaced. For optimum quality you should also use inks from the same manufacturer as the printer. There are cheaper alternatives available, but the quality is rarely as high and many photographers experience problems with blocked nozzles when using third-party inks.

An alternative is to convert your printer to accept 'continuous flow' inks which use bottles of ink and a series of tubes to feed the ink to the printer nozzles. If you make a lot of prints, this type of system will save money long term because the bottles hold a large volume of ink so the ink cost per print is much lower than if you use cartridges. The downside is that initial set-up costs are quite high.

Colour management

The most common problems photographers experience when making inkjet prints is that the image on the print does not match the image on the computer monitor. The usual reason for this is that the monitor is not giving a true representation of what the image looks like because settings such as brightness, contrast and colour temperature are incorrect. To remedy this the monitor needs to be calibrated on a regular basis, ideally using a proper calibration device such as a 'spider' which is attached to the monitor and, using special software, analyses each colour and then creates a profile that the computer uses to control the monitor settings so everything is optimized.

The next stage in ensuring perfect prints is to install an ICC profile on your computer for each paper/ink combination you work with so that Photoshop can match the colours accurately. Paper manufacturers often provide profiles for each paper type in their range as free downloads. You can also buy equipment and software that enables you to create your own ICC profiles, or pay for a profiling service.

Whichever system you use to obtain profiles, the idea is that when you decide to print on a particular paper, you can select the correct profile from a list in Photoshop's Print with Preview dialogue box so that it will handle colour management for that print.

It is tempting to ignore colour management, but do so at your peril as you will never achieve optimum print quality and you will also waste a lot of paper and ink.

Paper choice

The choice of inkjet paper available today is huge, with ranges available from Epson, Ilford, Hahnemuhle, Fotospeed, Forte, Lumijet, Olmec, Permajet and others.

If you are a keen black and white photographer the choice is especially good because some of the smaller, specialist paper manufacturers have finally managed to come up with products that have a similar look and feel to traditional fibre-based printing papers. For colour printing, you can choose from high-gloss to matte with pearl, lustre and other 'semi-gloss' finishes in between. Paper thickness (weight) also varies from lightweight materials around 100 gsm to heavy fine-art papers of 460 gsm or more.

The type you choose will depend on your needs. For contact prints, proofing and everyday printing, a basic gloss or matte paper will suffice, while more expensive specialist materials can be used if you are printing for a portfolio or exhibition. Papers with a weight around 250 gsm have a similar feel to traditional lab-made prints.

In terms of finish, that is purely down to personal preference. Glossy paper looks more like traditional photo paper and produces prints with rich colours and lots of punch. However, it also picks up glare and reflections so the images are not always easy to appreciate. At the other extreme, matte paper is dead flat so there are no problems with reflections but equally it can make colours appear painterly and muted.

The key is to experiment with different paper types and surface finishes to see which you prefer. Most paper manufacturers sell sample packs for this very reason.

Making contact sheets

Black and white photographers make contact sheets by laying the strips of negatives from a film on to a sheet of printing paper and exposing it under the enlarger. Once developed and fixed, this sheet provides them with a set of 'thumbnail' images the same size as the film format that they can analyse to decide which frames to print, mark cropping instructions and also file for future reference.

It is a good idea to do the same thing digitally, so that you are not always looking at images on a computer screen and you can also scribble ideas and notes on the sheets if necessary.

To create contact sheets in Photoshop, all you do is put the images you wish to include on the sheet/s in a folder then go to File>Automate>Contact Sheet II. A dialogue box will then open and give you numerous options in terms of the size of the contact sheet and the number of images to be printed on it. A good size to use is A4 as it means the sheets will not be too big. As for the number of images you put on it, 12–15 should be the maximum really, otherwise they will be too small to appreciate.

Once you have decided on the sheet size, the number of images and the resolution (choose 300 ppi), click on the Browse button so you can locate the folder containing the images you want to contact, and then click OK and Photoshop will do the rest. If there are too many images for one sheet, it will automatically create a second, third and so on until all the images have been contacted. There is no need to re-size the images for the contact sheets as Photoshop will scale them down automatically.

If you tend to back up images on DVD, smaller contact sheets can be made (12 × 12 cm) and inserted in the wallet or jewel case so you know which images are on the disc. (See DVD 16.02.)

The final print

So, your monitor is calibrated, your printer is profiled and you have decided to make your first inkjet enlargements. Here is a step-by-step guide to doing just that.

1 Open the chosen image in Photoshop then go to File>Page Setup. In the dialogue box, select the correct printer (you may have more than one set up) and also the paper size you intend to print on. Click OK.

2 If you wish to print a panorama on roll paper, you will need to create a custom paper size. To do this, click on paper Size in the set-up dialogue box and scroll down the menu to Manage Custom Sizes. Now click on + to create a new custom paper size and enter the required dimensions. The Width will be the width of the paper roll and the Height will be the length of the image you want to print plus a little extra to create a border. Click OK. (See DVD 16.03.)

3 Go to File>Print with Preview and another dialogue box will open showing how big the image will be at 100 per cent on the paper size selected. If the image is too big for the paper size you can scale it down by clicking on Scale to Fit Media or if you want the printed image to be a certain size you can

enter the required dimensions in the Height and Width windows.

4 Beneath the preview image you will see a Print window with Document and Proof options. Make sure Document is selected. You should also see Profile: Adobe RGB (1998) in brackets. This is the colour space being used and it is the preferred one over SRGB as it records a wider colour spectrum.

5 In the next box under Options you will see Colour Handling, Printer Profile and Rendering Intent. Make sure Colour Handling is set to 'Let Photoshop Determine Colours' and that Printer Profile is the correct ICC profile for the paper you are printing on (see above). The Rendering Intent is usually set to Relative Colour Metric, although with some profiles, Perceptual is recommended instead. (See DVD 16.04.)

6 Click Print and a Print dialogue box appears. In this, choose the printer you are working with then click on the window where it says Copies and Pages and scroll down to Print Settings. In Media Type select the paper type you are using – such as premium Glossy Photo Paper or Archival Matte. If you have had a profile created for a specialist paper you will know which Media Type to choose. (See DVD 16.05.)

7 In the Colour window make sure you have selected Colour for photographic printing. Some printers also have an Advanced B&W mode which you can select when printing black and white, although you can also print black and white images in Colour mode.

8 In Mode click on Advanced Settings then click on Print Quality. You have various options for print resolution which varies from printer to printer. The lowest is usually 360 dpi, then 720 dpi then 1440 dpi and with more sophisticated printers 2880 dpi and maybe even 5760 dpi. These numbers refer to the number of dots of ink that the printer will apply to every inch of the printed image. If you are making proof prints or contact sheets, 720 dpi will be fine, while for general use, 1440 dpi is recommended. You can print at higher resolutions than 1440 dpi but you won't really see a noticeable difference in print quality and it will take the printer much longer to actually make the print. If High Speed is selected, click on the box to turn this setting off when making final prints.

9 Click on Printer Colour Management. If you are using an ICC profile to manage colours, click Off (No Colour Adjustment) so the printer lets Photoshop manage colours.

10 Click Print. After a few seconds the printer should whirr into action and minutes later you will be admiring a perfect print.

11 If print quality is not as high as expected or there are obvious problems, refer to the Troubleshooting section of your printer instructions or go to the manufacturer's website and check the Help section. The most common printer problems are caused by blocked nozzles which mean that one or more colours won't be printing properly so you will see lines on the print. However, this is an easy problem to solve using the toolbox in the Printer Utility of the printer software installed in your computer.

Presenting and storing prints

There is little point going to the trouble and expense of creating high-quality prints if all you do is leave them lying around to get dog-eared and damaged or hide them away in empty inkjet paper boxes.

The best way to show off photographic prints is by window-mounting them behind thick card or mountboard. You can buy pre-cut mounts off-the-shelf in many art shops and then make prints to fit. Alternatively, make prints to the size you want and then either have mounts custom-made by a framer or buy a mount cutter and cut your own mounts. This latter option is the cheapest and most versatile, although it takes practice to cut perfect mounts, so expect to waste a few sheets of card when you first start. If you tend to print to a standard size and always need the same size of mount, it may work out cheaper to place a bulk order for 50 mounts or more with a framer – the bigger frame shops use computerized mount cutters so the unit price comes down considerably if you place a large order for the same mount/aperture size.

Stick with a neutral colour for the mount – white or off-white – and make sure the board is acid-free so it will have good archival properties.

To mount the print you should ideally use two simple 'T' hinges made from paper tape to attach the print to a backing board. The mount itself is then hinged to the backing board with more tape along the top edge. This means that the print can be removed quickly and easily from the mount if you wish to, and if you decide to frame the mounted print, the print itself will hang from the tape hinges.

If you do not intend to frame the mounted prints, store them in clear polyester sleeves. These not only look very professional but the sleeves also protect the mounted print from damage – matte fine art papers are particularly prone to marks and scratches.

Finally, store the sleeved prints in archival print boxes or portfolio boxes which are available from all leading art and photo stores. (See DVD 16.06.)

Make the most of your photographs

As well as printing and framing photographs, there are also numerous other things you can do with your work to show it off.

1 Print an album

The days of the traditional photo album are long gone thanks to digital technology. Most households now have a digital compact or SLR, a computer and an inkjet printer so instead of sticking small prints in albums, we can be more ambitious with our images.

One option is to buy an inkjet album which consists of 20 or so sheets of blank double-sided inkjet paper sandwiched between a stiff card or leather cover. All you do is dismantle the pages, run them through a printer, then put everything back together again. If you want to keep things neat and simple you can print just one image per page, but equally if you fancy something more creative you can have several images on each page and add text.

2 Photo books

Taking the idea of a photo album a step further, there are now many companies offering a photo book printing service. If you do an internet search you will find literally dozens – myphotobook, YoPhoto, Photobox, Album Factory, Bob Books... The list goes on. All operate in a similar way in that you design a book, usually using a template downloaded from the printer's website, upload the pages, pay, and a week or so later a colourful, hardbacked book arrives through the post. Quality varies, as does size, format, the number of pages you can have and how much control you have over the design of the book, but the concept is fantastic and it is a great way of collating a set of images – either your favourites from each year, as a portfolio, a record of a holiday or adventure or as a gift for someone else – to celebrate a birth, marriage or milestone birthday.

3 Publish a book

If you are feeling even more ambitious, you could design and publish your own book and make it available for sale to other people. This is a very expensive proposition if you have a bulk load of books printed and then have to set about selling them – you would need to print 500–1000 to make it even remotely viable and the print bill could run into thousands of pounds. However, there is an alternative route known as Print on Demand publishing (POD) where a book is printed literally one copy at a time and only when orders are placed, so there are usually no upfront costs and no financial risks involved.

The best-known name in POD at the moment is lulu.com. If you log on to the website you will find instructions on exactly how it works, but the basic idea is that you design your own book – or get someone to design it for you – convert the layout document to a PDF file and upload it to the lulu.com site. No payment is made to lulu unless you order copies of your book. However, the best part of all is that anyone around the world can also order a copy of your book if you want to make it available to the public, and you can tell lulu what the cover price is so that you actually make a royalty on each copy sold, which lulu sends to you every few months. You can even pay extra and have an ISBN number issued for the book so that it can be ordered through any bookstore or on-line store including retailers such as Amazon.

The potential here is vast and many photographers have already taken advantage of POD services, using it to produce photo books, portfolios and exhibition catalogues. (See DVD 16.07.)

3 Organize a slide show

Traditional slide shows always had a bad reputation simply because unless you had sophisticated equipment they were always rather dull – just pictures on a screen with a little commentary from the photographer. Fortunately, all that has changed now and anyone can create a polished audio visual display using a laptop computer and digital projector. Image management software such as Adobe Lightroom and Apple Aperture lets you do this, although there is also a number of specialist software options available, too, that allows you to create an entertaining show where multiple images can be projected at once. Background, text, music and commentary can also be added and you can use clever dissolve techniques to move from one image to the next. (See DVD 16.08.)

4 Get your work online

The Worldwide web now provides the biggest forum for photographers to show off their talents. There are dozens, if not hundreds, of image-sharing websites such as Flickr, Snapfish and Photobucket where you can create an account, upload images to your own galleries and then let other members access them and leave comments on your pictures. This is a great way to share your photography with a global audience, to find out what other photographers think about your work and gain ideas and inspiration.

Taking this idea a step further, why not consider creating your own website? Photography magazines often publish articles on how to create, upload and maintain your own website, although you can pay to have a website designed for you if you do not fancy doing it yourself, and the site can be used not only to show off your work but also to sell prints, sell use of the images for publication, promote events such as exhibitions and so on. (See DVD 16.09.)

5 Put on an exhibition

In pre-digital days, organizing a photographic exhibition was costly and time-consuming because you either had to make all the prints in your own darkroom or pay a printer or commercial lab to do the job for you. Consequently, only professional photographers tended to bother exhibiting.

Today, thanks to the advent of affordable inkjet printers, any photographer can exhibit because the most expensive part of the process – printing the images – is much more affordable and can be kept in-house.

You do not have to hire space in a proper gallery to exhibit your work – smaller venues such as cafés, clubs, libraries, local tourist attractions, museums, theatres and hospitals can all work well; basically, anywhere where members of the public go.

So, the first step is to make a list of possible local venues, then make an appointment to visit and show your work. A portfolio of the photographs you intend to exhibit can be taken along – ideally mounted and sleeved so they look professional. Keep the selection to no more than 20 images – any more than that and wall space will probably be an issue.

Most exhibition venues charge a commission on each sale – up to 30 per cent. With local venues you may not be asked to pay commission, but do not be surprised if you are.

The prints you exhibit should be offered as a limited edition – 50 is the usual number, although it can be higher or lower. Title, number and sign the prints prior to framing, and ask the framer to cut the mount aperture so it is big enough to show the title etc. This looks more effective than writing on the print.

In terms of price, you need to be sensible – go too high and the prints won't sell, but go too low and you won't make any profit for your effort. If you are exhibiting mainly as a means of showing your work to a larger audience, making lots of profit will not be paramount. However, photography is an expensive pastime so if you can make a little profit then so much the better.

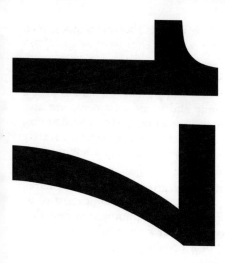

17

portraiture

In this chapter you will learn:
- about the equipment you need for portraiture
- how to put your subject at ease
- how to pose your subject
- about shooting indoor and outdoor portraits.

If a picture paints a thousand words, as the saying goes, then chances are it is a portrait.

People are without doubt the most accessible subject on earth, and as a result tend to be the most popular, too. The first thing most photographers do when they buy a new camera is take a few photographs of their family and friends. Cameras are also dusted off on special occasions such as birthdays, christenings, weddings and Christmas to record the people present. Rarely does a month go by that we do not take at least a few pictures of our fellow humans.

Once your interest in photography grows, you will probably want to take more serious portraits, at which point most of us realize just how tricky people can be to photograph and that there is a big difference between a quick snap taken at a party and capturing the character of a person who is posing for the camera.

Portrait photography demands little in terms of technical know-how – the techniques involved are quite simple and equipment can be kept to a minimum. But to succeed you must be a skilled communicator, and have the ability to capture the true personality of an individual by putting them at ease and drawing out their character naturally.

Pre-planning will put the odds of success firmly in your favour. If you already have a few ideas in mind about lighting, posing and locations it will save time once the shoot commences. Setting up your equipment beforehand is equally important, because if your subject has to wait ages while you fiddle around they will become nervous and bored very quickly. Being prepared and confident will also free you to concentrate totally on your subject, so you are always ready to capture interesting expressions as they appear. (See DVD 17.01.)

Equipment for portraiture

Lots of expensive equipment is just not necessary for portraiture. In fact, the less you have the fewer decisions you will have to make about what to use, and the more time you will have to spend concentrating on your subject which in turn means that you end up with much better portraits.

A compact camera is ideal for candid shots, allowing you to make the most of fleeting opportunities by simply pointing and shooting. For more serious portraits an SLR is a better choice though, giving you more control over the exposure, depth of field and the option to use a variety of different lenses.

For traditional head-and-shoulders portraits, the ideal lens is a short telephoto with a focal length between 85 and135 mm – most photographers prefer an 85 mm or l05 mm. The beauty of this type of lens – often called a 'portrait' lens – is that it flatters facial features by slightly compressing perspective. The magnification also allows you to fill the frame with your subject's face from a comfortable working distance, and the shallow depth of field you get at wide apertures such as f/2.8 and f/4 means distracting backgrounds are reduced to an indistinguishable blur so your subject stands out and takes centre stage. (See DVD 17.02.)

Longer lenses come into their own for candid shots. A 70–200 mm or 75–300 mm telezoom will allow you to fill the frame from further away, thus reducing the chance of your subject realizing you are there. A standard 50 mm lens or standard 28–70 mm zoom is also fine for half- or full-length portraits, but focal lengths less than 70 mm should be avoided for headshots because they will distort your subject's face, making their nose and chin look too long. (See DVD 17.03.)

Distortion is even more apparent with wide-angle lenses, so extreme care is required. A 24 mm, 28 mm or 35 mm wide is ideal for environmental portraits that include your subject's surroundings in the shot to offer clues about who they are and what they do, but you should keep your subject away from the edge of the frame, where distortion is at its greatest. (See DVD 17.04.)

Although by no means essential, a tripod can be an invaluable ally when shooting portraits. Not only will it keep your camera steady in low light, but once you have composed and focused a shot you can take your eye away from the viewfinder, chat to your subject and be ready to capture interesting expressions by tripping the shutter with a cable release.

For daylight fill-in (see page 227), or providing illumination in dimly-lit interiors, a flashgun is worth its weight in gold. Avoid using the flash direct though – bounce it off a wall or ceiling, or fit a diffuser, so the light is softened to give more flattering results.

Finally, it is worth keeping a few filters to hand. The 81 series warm-up filters are good for making skin tones looks healthy and attractive when you are shooting in overcast weather or in the shade. A soft-focus filter can also be used to add a touch of atmosphere and romance to the odd portrait, while a centre-spot will soften just the edges of the picture to make your subject stand out – though any of these effects can be added afterwards if you are shooting digitally, and skin blemishes can easily be cloned out if necessary.

The informal approach

The main problem with people – particularly adults – is they tend to 'put up a front' at the first sign of a camera, so capturing their true personality can be difficult. Either that or they become nervous and embarrassed.

An easy way around this is by taking informal portraits, where your subject is aware of the camera but too occupied by other things to feel intimidated or nervous. Hobbies are ideal, because as well as providing a suitable distraction for your subject they also tell the viewer something about them. You could photograph your neighbour throwing a pot on his potter's wheel, or your father putting the finishing touches to a new coffee table on his workbench. Alternatively, keep your camera ready when you are spending time with family and friends. Picnics, barbecues, holidays, parties and walks provide lots of opportunities to capture people enjoying themselves, and even if you are spotted doing your David Bailey bit, most people won't mind.

Putting your subject at ease

In a formal portrait situation, having your picture taken is rather like phoning a friend only to reach an answering machine. Even the chattiest people turn into blithering wrecks when they have to think about what to say. The same problem is encountered when you expect your subject to look relaxed and composed while staring into the black hole of your camera lens.

Volumes have been written about how to relax a nervous sitter, but at the end of the day it all boils down to communication. If you hide behind your camera and do not say a word your subject will feel terribly uneasy and you are not going to bring out their character. But if you chat to them and make the shoot enjoyable they will soon forget about the camera, giving you the opportunity to capture relaxed and natural expressions.

Talk about their hobbies, politics, news, music, the weather. Anything makes a good starting point, because once you break the ice the conversation will naturally progress and a friendly rapport will quickly be established. While chatting, keep a close eye on your subject so you can trip the shutter whenever they strike an interesting expression.

Equally important is feedback and direction. Your subject needs to be told if what they are doing is right, so talk them through poses, offer suggestions for facial expressions if you want to capture a certain look, and bolster their confidence by paying them regular compliments.

Poser's guide

Posing is a vitally important aspect of portraiture, because the way your subject presents their body to the camera says a lot about their personality and feelings. Body language is a potent form of non-verbal communication, so if a person is feeling tense it will be reflected in the way they stand, or what they do with their hands. Equally, if they are confident and relaxed, that will shine through, too.

As most people find having their portrait taken difficult, they tend to become very stiff and wooden in front of the camera, and do not really know what to do with themselves. Even if you are shooting head-and-shoulders portraits, the pose adopted by your subject is important because it will influence how comfortable and relaxed they feel and this will show on their face.

The worst thing you can do is expect a person to just stand there while you fire away – at least provide a chair, table or something for them to lean on. Even more care needs to be taken if your subject is sitting down. Hands can be a problem floating around the frame doing nothing, so give your subject something to hold, ask them to fold their arms, place both hands on their lap, or suggest they rest their chin on one hand.

The hands-on-chin approach is very popular, but should not be overused. A flat hand looks more attractive with women, while a clenched fist suits men. In either case, make sure the hand does not distort the side of your subject's face or dominate the shot. Cupping the face with both hands can also work well occasionally, because your subject's arms will create a triangle that directs attention towards their face.

Avoid shooting your subject head-on if they are seated as this tends to produce very flat, static-looking portraits and exaggerates the width of their shoulders. Instead, position the chair at an angle of about 45° to the camera and ask your subject to turn their head to face you. Younger people may decide to sit on the chair the wrong way round so the back provides a convenient rest for their arms. This, too, produces a relaxed, comfortable pose.

What you should never do is ask you subject to hold a pose they find uncomfortable, or stick with the same pose for too long. Professional models are encouraged to switch poses after every few frames so a variety of different pictures result. Your subject should not be expected to do this, but the old saying 'A change is as good as a rest' still rings true, and working through a variety of poses will keep the shoot relaxed and enjoyable.

Lastly, do not force your subject to wear certain types of clothing – leave the choice to them, as it reflects their personality. At the same time, do not be afraid to make suggestions if you have specific ideas in mind. Bright, detailed or unusual clothes take attention away from your subject's face so they should be treated carefully. The same applies with jewellery. Beware of earrings, hair clips, rings, watches and brooches that reflect the light to create distracting hotspots. If your subject does not want to remove them, change the camera angle or pose so they do not cause problems. (See DVD 17.05–17.10.)

Outdoor portraits

Most enthusiast photographers tend to shoot their first portraits outdoors, simply because there are no lights or backgrounds to set up and the informality of the situation is more relaxing for both photographer and subject. Where you decide to shoot is up to you. Your garden on a sunny afternoon is as suitable as anywhere. A chair can be placed in a spot where the light is at its most attractive, and the whole session need not take longer than half an hour to complete.

The main thing you need to think about is the quality of light, as this plays an important role in determining the success or failure of your portraits. Early morning and late afternoon are ideal times to shoot, because the warm sunlight enhances your subject's skin tones to give them a healthy, glowing appearance. (See DVD 17.11.) Keep the sun slightly to one side of the camera rather than shooting with it behind you. Not only does this prevent your subject squinting into the light, but shadows cast across their face will reveal texture and add modelling. With the sun low in the sky you can also create beautiful backlit portraits. Just position your subject with the sun behind them, so a halo of light is thrown onto their hair, and light their face using a reflector or burst of fill-in flash (see below).

Many photographers hang up their camera in bad weather, but the soft, diffuse light of an overcast day is actually very attractive. Contrast is low and shadows are very weak, so you can emphasize the softness of your subject's skin and accentuate modelling. (See DVD 17.12.)

Care needs to be taken if you shoot around midday in bright sunshine as the harsh light is far from flattering. With the sun almost overhead, shadows are cast under your subject's nose and chin, and their eye sockets tend to look like dark, lifeless holes. Posing your subject in the shade of a building or tree is advised, as the light is much softer.

The background should also be given plenty of thought – it is so easy to end up with a lamp post or tree sprouting from the top of your subject's head if you are not careful. Neutral backgrounds created by foliage, a fence or a wall work well, especially if you select a wide lens aperture to throw it out of focus so it does not compete for attention with your subject.

Fill-in flash

Fill-in flash is often used by portrait, wedding and glamour photographers to light their subject when shooting against the light, or to soften the harsh shadows created by bright sunlight. An added benefit is the flash also puts attractive catchlights in your subject's eyes.

The key with fill-in flash is to provide enough light to soften shadows and lower contrast, without letting it dominate the whole shot. This is done by setting up your flashgun so it only fires at half- or quarter-power, rather than full power. If your flashgun has a variable power output, as many dedicated flashguns do today, you can do this simply by setting it to a quarter or half to achieve a flash-to-daylight ratio of 1:4 and 1:2 respectively. Alternatively, if your camera has a flash exposure compensation facility, simply set it to −1 stop to achieve the same effect as half-power, or −2 stops to achieve quarter-power.

If you have a more basic automatic flashgun, set the auto aperture setting to an f/number two stops smaller than the f/number your lens is set to. This fools the flashgun into delivering less light and gives the same effect as setting it to quarter-power. If you set the auto aperture one stop smaller than the f/number set on your lens, you will effectively reduce the output of the gun to half-power. (See DVD 17.13 and 17.14.)

Using window light

The daylight flooding in through the windows of your home is perfect for flattering portraits. In fact, window light is so effective that many leading photographers create daylight studios so they can take advantage of it.

By positioning your subject close to an average-sized room window an attractive side-lit effect will be created that reveals half their face and partially hides the other half in shadow. If you want more even illumination, place a large white reflector board opposite the window to bounce stray light into the shadows, or ask your subject to face the window so the light strikes them head-on.

For the most flattering effect use a north-facing window, which only admits reflected light, and shoot in bright but slightly overcast weather. If the light is too harsh, tape a sheet of tracing paper or muslin over the window to diffuse the light even further. Early or late in the day you can also make use of warm sunlight raking in through the window. Net curtains will cast a dappled pattern of shadows across your subject's face, or you can create unusual shadow patterns by cutting shapes out of black card and then fixing the mask over the window. (See DVD 17.15.)

Studio lighting techniques

The range of lighting effects possible with studio flash units is limited only by your own imagination. Having said that, the majority of portraits are taken using just a handful of different lighting set-ups, and rarely involve more than three separate sources. So do not be misled into thinking you need to re-mortgage your house to equip yourself with the right gear – keep things simple in the beginning and you will benefit greatly.

Tungsten spotlights were once a popular choice for portraiture because they were relatively inexpensive and provided a continual source of light so you could always see the effect it was having on your subject. However, electronic studio flash units have all but replaced tungsten now, in the same way that digital cameras are gradually taking over from film.

Despite being more expensive than tungsten, studio flash is a much more versatile option. For a start, flash is daylight-balanced so you can shoot digitally without having to play around with your camera's white balance to cancel out any colour casts, or use normal colour film. Tungsten lamps also generate a lot of heat and the bulbs are not nearly as intense as a burst of flash, so you will be forced to use wider lens apertures, slower shutter speeds or higher ISOs. Electronic flash is more intense so you can shoot at smaller apertures, and although it is not a continuous source, studio flash units employ a tungsten modelling lamp which allows you to assess the direction and quality of the light produced.

If you do decide to use flash you will need a flash meter to measure the exposure required. To use the meter simply hold it close to your subject, point it back towards the light source and press the button so a reading is displayed. When using more than one flash unit a separate reading should be taken for each in turn so you can assess the lighting balance. (See DVD 17.16.)

Using one light

The best way to learn about lighting theory is by starting off with just one light and using it in different positions around your subject. You could use a tailor's dummy for this if you cannot find a 'live' subject willing to sit around while you experiment.

With the light placed next to your camera you will see the illumination is very even, but your subject lacks modelling as most of the shadows are cast behind them and out of sight. Placed at 90°, texture is revealed and half your subject's face will be plunged into shadow to give a very dramatic feel. Using the light at 45° provides a more sensible balance between highlights and shadows. This approach – known as three-quarter lighting – is often used by portrait photographers.

The problem with using a single bare flash is that the light is very harsh and shadows are dense, making it difficult to achieve flattering results. The solution involves diffusing the light in some way, so contrast is lowered, shadows are weakened and the overall effect is more pleasing.

The two most popular diffusers used in the studio are brollies and softboxes (the latter also being known as 'windowlights' or 'squarelights'). Both devices increase the apparent size of the source, so the light is spread over a wider area and its harshness is reduced. If you fit a brolly or softbox to your one light you will see an immediate improvement in the quality of illumination. Attractive catchlights are also added to your subject's eyes.

All portraits, no matter how cleverly lit, are based on this one light – known as the 'key' or 'main' light – which provides most of the illumination and establishes the exposure for the shot. Further lights are only used to control shadows, light the background or add effects.

Adding more lights

Once you have mastered the art of using one light, further flash units can be added to the set-up to give you more flexibility. A second flash unit positioned at 45° on the other side of the camera, for example, will fill in the shadows cast by the 'key' light. This unit should be switched to half-power so it does not create shadows of its own – studio flash units have a variable power switch for this purpose. Alternatively, by filling in the shadows with a reflector you can use the second light more creatively: as the background light, or as a clip or halo light to catch your subject's hair and make it stand out.

When using one light on the background you can either place it on the ground and shine it upwards, so a graduated effect is obtained from bottom to top, or you can place it on one side so the brightness of the background falls off from side to side. If you want to light the background evenly, two lights are required, one either side and at 45°. Coloured gels can also be fitted over the flash to colour a white background.

To create a halo of light around your subject's hair, the flash unit is fitted with a standard reflector and is placed behind the subject, pointing back towards the camera. Set the output of the light so it overexposes by about a stop, and make sure the unit is not visible in the shot – shining it through a hole in the background paper prevents this. If you just want to light part of your subject's hair, the flash unit is usually fitted with a conical attachment known as a 'snoot'. This produces a narrow beam of light that can be directed exactly where you want it – usually onto the top or side of your subject's head.

As your experience grows you can experiment with three or more lights to create more complicated lighting effects. To get you started here is a selection of popular set-ups. (See DVD 17.17–17.22.)

1 For a moody effect similar to that obtained using window light, place a single flash unit fitted with a softbox (a) at 45° or 90° to your subject.

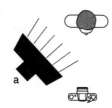

2 If you prefer more even illumination and are restricted to one light, place it at 45° to your subject (a) and use a white reflector on the other side to fill in the shadows (b).

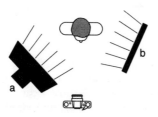

3 Place a single flash fitted with a brolly or softbox to the side and slightly behind your subject, so it emphasizes the side of their face and shoulder (a). Use a reflector near the camera to bounce light onto the shadow side of their face and reduce contrast (b). See the diagram overleaf.

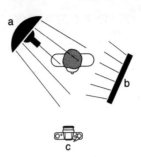

4 A traditional set-up for head-and-shoulders portraits uses one main light fitted with a brolly or softbox (a), a fill-in light set on half-power and bounced off a reflector or fired through a brolly (b), a snooted clip light directed on the subject's hair (c) and a fourth light on the background (d). A reflector can also be placed under the subject's chin to fill-in any shadows created (e).

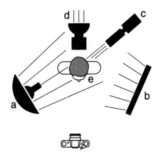

5 For very clean, even lighting, place large white reflectors either side of your subject and bounce light onto them from two flash units (a) and (b). A third light can be used on the background or to create a halo around your subject's hair (c).

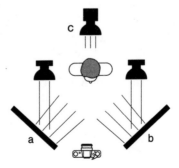

Choosing a background

All sorts of materials can be used to create a background when shooting studio portraits, although whatever you choose it should be kept simple and uncluttered.

Rolls of background paper are available in a range of different colours and can be suspended on a framework behind your subject. Pale colours work well, but tend to go dark and muddy unless they are lit separately. Dark backgrounds do not suffer in this way, and are ideal for creating a dramatic result or making your subject stand out – they work particularly well if you are using a halo light. A sheet of black card or velvet makes a perfect backdrop.

More elaborate backgrounds are available from manufacturers such as Lastolite, including 'Old-Master', splatter and cloud effects. Alternatively, you can make your own by painting or spraying sheets of hardboard, paper, canvas and other materials. Existing background can be used, but should be kept plain and simple. Patterned or stripy wallpaper will take attention away from your subject, so avoid it at all costs.

Portrait tips

- Always focus on your subject's eyes, particularly when using a wide aperture which limits depth of field. A person's eyes reveal a lot of information about how they are feeling, so if they are unsharp the portrait will lose its appeal.

- Never be afraid to take lots of pictures during a portrait session. If you try to wait for the perfect moment you could wait forever, whereas if you take pictures steadily throughout the shoot you can select the most revealing shots afterwards.

- Do not ask your subject to adopt an uncomfortable pose or do anything they object to, and if the shoot is not proving too successful take a break, talk things through and then resume later. The more you try to force the issue when taking someone's portrait the less likely you are to produce a successful result.

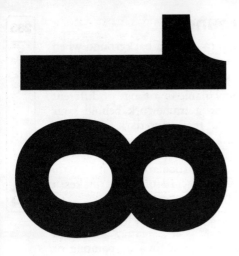

18

photographing children and babies

In this chapter you will learn:
- how to deal with children of different ages
- about keeping your subject occupied
- about formal portraiture and lighting
- about equipment needs when photographing children.

Children are the most challenging, rewarding and frustrating subject all rolled into one. They are infinitely photogenic, totally unselfconscious and lack the inhibitions of grown-ups. But as you will know to your peril if you have ever tried photographing them, at the first sign of a camera most children will decide to play a little game of 'Annoy The Photographer'.

Ask them to sit still and they will jump up and down. Try to coax a smile and they will pull horrid faces. Then when you have at last got their attention and are poised to take a winning portrait, they decide to lose interest and do a vanishing act.

Children are naturally mischievous – that is what makes them so appealing. So instead of tearing your hair out with frustration when things do not go according to plan, go with the flow and make the most of their antics. By doing this you will be able to capture natural, relaxed pictures that sum up the joys of being young, whereas if you try to impose your will on them the whole shoot will crumble at your feet.

Patience, it has to be said, is something you need lots of if you want to photograph children and remain sane. Lightning-quick reflexes also come in handy, because the most rewarding photo opportunities tend to occur when you least expect them. That is why it is always a good idea to keep a camera loaded and ready so you can grab it and fire without hesitation.

Equally important is that you let photographing your children be an enjoyable part of family life rather than a special occasion which involves dressing them up in their Sunday best. If you fail today there is always tomorrow or next week – adopt that philosophy and you won't go far wrong. (See DVD 18.01.)

The changing faces of childhood

The way you photograph children depends upon their age, as this not only dictates the type of pictures you will be able to take, but the way your subject reacts to the camera and how much help they need from you.

Make an effort to photograph your children on a regular basis, so that over the years you create a revealing documentary of them growing up and record the many milestones in their life, from the moment they come into the world to the day they leave home for college.

The birth of a child is one of the most treasured moments in your life so do not let the opportunity slip by. A compact camera is all you need – do not take a bag full of equipment into the delivery room. Avoid using flash if possible as it destroys the atmosphere of the moment. Instead, increase the ISO of your camera to 800 or 1600 or, if you are shooting film, load a roll of ISO 1600 so you can take handheld pictures in available light.

At the time of the birth itself the mother will need your support, but be ready to capture the first seconds of the baby's life, and the elation on the mother's face as she is presented with her newborn offspring – these pictures will be treasured possessions for the rest of your life.

Pictures of mother and baby sleeping after the birth, the first feed, first wash and weigh-in are other events worth capturing. Pictures of the newborn's tiny hands, feet and crumpled face are also very poignant.

Babies are a joy to photograph, simply because they are not fully aware of what you are doing so they cannot lose interest and start playing up to the camera. At the same time, however, this makes it tricky to capture an interesting expression – most babies are either asleep or crying! Try making funny noises, pulling faces or shaking a rattle so your subject looks at the camera. If you are lucky you may be able to capture a smile, or a look of dismay. Nappy changing, feeding and bath time also provide opportunities to take interesting pictures. (See DVD 18.02.)

Toddlers tend to make the most of the fact they can walk, and enjoy nothing more than wobbling around the house – from the sofa to the TV, to the chair, to the door... Get down on your hands and knees and follow them around, snapping away as you go. They will be amused by your antics, so you should be able to capture lots of natural, relaxed expressions as they try to work out what you are up to. (See DVD 18.03.)

By the age of five or six, children have developed a mind of their own and personalities really begin to show. They are also incredibly mischievous and do not like being told what to do, so an informal approach is recommended. Attention spans are short, so do not expect total cooperation for more than a few minutes, but their basic lack of inhibitions will help you to capture happy expressions. Be patient, let your subject have fun, provide something to keep them occupied and you should come away with some super pictures.

Older children aged nine or ten need to be dealt with more tactfully. They won't take too kindly to being bossed around, or dragged away from what they are doing, so take the camera to them rather than vice versa. If you want their full attention, treat them as an equal rather than a baby and take an active interest in what they are doing. Talk to them about school, TV, sport and hobbies, and let them get involved in the shoot by contributing ideas for locations, poses, props and so on. (See DVD 18.04.)

Adolescents are at a stage in life when they are undergoing many changes, both physically and emotionally, so they tend to be the most sensitive group to photograph. You need to tread very carefully and treat your subject with respect and understanding. Both sexes are concerned about their image, and may find posing for the camera quite daunting in all but the most informal situations. Let them decide what to wear, discuss the type of pictures you would like to take, choose sympathetic lighting, keep the shoot relaxed by chatting and playing music and you should be able to capture some very sensitive, revealing portraits.

Be prepared

The most important aspect of child photography is always making sure you have a camera handy to record all those special moments, such as baby's first smile or first bath. Mundane tasks like feeding and nappy changing can also be very rewarding.

As your children get older other achievements should be captured – the first bike ride, kicking their first football, catching their first fish, dressing up, cooking their first cake or playing with a doll's house, coming home covered in mud after playing war in the local swamp, or nursing a grazed knee after falling off their skateboard.

If you are prepared you will also be able to capture touching moments, such as a toddler meeting his baby brother or sister for the first time, children interacting with their grandparents, or playing with pets and friends.

It takes a while to get into child photography mode on a day-to-day basis, because the task of running a family leaves little time for anything else. However, digital cameras do make things easier because you can see the results instantly and most of us have computers and printers at home so we can do things with the pictures immediately. So make taking family snaps a natural part of daily life and your efforts will be rewarded many times over. (See DVD 18.06.)

Keeping your subject occupied

Because children have a short attention span – particularly toddlers and infants – it is vital you give them something to keep their active minds occupied. If you just expect them to stand around while you take pictures they will quickly lose interest and it will show on their faces, whereas if you provide a distraction they will forget about the camera, leaving you to get on with the task of capturing natural expressions.

Often all you need to do with toddlers is take them into the back garden and give them a favourite toy to play with, or an ice-cream to lick. Pets can also work wonders – a cuddly rabbit, mischievous kitten or puppy will keep a young child occupied for hours, as well as providing a source of wonder and surprise.

Older children need something more exciting to do such as kicking a football around, riding their bicycle, dressing up for the camera, playing house or cooking. All these things can be used as the basis for your pictures. But rather than set up the situation specially, suggest it and then step back and give your subject a free reign to have some fun. This semi-candid approach tends to work far better than posed portraits.

If all else fails, involve other children in the shoot. A brother, sister or friends will provide the necessary distraction, and although they are likely to play up to the camera – making your job even harder – you should be able to take some great pictures of your subjects interacting like all children do. (See DVD 18.05.)

Formal portraits and lighting

If you decide to take some posed portraits of your children a little thought and preparation will go a long way to ensuring success. As soon as a child is placed in a formal photographic environment they easily become bored, restless and uneasy. To prevent this there are various steps you can take.

First of all, have a think about the type of pictures you would like to take, so you have a few ideas in mind. Do not stick to them religiously though – once the shoot is underway your subject may offer much better suggestions if you get them involved.

Next, decide on the type of lighting you want to use and get everything set up beforehand. If your subject has to sit around while you fiddle with your equipment they will be bored to tears by the time you are ready to start, and all you will end up with is wooden poses and false expressions. Do not force your subject to put on their best clothes and have a wash and brush-up. Children are rarely squeaky clean, so let them decide what to wear and how to look – it is all part of their personality after all.

Once the shoot is underway, explain what you want your subject to do. Suggest poses and offer lots of feedback so they know if things are going well. To capture your subject's character they need to be fully relaxed and at ease in front of the camera, so chat to them about their hobby, or what was on TV last night, tell jokes, lark about a little and make them laugh.

The lighting itself should be kept fairly simple. Window light is ideal for moody portraits, and with a reflector or two to fill in the shadows you can create surprisingly attractive results. If you want to use flash, bounce the light off a ceiling or wall rather than firing it directly at your subject, as this produces harsh, unflattering light.

For those of you with proper studio lighting equipment all sorts of different effects can be created (see Chapter 17). You should still keep things simple though, as too many lights could prove rather daunting for your young subject. (See DVD 18.08.)

Equipment for children

Quick reflexes, patience and enthusiasm are far more important when photographing children than the amount of equipment you possess. A compact camera is ideal for keeping handy because you can grab it and shoot in an instant, knowing that 99 per cent of the time you end up with a sharp, well-exposed picture.

If you use an SLR, make sure you are familiar with the controls and keep it set in an automatic mode such as program of aperture priority, so you do not have to worry too much about the exposure before firing away. In terms of lenses, everything from wide-angles to telephotos can be used successfully. For head-and-shoulders portraits a short telephoto or zoom setting around 85–135 mm is ideal, while a standard 50 mm lens is suitable for full-length shots.

If you want to capture candid or action pictures of your children a 200 mm lens or the top end of your 70–200 mm telezoom will allow you to fill the frame from a greater distance. Set the lens to a wide aperture such as f/4 and f/5.6, so the shallow depth of field throws the background out of focus to make your subject stand out.

Wide-angle lenses should be avoided for conventional portraits because they distort facial features when used at close quarters. However, if you exaggerate this characteristic by shooting from just a few inches away you can take some highly amusing portraits, with your subject's face stretched, their eyes bulging and their nose looking much longer than normal. They will also think you are potty! (See DVD 18.09–18.14.)

Tips when filming children

- Always shoot from the child's eye level or below, rather than towering above them like a giant. Not only will this make your subject feel relaxed, but your pictures will look more natural.

- Never be afraid to fire off lots of frames when photographing your children – it is better to waste a few and get one brilliant shot, rather than hold back and end up with nothing of merit. Digital images cost nothing.

- Do not lose heart if your first few attempts are not very successful – it takes a lot of practice to become a skilled child photographer, but eventually you will get there.

- Family outings and special events are a great time to take candid pictures of your children having fun, so keep a camera handy when you visit the zoo, funfair, park, go on holiday, have a picnic, visit grandparents, walk the dog, clean the car, mow the lawn, have a birthday party, visit Santa Claus at Christmas, build a snowman, go swimming, play games, decorate the house, clean out the garden shed, visit a bonfire and firework display... Anything and everything in other words!

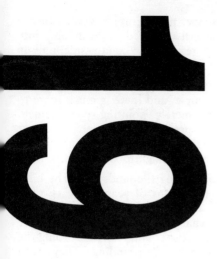

19

landscapes

In this chapter you will learn:
- how to make the most of light
- how to compose great landscapes
- how to make a feature of the sky
- how to use filters to perfect your shots.

On the face of it, landscape photography seems like a ridiculously simple discipline. All you need to do is jump into your car, drive to the nearest area of open countryside, pull up in a lay-by and snap away to your heart's content. At least that is what most photographers are misled into thinking.

Unfortunately, life is not so simple, and there is much more to landscape photography than merely pointing your camera towards a beautiful scene and pressing the shutter release. At least there is if you want to do the landscape justice, and capture its character rather than just taking straightforward record shots.

Patience is the key to photographing the landscape. The hills, rivers and valleys have taken millions of years to reach their present glory, so you should be prepared to spend more than just a few minutes recording what you see. Successful landscape photographers love being out in the countryside, absorbing the peace, tranquillity and beauty of their surroundings. They spend hours walking around, looking at the scenery and getting to know the landscape intimately, so the pictures they take come from within rather than just being a passive response to something that caught their eye.

An understanding of light is vitally important, because the mood and character of the landscape is totally dependent upon this single factor. From the minute the sun comes up in the morning, to the minute it sets in the evening, the landscape undergoes a myriad of wonderful transformations as the colour, harshness and intensity of daylight changes. You also need to think very carefully about the way your landscapes are composed, because it can make all the difference between a picture that transports the viewer from their armchair into the heart of the countryside, or demands nothing more than a furtive glance. (See DVD 19.01.)

Make the most of light

The quality of light should never be underestimated in landscape photography, simply because the success of your pictures hangs on it more than anything else. It is tempting to start firing away the minute you come across an interesting scene, but by doing this you are not giving yourself the opportunity to see if its appearance could be improved. Nine times out of ten it can, because rarely is the landscape looking its best the very moment you want to photograph it.

Often, all you will need to do is wait ten minutes until a cloud moves from in front of the sun and the landscape is once more bathed in attractive light. But sometimes you will need to return several hours later, when the sun has moved to a different part of the sky, or on another day when the weather has improved.

For this reason it is a good idea to carry a compass, so you can plot the path the sun will take throughout the day and estimate when it is likely to be in the best position. Equally useful are Ordnance Survey maps, for checking the topography of an area before you leave home and getting an idea of what you are likely to encounter when you arrive.

Generally, the best time to photograph the landscape is early in the morning or late in the afternoon. (See DVD 19.02 and 19.03.) During these periods the sun is low in the sky, the light has a beautiful warmth to it and raking shadows accentuate texture and form which brings the landscape to life. During the summer months you are advised to avoid shooting between 10 a.m. and 4 p.m. because during this period the light is very harsh, contrast is too high, and with the sun overhead the landscape looks flat and lifeless. Fortunately, the sun never climbs too high in the sky during autumn and winter, so you can happily shoot throughout the day without having to waste valuable hours waiting for the light to improve. (See DVD 19.04.)

Handsome rewards can also be reaped by photographers willing to brave the elements. Bad weather does not exactly make for comfortable shooting, but it creates exciting conditions for landscape photography. Dark storm clouds rolling across the heavens add drama to your pictures, and if the sun happens to break through during a storm the landscape looks stunning as shafts of sunlight pick out features against the brooding sky. The light after a storm is worth waiting for too – rain has a cleansing effect on the atmosphere, so everything appears to be very clean, crisp and fresh.

The importance of composition

Composition is on an equal footing with light when it comes to creating successful landscapes. No matter how attractive the light is, your pictures will still fail if they are poorly composed, just as an excellent composition is not enough to sustain a picture if the light is poor.

The temptation is to try to include too much in a picture. That sweeping vista before you may look impressive to the eye, but simply fitting a wide-angle lens to your camera and tripping the shutter rarely captures the glory of the scene. Quite the opposite in fact – usually all you will end up with is an empty and boring composition.

What to do? Well a good place to start is by including some foreground interest in your pictures, to add a sense of depth and perspective to the scene, as well as providing the eye with a logical entry point into the picture. All sorts of things can be used as foreground interest: a river, wall, hedgerow, boulders on the shore of a lake, driftwood, a tree, gate, even a mound of earth. If you look around you are bound to find something. If not, you could always ask a person to pose in the foreground.

A 24 mm or 28 mm wide-angle lens is ideal for emphasizing the foreground. By moving in close to the features being used you can make them dominate the picture to create a dramatic feeling of distance, as well as filling the frame to tighten up the overall composition. For the best results, mount your camera on a tripod, and stop the lens down to a small aperture, such as f/16 or f/22, so you have got enough depth of field to ensure the whole scene comes out sharp.

Telephoto lenses are equally useful for landscape photography, allowing you to isolate interesting sections of a scene like the patterns created by dry stone walls, the play of light on a hillside, or a remote cottage perched at the foot of towering cliffs. The 'stacking-up' effect created by telephotos due to the way they compress perspective can also be used to great effect. Mountain ranges suddenly appear like cardboard cut-outs rising from the dawn mist, and distant hills can be pulled in to create simple, uncluttered backgrounds.

Any telephoto between 80 and 300 mm can be used successfully for landscape photography. So make sure you do not leave them at home when you go off for a day in the countryside, and keep your eyes peeled for interesting details when you are wandering around.

Another way of completely transforming the composition of a picture is by turning your camera on its side. The horizontal format tends to be used most often for landscapes – it is even known as the 'landscape format' – but that does not mean you have to restrict yourself. The advantage of taking upright pictures is that you can make better use of foreground interest – using a path or track to lead the eye up through the scene for instance. Because the eye has further to travel the composition also tends to be more active and dynamic.

Using your feet

Laziness is without doubt the biggest obstacle standing in the way of photographers when it comes to shooting the landscape. It is all too easy to start firing away the minute you come across an interesting scene, but while this approach is convenient, it rarely produces the best pictures.

The thing is, you cannot expect to make the most of a scene by accepting the first viewpoint you come across – particularly if all you have done is stopped the car and started shooting from the side of the road. You need to wander around and explore your subject from all angles and viewpoints. There is only so much you can see from where you are standing, and the most interesting aspects of the landscape tend to be in the more out-of-the-way places that you can only discover if you make the effort to look.

Include the sky

The sky adds character to the landscape just as much as trees and fields, so never be afraid to make a feature of it in your pictures. Bland, grey sky or acres of empty blue sky is not particularly inspiring, but attractive cloud formations floating across the heavens look beautiful – so much so that it is often worth tilting your camera upwards to make them the most dominant element in the shot.

The sky also needs to be considered for another important reason – it can cause exposure problems. Being much brighter than the foreground it has a tendency to fool your camera into thinking the whole scene it bright, so the landscape itself will be underexposed. To avoid this, tilt your camera down to exclude all or most of the sky from the viewfinder, and take a meter reading for the foreground. Use your camera's memory lock if it has one, to hold the exposure obtained while you re-compose the shot, or switch to manual mode. Alternatively, if your camera offers spot metering you can simply take a reading from a small part of the scene and ignore the sky. Well-lit green grass or foliage is ideal, because it is neutral in tone and gives an accurate exposure.

Should you decide to include the sun in the frame – just before sunset, for example – even greater care is required when metering, because brightness levels in the scene will be much higher and the risk of underexposure increases dramatically.

Your best bet is to follow the advice given above, but it is also worth bracketing the exposures to at least a stop over the metered exposure.

If you are shooting digitally, a quick check of the preview image and histogram will tell you if the exposure is accurate or not.

Improve things with filters

Filters are essential for landscape photography, allowing you to balance contrast, improve colour saturation and clarity and enhance the light. Here are the three main types you need. For more information on filters see Chapter 05.

1 Polarizer

As well as deepening blue sky, the polarizer also reduces glare on foliage and other non-metallic surfaces so colours appear much richer. It also removes unwanted reflections from water. When all three effects are combined, it can vastly improve a landscape picture. Polarizers work best in bright, sunny conditions. They are also ideal for increasing colour saturation when shooting woodland scenes in overcast or wet weather. To obtain optimum deepening of blue sky, keep the sun at 90° to the camera.

2 Warm-ups

The 81-series of amber-coloured warm-up filters is used to enhance the warmth of natural daylight when shooting at dawn or dusk. They are also handy for balancing the cool cast created in dull weather, when taking pictures in the shade, or in full sun on a cloudless day – especially around midday. The 81B is ideal for general use, while an 81C or 81D will give a stronger warming effect.

3 Neutral-density (ND) grad

A common problem when shooting landscapes is that if you correctly expose the landscape, the brighter sky often washes out and loses its impact. Neutral density (ND) graduate filters overcome this by darkening the sky so it requires the same exposure as the landscape and records as it appears to the naked eye. A 0.6 density ND grad is dark enough for general use, but it is also worth buying an even darker 0.9 grad as well, to use when shooting into the sun or if the sky is very bright.

Keep your ISO low

Landscape photographers generally like to keep image quality as high as possible so that the images they make look natural and large prints can be made without a significant loss of image quality. When using film they tend to stick to slow brands with a speed of ISO 50–100. Fujichrome Velvia is by far the most popular colour slide film used for landscape photography because it not only produces rich, vibrant colours, but it is also very sharp and fine-grained and able to resolve amazing detail.

The digital equivalent would be to keep your camera's ISO setting to its lowest speed – usually ISO 100, but in some cases only ISO 200 and in a handful of models just ISO 50.

The main drawback with slow film and low ISO settings is that often you will be forced to use a tripod to avoid camera shake – especially if you want to stop your lens down to a small aperture such as f/16 for optimum depth of field, use a polarizing filter, which loses two stops of light, or take pictures in low light conditions at dawn and dusk. This extra effort will pay handsome dividends though, so do not compromise.

Of course, there is nothing to stop you using faster film. The coarse grain and muted colours of ISO 1600 film provide the perfect ingredients for creating atmospheric, painterly landscapes, or stark, gritty images in black and white. Many photographers, myself included, use this technique on a regular basis.

If you shoot digitally, increasing the ISO to 1000 or above will not have the same effect as using fast film in terms of contrast and grain. However, you can add amazing grain effects afterwards (see page 198), and convert images to black and white.

20

holidays and travel

In this chapter you will learn:
- about the importance of research
- about the right equipment for travel
- how to make the most of famous sights
- about shooting travel portraits.

Annual holidays provide the perfect opportunity to dust off your camera gear and indulge in an orgy of picture-taking. You may only take a few dozen photographs during the rest of the year, but come your fortnight of well-earned sabbatical, photography suddenly takes on a whole new meaning and everyone starts burning film and filling memory cards at a rate of knots.

The reason for this is simple. Faced by completely fresh surroundings – often far more exotic than anything you are used to at home – the urge to capture everything in glorious Technicolor is irresistible; if only to turn your neighbours green with envy when you return.

Unfortunately, despite all the promising signs, most holiday pictures fail miserably in their attempt to faithfully capture the spirit of the place depicted. Instead of making you the envy of your friends and neighbours, they provide an instant cure for insomnia. In short, they are boring. Why? For exactly the same reason you took them in the first place. Being hundreds of miles from home in a strange place – often a strange country – even the most mundane scenes seem beautiful simply because they are unfamiliar. So another half a dozen frames are exposed without a care in the world, to add to the millions of tedious holiday snaps already taken by other people.

At the time you thought you had created a masterpiece of photographic art, but from the comfort of your armchair back in suburbia you cannot imagine what possessed you to bother snapping so many tedious subjects and scenes, and the memories you thought those pictures would rekindle in an instant just do not seem to materialize.

Of course, this does not have to be the case. With a little thought for what you are doing, your holiday pictures can indeed be masterpieces. But it is no good waiting until you are lying on a beach before doing that – you need to start preparing well before you leave home... (See DVD 20.01.)

Do your homework

The more you know about a place before you arrive, the better equipped you will be the make the most of it photographically. So once you have decided where you are going to spend your holiday, the next thing on the agenda is to do a little research.

A good place to start is at the travel agents where you book the holiday. Ask the rep if they have any details of special events, celebrations, interesting sights for visitors, and so on. If they do not, your local library is sure to contain a few guidebooks giving essential information on all sorts of things. Websites are another invaluable source – just type the name of your holiday destination into a search engine such as Google and see what comes up.

People themselves can also supply invaluable advice. You may have a friend, relative or colleague who has been to the area before and can give you lots of useful tit-bits they picked up through trial and error; where to capture a wonderful sunset, what you will discover if you go wandering off the well-worn tourist track and so on. (See DVD 20.02.)

Take the right equipment

The next consideration is to decide what equipment to take, and to make that decision you first need to think about how big a part photography will play on your holiday. If you are mainly interested in soaking up the sun and taking snaps of your family having fun, a decent compact camera is all you really need – ideally a zoom model so you have got the flexibility to shoot a range of different subjects.

Chances are most of you will want to do much more than that, however, so you need to think carefully about the contents of your gadget bag.

Cameras One SLR body is sufficient, but if you have a second it is worth taking as a back-up in case the main camera decides to stop working. If you still shoot film it also means you can use two different types at once, such as colour and black and white, or slow and fast film or normal and infrared.

Lenses When it comes to lenses, focal lengths from 28 to 200 mm should cope with 99 per cent of your needs, and can be covered using various combinations. The ideal one is probably a couple of zooms, say, 28–70 mm and 70–200 mm, mainly because it cuts down on weight and bulk. Zooms are also quick to use and allow you to compose your pictures precisely. If you like to use wider or longer lenses by all means take them along, but remember the weight factor. A good policy to adopt is if you are unlikely to use a lens at least once every day, leave it out.

Flashgun You may not use a flashgun very often at home, but on holiday it will prove essential for taking pictures in dimly-lit interiors, or illuminating people outdoors at night. Your camera's integral flashgun will be fine for close-range shots, but a more powerful accessory flashgun with a guide number around 35 (m/ISO 100) will give you more options.

Filters As far as filters go, a polarizer is an absolute must. It will deepen blue sky, reduce reflections on the sea and increase colour saturation to make the scenes you capture look better than they did in reality. An 81A or 81B warm-up should also be included, for enhancing the light, and a couple of neutral density grads (0.6 and 0.9 density) to tone down the sky so it does not wash-out.

Tripod The very thought of carting a tripod halfway around the world may not exactly fill you with excitement, but if you want to make the most of the photo opportunities that you encounter it is an essential tool. Rather than taking a large tripod, compromise by purchasing a smaller model that is easy to carry but stable enough to keep your camera still during long exposures. Even a table-top tripod is better than nothing, although it does not offer as much flexibility because you need to find an existing support such as a wall or post to stand it on.

Cable release Tuck one of these away in your backpack so you can trip the camera's shutter when it is mounted on a tripod, without touching it and causing vibrations.

Cleaning kit Sand, salty air and general day-to-day use play havoc with cameras and lenses, so regular cleaning is necessary if you want to keep everything in tip-top condition. Essential items include: a stiff brush for the camera body and lens barrels, a soft blower brush to remove dust from filters and lens elements, and a microfibre lens cloth for removing marks and fingerprints from filters and lenses.

Finally, be sure to pack spared batteries and battery chargers for your cameras and flashgun – this is an absolute must if you are shooting digitally.

All this gear should be carried in a photo backpack that has plenty of pockets and partitions to give easy access, but can be closed securely to protect the contents from sand, wind, rain and thieves.

Film and memory

One of the great joys of digital photography becomes apparent when you travel – no need to pack lots of film! Memory cards are small but with storage capacities up to 8GB they now allow you to take and save thousands of images.

Take enough memory cards so that ideally you do not have to erase the contents of any until you get home. Stick to relatively small capacities so that you do not have too many images stored on any one card that could be lost forever if a problem suddenly developed. Pack a storage device so that you can copy the contents of each memory card and get into the habit of downloading images either every evening or at intervals throughout the day if you are taking lots of pictures. You can also use this time to assess the images on-screen.

If you are still shooting film you do not have to worry about corrupt cards or back-up devices, but you do need to make sure you take the right stuff and enough of it. As a guide, reckon on shooting at least three rolls per day, preferably more if your intentions are serious. It is easy to use 40 rolls of film on a fortnight's holiday, without even thinking about what you are doing.

It is a good idea to buy all this film before you go on holiday, rather than relying on locating an available source when you get there. In many countries you will have difficulty finding exactly the film you want, and in touristy areas you will pay way over the odds even if you do find the brand of your choice.

In terms of speed, use film with an ISO rating of between 50 and 100 for your general shots – it is easily fast enough in the sunny weather you will be expecting. Also take along a few rolls of ISO 400 film so you can take handheld pictures in low light or inside buildings where tripods are not permitted.

x-rays

One subject that confuses millions of holidaymakers every year is whether they should allow their films to be x-rayed or not. Due to a rise in terrorism, all airports insist on x-raying everything, so you have no choice. But do not let this bother you – modern x-ray units are completely safe and will not harm your film. The main thing is to carry all film in your hand luggage.

Never pack it in your hold luggage as this will be subject to higher doses of x-ray and fogging will probably occur.

Fast film of ISO 400 and above is more susceptible to x-ray damage so if you are carrying a lot of fast film and your hand luggage is going to be x-rayed many times during a single trip you could ask for your bag to be hand-searched.

If that is your intention, make the job of airport security personnel as easy as possible by removing each roll of film from its box and tub, unless they are clear, then place it all in a clear plastic bag. This allows fast inspection, and stands you in much better stead of a hand-search being granted.

When you arrive

So finally, after long delays at the airport and hours in the air, you have arrived at your destination, tired, hungry and more in need of a holiday than when you left home!

Now what? Well, you are going to be eager to start shooting as soon as possible, so a quick wander around the area is in order. Do not get overexcited at this stage though. Instead, take a look around you, absorb the news sights and sounds, and earmark things you see that are going to be worth closer inspection once your jetlag has subsided.

The quality of light is important in your pictures, so try to work out where the sun is going to rise and set, and what time of day the light is likely to be at its most attractive to the things you see, such as buildings, harbours, hills, monuments, sea views and so on.

While you are out, have a glance at the postcard stands to get an idea of what subjects are at hand. I am not suggesting you buy a fistful of postcards and then make your own pictures look exactly the same, but they will give you a good idea of attractive locations that you can look for. Something else you should get hold of is a map of the area, so you can work out the lie of the land and pinpoint places of interest – including those you researched before leaving home.

Within a day or two you will become familiar with the area, and that is when your photographic exploits should really begin to bear fruit.

Make the most of famous sights

The Eiffel Tower, The Taj Mahal, The Leaning Tower of Pisa, The Statue Of Liberty, Big Ben, The Houses Of Parliament, The Pyramids at Giza... All these places and many others around the world are photographed by millions of people every year. The trouble is, just about all the pictures look the same. Tourist sights usually have recommended viewpoints and that is where the vast majority of visitors take their snaps from, or they start firing away the minute they tumble off the coach, not worried about all the other tourists in the way.

As a keen photographer, rather than a snap shooter, you will want to come away with something better and different from everyone else, so you need to think carefully about what you are doing. First, avoid the clichés and popular viewpoints. Instead, wear out a little shoe leather looking for alternative camera angles, and look at your subject through different lenses. Get up really close with a wide-angle lens, or wander down the street and shoot with a telephoto.

The actual camera angle can also make a big difference to your pictures. While most folk are snapping away with the camera at eye-level, try capturing a worm's eye view by stretching out on the ground, or find a higher viewpoint so you are looking down at your subject.

Getting up early so you are there before the tourist crowds arrive is a great idea because you will have the place to yourself. Similarly, staying late can be productive because most tourists will have headed back to their hotel for a sundowner. Many monuments are also lit up at dusk and make stunning photo subjects.

Once you start to think about it, there are countless ways in which you can take original, imaginative pictures of much photographed scenes. (See DVD 20.03.)

Photographing local people

The people you meet on your travels are as much a part of the country as the buildings and landscape, so remember to shoot a few local portraits for your picture collection.

The best way to photograph strangers is by approaching them and asking permission, rather than sneaking pictures from behind a lamppost with a long telephoto lens. That way if they object, either for personal or cultural reasons, you will avoid the embarrassment of a confrontation. Your pictures will also be far more intimate because you are closer to your subject, and you will have more control over the final result.

Before taking any pictures, try to show some genuine interest in your subject by making conversation. Hand signals and facial expressions go a long way if you do not speak the local language. If nothing else, they will amuse your subject and you will be able to capture relaxed and happy expressions.

A short telephoto lens with a focal length between 85 and 135 mm is ideal for head-and-shoulders portraits – remember to set a wide aperture so the background is thrown out of focus. Alternatively, switch to a wide-angle lens and include your subject's surroundings in the frame so your pictures tell a more vivid story.

In many countries the local population have realized that they can make money by posing for tourists. Whether you feel it is right to pay for pictures is a personal decision, but if you approach someone and they ask for money, be sure to agree a price first if you are to avoid problems later.

Most important of all, you should treat your subject with dignity and respect. A ragged shoeshine boy may look like an ideal subject to you, but he will still be a ragged shoeshine boy working hard to earn a meagre living when you are back home enjoying your holiday photographs and duty-frees. (See DVD 20.04.)

Travel tips

- Make sure all your equipment is insured under a 'new for old' policy against loss, damage of theft before you leave home.
- Never advertise the fact that you are carrying lots of expensive camera gear – there are always some individuals who would be quite happy to relieve you of it.
- Avoid having your films processed locally, unless you are staying with friends who know a reputable lab. It is tempting to want to see your pictures immediately, but excitement can turn to bitter disappointment if they are ruined.
- Keep your film and cameras out of the heat, otherwise the rise in temperature can cause colour shifts. Many people store their camera in the car's glove compartment, but this is the worst thing you can do.

- Keep your camera bag zipped up when you are on or near the beach. Fine particles of sand and salt in the air can find their way into the tiniest nooks and crannies and cause irreparable damage.
- Never take photographs of, or anywhere near, military installations, police stations, airports, soldiers or any other members of the security forces. In many countries this is tantamount to spying, and you could find yourself being dragged off to jail – without passing Go or collecting £200!
- The light is at its most attractive during early morning and late afternoon/evening, but it is far too harsh between 10 a.m. and 3 p.m. during summer. Use this period to soak up some sun, or better still, discover new locations that can be photographed when the light improves again.
- Take a pocket guide to photography with you – such as this very book – so you can find out how to solve any problems, or tackle subjects that you come across for the first time.
- Do not get so involved in photography that you forget to take lots of snapshots of your family having fun. It will be these pictures that bring the memories flooding back in years to come.

(See DVD 20.05–20.21.)

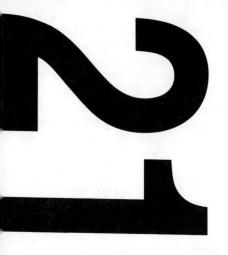

21

night and low-light photography

In this chapter you will learn:
- about keeping your camera steady
- how to photograph night scenes
- how to shoot traffic trails
- about capturing firework displays.

Most photographers put their camera away and head for home once the sun has set, but by staying outdoors and waiting until nightfall you can take stunning pictures as the world is transformed into a dazzling light show courtesy of man-made illumination.

Once daylight fades away streets come alive under the cosy glow of artificial lighting. Shop windows beckon you inside, floodlit buildings stand out vividly against the velvety blue sky, and neon signs flicker outside pubs, clubs, hotels and cinemas.

All these things make perfect subjects for the enthusiastic photographer, and even the most mundane urban scenes by day look far more inspiring by night. (See DVD 21.01.)

Keeping the camera steady

The main thing you need to bear in mind is that light levels fall rapidly once the sun sets, so long exposures – often ten seconds or more – are commonplace.

For this reason you need some kind of stable support for your camera if you are to avoid taking shaky pictures. A sturdy tripod is ideal for the job, and in windy weather you can increase its stability by hanging your gadget bag over it to increase the weight. Alternatively, use a table-top tripod and rest it on a wall, pillar-box or post to provide the necessary height.

A cable release will also come in handy, allowing you to trip the camera's shutter without actually touching it, so there is no risk of vibrations being introduced during long exposures. This is particularly important if you are using your camera's B setting, and need to keep the shutter release depressed during the whole exposure.

Another cause of vibration when you take a picture is the reflex mirror flipping out of the light path. On many SLRs the mirror can be locked up before the shutter is tripped, to reduce vibrations. If your camera has one it is a good idea to use it.

Getting the exposure right

Although low-light and night shooting may seem much trickier than daytime photography, modern camera metering is so good that it will be able to produce perfectly exposed results with little or no help from you. So, instead of making life more complicated than it needs to be, use your camera exactly as you would during the day – set it to aperture priority mode so that the exposure time is set automatically and you select the aperture to control depth of field, make sure the metering is set to multi-zone and simply fire away. You can check the preview image and histogram to assess exposure and make any adjustments as necessary, though chances are you won't need to make any changes because your camera will get it right.

If you are using film, one thing you need to be aware of is a phenomenon known as Reciprocity Law Failure, which is where film becomes less sensitive to light as exposure times increase. You will therefore need to compensate to avoid underexposure. This is not such a problem with negative film which has wide exposure latitude, but is more of a problem with colour slide film which does not. As a guide, if your meter suggests an exposure of 2–5 seconds, increase the exposure by half a stop and if it suggests 6–30 seconds, increase exposure by one stop.

Because these increases are only approximate it is always a good idea to shoot a sequence of exposures, just to be on the safe side. For example, if your meter suggests an exposure of ten seconds, take pictures at ten, 15, 20 and 30 seconds.

If you are shooting digitally, reciprocity failure is not an issue, and because you have the benefit of instant feedback you can detect any major exposure blunders anyway and deal with them immediately.

However, with both film and digital, one thing that might confuse you is if your camera meter seems unable to give you a reading because there is not enough light around. Most SLRs have a maximum timed exposure of 30 seconds, but if you are shooting at a low ISO and small aperture you may find that the exposure required is more than 30 seconds.

The solution is this: keep setting the lens to the next widest aperture until the required exposure time falls within the camera's range. For example, if you can get a reading at f/16, you may be able to at f/8. Once you have that exposure time, you can calculate the one required when the lens is stopped down again by back-tracking – if the correct exposure time at f/8 is 20 seconds, it will be 40 seconds at f/11 and 80 seconds at f/16. All you do then is set the camera to bulb (B), open the shutter with a cable release and close it after 80 seconds.

The table below will give you an idea of the exposures you should be using for common night subjects at ISO 100. (See DVD 21.02.)

Suggested exposure (seconds)				
Subject	Aperture f/5.6	f/8	f/11	f/16
Cityscape at night	4	8	16	32
Cityscape just after sunset	1/4	1/2	1	2
Fairground rides (e.g. big wheel)	3	6	12	24
Floodlit building (e.g. church)	2	4	8	16
Brightly-lit city street	1/4	1/2	1	2
Neon signs	1/15	1/8	1/4	1/2
Landscape by moonlight	2 m	4 m	8 m	16 m
Bonfire	1/8	1/4	1/2	1
Fireworks (aerial)	Bulb (B) at f/16			
Traffic trails	Bulb (B) at f/16			

Choosing film

Many photographers automatically assume that because light levels are low at night it is necessary to use fast film or, in the case of digital, a high ISO setting. However, with your camera mounted on a tripod it does not matter how long the exposure times are so you might as well use a low ISO to maximize image quality. Films with a high ISO are grainy while high ISO settings on digital cameras result in Noise where random pixels in the shadows appear bright or 'hot'. Keeping the ISO down avoids these issues and results in sharper more vivid images.

The only time fast film or a high ISO setting is worth using is if you want to take handheld pictures in low light – such as under the glow of a street lamp. The fastest colour film available is ISO 1600 but there are ISO 3200 black and white films that can be uprated to speeds as high as ISO 25 000! Digital cameras cannot go this high, but an increasing number do have an ISO range to 3200 or even 6400.

Photographing traffic trails

One of the most popular and accessible night subjects is the colourful trails of light created by photographing moving traffic with a long exposure – the headlights of on-coming traffic records as white streaks, while tail-lights come out red.

For the best results, find a location which gives you an elevated view of a busy dual carriageway, motorway or roundabout – bridges, walkways, multi-storey car parks and office windows are ideal. Then all you have to do is mount your camera on a tripod, compose the scene and wait for traffic to appear.

The way you expose the picture will depend upon what is included in the scene. If there are buildings and other features visible, take a meter reading from them so they are correctly exposed but stop your lens down to f/11 or f/16 to ensure the exposure time is nice and long. If you are only capturing the road and traffic trails, stop your lens down to a small aperture such as f/16, set your camera to bulb (B), and hold the shutter open with a cable release for around 30 seconds while traffic passes by.

Should the traffic run out, simply cover the lens with a piece of black card or your hand while still holding the shutter open, stop counting, then move it away to add more traffic trails when the traffic re-appears and resume counting down the exposure. By repeating this you can build up the colourful trails gradually to produce striking results. (See DVD 21.03.)

Using flash at night

It is amazing how many photographers think the small flashgun built into their compact camera can be used to illuminate vast night scenes. Unfortunately, it can't, and all you are likely to end up with is a black frame with a few specs of light in the background. Flash can be used successfully at night to add impact to your pictures, but you need to think carefully about what you are doing.

One technique you may want to try is illuminating a person standing in front of a floodlit building or seaside illuminations with a burst of flash. The latest digital compacts and SLRs can take pictures like this with ease – many even have a flash setting for taking pictures at night, though a slow-sync mode will work, too, because basically what you want to ensure is that the camera sets a long exposure to record the lights while the flash fires to illuminate and freeze your main subject.

This technique can be used to light other foreground features, such as gravestones in front of a church, or driftwood on a beach. If you are feeling really adventurous you could even put a filter or gel over the flashgun to colour the foreground so it contrasts with the rest of the scene – red, blue, orange and green filters work well.

Your flashgun can also be used to 'paint' buildings such as old churches with light. All you have to do is lock your camera's shutter open on the B setting then dash around the scene, popping the flash with the test button from close range so it lights selected areas. To give you enough time to light the whole scene use an exposure of at least one minute – preferably longer – and take a friend along with a second flashgun if possible, so you can both work on different areas and build up the light much quicker. (See DVD 21.04.)

Capturing fireworks

Aerial firework displays look stunning captured on film, and taking successful pictures is not as difficult as it sounds.

The technique is very similar to that used for capturing traffic trails. First, you need to mount your camera on a tripod and point it towards the area of sky where the fireworks will be exploding. If you are at a communal firework display, ask one of the marshals where the rockets will be launched, then watch the first few go up to ensure you have got the best composition.

A 24 mm or 28 mm wide-angle lens is ideal for photographing large displays because it will allow you to include buildings or spectators in the shot to add scale. Alternatively, fit a telephoto or telezoom lens so you can home in on the firework bursts to create colourful abstract images.

Once the rockets start going, lock the camera's shutter open on bulb (B) with a cable release so the explosions are recorded as colourful streaks. One or two rockets will not provide enough colour, so between explosions cover your lens with a piece of black card and then uncover it when the next rockets are launched. By repeating this you can capture half a dozen or more explosions on the same frame of film.

Again, the exposure should be based on any buildings in the scene, or the sky if there is still an afterglow present. Expect something in the region of 30 seconds at f/11 on ISO 100.

You will also find lots of other subjects to photograph at firework displays. Silhouettes of people warming themselves by the roaring fire, poor old Guy Fawkes being consumed by flames and children writing their names in the air with sparklers, to name but a few. They all make great pictures. (See DVD 21.05.)

Shooting the moon

Although it is thousands of miles away, you can take striking pictures of the moon glowing brightly in the night sky.

The main requirement is a long telephoto lens to get it a decent size in the frame. The minimum focal length worth using is 300 mm, although a 500 mm lens or longer is preferable. For every 100 mm of focal length the diameter of the moon is increased by roughly 1 mm on a 35 mm frame of film or full-frame digital sensor, so if you use a 1000 mm lens it will measure 10 mm across. On smaller digital sensors it will appear quite a lot bigger because focal length is increased – a 500 mm lens becomes 700 mm, for example, if your camera has a multiplication factor (mf) of 1.4.

If you do not have such a long telephoto, double the focal length of your longest lens with a 2× teleconverter. You could even use two converters to quadruple the focal length, so a 300 mm telephoto is converted into a 1200 mm for example. Alternatively, increase the size of the moon by cropping and enlarging the original image.

In terms of exposure, use 1/125 sec at f/8 on ISO 100 film when photographing the full moon. If you want to include the moon as part of a night scene, do so by adding it via a double exposure or superimposing it digitally. This is necessary because the moon moves, so it will blur when you use a long exposure for the rest of the scene, and being very bright it will burn out so no detail is captured. (See DVD 21.09.)

Night tips

Here are a few final words of advice to help you get the best results from your night-time exploits.

- The best time to take 'night' pictures in during the hour or so after sunset, when there is an afterglow in the sky. Do not wait until the sky is totally black as it tends to look uninteresting and contrast will be too high.

- Avoid including bright light sources such as street lamps or spotlights in your pictures at close range, and use a lens hood to minimize the risk of flare.

- Do not just shoot the obvious subjects. Colourful reflections in puddles, car paintwork, water and windows can look stunning, but they tend to be ignored. You can also take eye-catching pictures at fairgrounds by using a long exposure so rides such as the big wheel and carousel are reduced to colourful streaks.

- Wrap up in warm clothing before venturing outdoors at night – fingerless gloves will keep your hands warm but still allow you to operate your camera.
- Do not worry if there are people walking across the scene you are photographing. By using an exposure of ten seconds or more they won't appear on the picture unless they stop and remain stationary for part of the exposure, in which case a ghostly image of them will record.

(See DVD 21.06–21.08.)

22

animals and pets

In this chapter you will learn:
- how to take great pictures of family pets
- about photographing zoo animals
- about shooting from a hide
- about capturing garden birds and wild animals.

As a nation of animal lovers it is natural that at some stage you will want to try photographing the wonders of Mother Nature, not least the many species of birds and animals that inhabit our world.

The path you follow will mainly depend upon how interested you are in nature and the amount of time at your disposal. True nature photography demands much knowledge and patience, because wild animals are not renowned for being cooperative when it comes to posing for enthusiastic photographers. But if you do not fancy the idea of spending many hours waiting silently in a hide for a fox or badger to make an appearance, or stalking big game with a long telephoto lens, there are other options open to you.

Family pets make fascinating subjects, and are by far the most accessible animals. Or a visit to your local zoo will give you the opportunity to capture all sorts of species, from the common to the exotic, in a controlled environment that makes life much easier.

Photographing pets

Most families own a pet of some sort, from common animals such as dogs and cats, to rabbits, guinea pigs, hamsters, a parrot or canary, and exotic reptiles.

The techniques you use will depend very much upon what your subject is. But one thing all pets have in common is they are not going to sit patiently while you take their picture, so patience and the willingness to adapt are prerequisites to success. Treat pets like children and you will not go far wrong.

Dogs are highly intelligent pets, and as such the easiest to photograph. Most will respond to commands, so you can usually position them in the right spot and make them stay put.

To get your dog in a cooperative mood, take it for a walk and let it run around to burn off excess energy. You can use this opportunity to take some action pictures – try panning with a slow shutter speed as your subject bounds along, freeze it in mid-air as it jumps for a stick, or capture it rolling around in the long grass. Dogs also like water, so let your subject go for a paddle then photograph it shaking the water off afterwards – a shutter speed of l/500 sec or above will freeze the spray of water droplets.

For posed portraits ask the dog to sit and stay while you back off – taking a companion along will provide a suitable distraction. Making sudden noises, calling the dog's name or clicking your tongue will generate an alert response that will add character to your portraits, so make sure you are ready to capture it. You can also take successful pictures of dogs interacting with people – children and puppies are a perfect combination.

Use a telezoom lens for headshots, and focus on the dog's eyes. An aperture of f/5.6 or f/8 will provide enough depth of field to keep the whole of its head sharp, as well as throwing the background out of focus to reduce distractions. (See DVD 22.01.)

Cats have a mind of their own, so it is almost a waste of time trying to control them. Kittens can be kept occupied with a ball of wool or a furry toy, leaving you to fire away from close range with a standard or short telephoto lens. Alternatively, take your subject into the garden, stretch out on the ground and photograph it peering at you through the grass. Rustling your hand on the ground will provide a response. Kittens playing with their brothers and sisters, or curled up next to their mother, make interesting pictures.

With adult cats your best bet is simply to follow them around. Most have a favourite resting place, like the back of the sofa, the garden fence or a sunny window sill, so you will often find them curled up asleep – the perfect time to grab a few pictures. (See DVD 22.02.)

Rabbits and guinea pigs are quite docile, and will stay in position for long periods. The garden is again a good place to photograph them because the setting looks natural. You can also take pictures through the wire mesh of their cage or hutch – capture them eating, sleeping or scurrying around. (See DVD 22.03.)

When photographing smaller mammals such as hamsters, gerbils and mice you need the help on another person, just in case your subject decides to scamper off. You could take a picture of a mouse curled up on the palm of someone's hand, for example, or a hamster sitting on a child's shoulder. When shooting through the cage bars, wait for your subject to go to its food box or water bottle. Great shots can also be taken of small animals running around on their exercise wheel, curled up in their nest or peering at you through the wire mesh.

Birds are best photographed sitting on a perch rather than behind the bars of a cage. Position the perch close to a window so the bird is attractively lit, or use bounced flash for the illumination. Make sure the background is nice and simple – a sheet of card taped to the wall will do. To get really close and fill the frame with your subject use a macro lens or the macro facility on your zoom lens. (See DVD 22.04.)

A day at the zoo

Zoos offer the best of both worlds. You can photograph exotic animals and birds that are normally found in far-flung corners of the world, and because their movements are restricted, you can get much closer and fill the frame with shorter lenses.

Most zoo animals are at their most active when it is cool, so arrive early in the morning. That way you will miss the crowds and have the opportunity to shoot from the best positions. Feeding times can also provide lots of opportunities to get excellent pictures, so it is worth phoning the zoo to find out when the keepers will be handing out dinner.

To make your pictures look as though they were taken in the wild avoid including man-made features in the background, such as nest boxes, fences or other people. Most of the time you will be forced to shoot through wire mesh or bars, but that need not pose a problem. All you have to do is get as close as possible to the obstruction, then use a telephoto lens set to its widest aperture and carefully focused on your main subject. The mesh or bars will be thrown so far out of focus that they do not appear on the final picture. The background will also be nicely blurred by the shallow depth of field, making your subject stand out strongly. (See DVD 22.05.)

To photograph animals and reptiles behind glass, fix a rubber hood to your lens and press it against the glass to cut out any reflections. The enclosure will probably be lit by tungsten or fluorescent lighting, so to prevent problems with colour casts use a portable flashgun. This should also be pressed against the glass and held a few inches to one side of your camera. (See DVD 22.06.)

It is tempting to fire away without really thinking about what you are doing when you are faced by such a wide range of exotic animals, but resist the temptation. Instead, wait patiently for the subject animal to strike an interesting expression, or do something that will add an extra dimension to your picture.

Shots of young animals with their mother have great appeal, so ask one of the wardens on duty if there are any new arrivals on show that you can photograph.

In terms of equipment, a 70–200 mm or 75–300 mm telezoom should be long enough for most subjects, although it is worth taking a longer lens or a teleconverter along if you have one.

Going wild in the country

You need not go on an expensive African safari to shoot stunning wildlife pictures – the British Isles is home to many beautiful species of animals and birds, and although stalking a fox may not seem as exciting as stalking a big cat in the Serengeti, the thrill of the hunt and the primitive sense of adventure is just as great.

The main attributes you need to succeed are a genuine fascination for nature and a love of the countryside. Serious nature photographers tend to be dedicated naturalists who spend many hours studying different species to learn more about their behaviour patterns, favourite habitat and food. This is important because the more you know about your subject the better chance you have of taking good pictures of it – foolhardy is the photographer who thinks he can buy a long telephoto lens, wander off into the local woods and return home with award-winning images.

In the beginning stick to more accessible species, such as rabbits and squirrels. Common garden birds also make challenging subjects (see below), while your local riverbank is worth exploring for frogs, toads, newts, water voles, moorhens, coots, kingfishers, herons and swans, to name but a few. (See DVD 22.07.)

Once you have cut your teeth closer to home you can then become a little more ambitious and look for less common species such as badgers, deer, otters, owls and birds of prey.

A 75–300 mm telezoom will be powerful enough for animals and birds that you can get close to. Timid species will have to be captured from further away though, so you will need a longer lens to get your subject a decent size in the frame. Anything over 300 mm is suitable, but professional wildlife photographers tend to use a 500 mm or 600 mm almost as their standard lens. If you cannot afford the expense of such a long lens, buy a 2× teleconverter and double the focal length of the longest lens you already have.

Using a hide

Working from a hide is an excellent way to photograph timid animals and birds, because it allows you to get close to your subject without them being aware of your presence.

Hides can be made by draping a large sheet of camouflaged or drab canvas over a framework of poles. A selection of holes in the sides will allow you to poke the lens through, and undergrowth can be added as further concealment if necessary. For those of you with money to spare, purpose-built hides are available that collapse into a small storage bag for easy carrying and can be erected in a matter of minutes.

Before using the hide you first need to find a suitable location where wildlife activity takes place. This could be the nest site of a blackbird or a kingfisher's hunting perch, a badger run or a deer's favourite watering hole.

So the animals and birds are not alarmed by the sudden appearance of the hide, you should erect it quite a distance away at first, wait a few days, move it closer, wait another few days, move it even closer and so on until it is in the desired spot. Patience is the key – if you try to rush this process you will end up with no wildlife to photograph. Once you are ready to enter the hide, take a friend along to act as a decoy – he can leave when you are inside and this will fool most animals and birds into thinking no-one is there.

It may take many hours of waiting quietly and patiently before any activity begins, so make sure you have food and drink at hand to sustain you throughout your stay, plus warm clothing to keep you comfortable if the temperature drops.

Animals have a habit of appearing without warning, so make sure you are ready to respond by mounting your camera on a tripod, setting the exposure and focusing your lens on the area you expect to be covering. The lens you need will depend upon the subject you are hoping to capture and how close you are. A 70–200 mm telezoom may be powerful enough to fill the frame with a small bird if you are only a couple of metres from its perch or nest, but for rabbits, deer, foxes and other animals you may need anything from a 300 mm to a 600 mm telephoto.

On a more everyday level, your car can be used as a temporary hide, allowing you to shoot common animals and birds from the roadside. Car parks and picnic sites in woodland or parks tend to attract all sorts of species in search of food, so if you stay put and wait you could be handsomely rewarded. Just wind the window down, and place a jacket or beanbag over the frame to support your lens. You could even put out morsels of food on the ground to attract common animals and birds. (See DVD 22.09.)

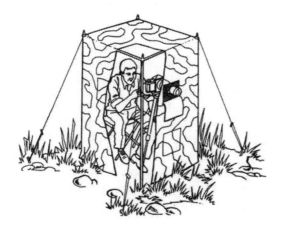

figure 22.1 Shooting from a hide will allow you to photograph timid animals and birds from close range without being spotted.

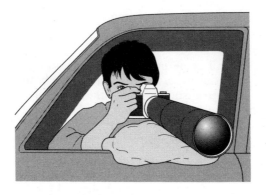

figure 22.2 Your car can also double as a useful temporary hide if you see any animals as you are driving through the countryside or sitting in a woodland clearing.

Stalking wild animals

Another common approach to wildlife photography involves carefully stalking your subject until you are close enough to get a decent picture. Most photographers use stalking for deer and other large mammals whose whereabouts are known or can be traced by any signs left.

The key to success with stalking is moving very quietly and carefully so your subject does not realize you are nearby. Any sudden movements, such as the crunching of leaves underfoot or the cracking of twigs will make the animal immediately aware of potential danger and, although the alert response can lead to excellent pictures, the animal will more than likely disappear out of sight. If your subject does stop and look around, remain perfectly still – stationary objects are far more difficult to spot than moving ones.

Blending in with your surroundings is vitally important, so wear drab clothing – army-surplus garments are ideal and can be purchased cheaply. You should also avoid wearing shiny jewellery or watches that create reflection and make a lot of noise, or aftershave and perfume which animals will pick up immediately with their keen sense of smell. Staying down wind will also help reduce the risk of you being spotted.

Equipment should be kept to a minimum so you can travel lightly and quietly. A 35 mm SLR body and a single telephoto lens is all you really need in terms of hardware – make that lens at least a 300 mm telephoto so you do not have to get too close, especially if you are photographing potentially dangerous animals on safari. Film and other accessories can be carried in your jacket pocket.

A monopod will come in handy for supporting the lens and preventing camera shake. Alternatively, take a beanbag along so you can turn tree stumps and other natural features into convenient supports. Use a shutter speed of at least l/500 sec to freeze any subject and camera movement, plus a wide aperture of f/4 or f/5.6 to throw distracting background details out of focus.

Finally, if your camera body is chrome, cover the shiny bits in black tape to prevent reflections. A sheet of green netting will also prove useful as a temporary hide once you are in position, and can be covered with foliage to provide extra cover. (See DVD 22.10.)

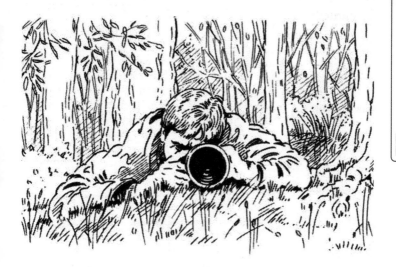

figure 22.3 To put the odds of success in your favour when stalking animals, wear drab clothing and use natural features such as tree stumps and banks to provide plenty of cover.

Photographing garden birds

Photographing birds in the wild is notoriously difficult. Not only are most species small, meaning you need to get close to fill the frame even with a powerful telephoto lens, but their senses are also highly tuned and they are very timid, making this task all the more tricky.

An easy way around this problem, and an ideal introduction to the joys of photographing wild birds, is to concentrate on the species that visit your back garden. Robins, blackbirds, thrushes, sparrows, blue tits and starlings are the most common, but if you have large trees in your garden you may also see magpies, jays, jackdaws, pigeons, doves, even the odd woodpecker or two.

To attract plenty of birds into your garden, put food out on a regular basis. Bacon rind, breadcrumbs, suet and nuts work a treat. You can also buy packets of wild bird seed containing the favourite food of many different species.

If you scatter food on the ground close to your house you may be able to take successful pictures by hiding behind the curtains and poking your lens through an open window. A much better way, however, is to erect some kind of perch from an old branch driven into the ground. That way you can hide morsels of food out of sight so they do not appear in the picture, and the birds will be on your level, giving more pleasing results. A fork or spade stuck in the ground works well too – robins can often be seen sitting on a garden folk waiting for worms to appear in the soil below. Make sure the background is nice and simple –

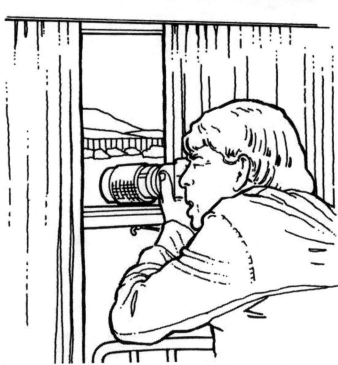

figure 22.4 Shooting through an open window with a telephoto or zoom lens can produce excellent pictures of garden birds. If you cannot get close enough, position the camera close to a suitable perch and trip the shutter from a distance using a remote release.

a hedgerow, fence or shrubs work well – and throw it out of focus by setting your lens to a wide aperture.

If you do not have a long enough lens to fill the frame with the bird from a distance – a 200–300 mm lens will be required – you can try your hand at remote photography. This involves mounting your camera on a tripod close to the perch, focusing on it, setting the exposure controls, then tripping the shutter from a safe distance using a long cable or air release.

Covering the camera with a sack or sheet or drab canvas will disguise it and dampen the noise of the shutter and winder, as well as protecting it from any little presents the birds leave behind if they decide to use it as an impromptu perch! (See DVD 22.08.)

Nature tips

- Learn as much as you can about the animals and birds you would like to photograph. The more knowledge you have of their habits the more likely you are to take successful pictures.

- Wild animals tend to be more active at dawn and dusk, so time your shoots at these periods rather than searching in vain when they are hidden away.

- Even if you live in a busy city it is still possible to photograph wildlife – foxes and badgers can often be seen rummaging around for food, while starlings, kestrels, pigeons and other birds are common visitors to urban areas.

- There are various courses you can go on to learn more about the techniques of wildlife photography. Check photographic magazines for details.

23

close-up photography

In this chapter you will learn:
- the right equipment for close-up and macro photography
- controlling depth of field
- using flash for close-ups
- shooting in available light.

Exploring the world in miniature is a fascinating area of photography, and one that you won't be able to leave behind once you sample the many delights it holds in store. Being able to peer through your camera's viewfinder and see things that are too small to appreciate with the naked eye is an exciting experience.

There is an endless range of subjects out there waiting to be captured, from butterflies, bees and spiders, to dragonflies, flowers, and the many intricate patterns and textures created by Mother Nature. You can also take interesting pictures of everyday items, such as the minute workings of a wristwatch, the bristles of a toothbrush, the veins and cells in a leaf, or the tiny fingers of a newborn baby's hand.

Many photographers avoid shooting close-ups because they are misled into thinking you need expensive specialist equipment to have a go. This is half true, simply because conventional lenses will not focus close enough to fill the frame with small subjects. However, you can set yourself on the road to successful close-ups for only minimal investment.

Another misconception is the complexity of the techniques involved. Admittedly, close-up photography does demand a different approach from most other subjects, but the difficulties are no greater and with a little practice you will be taking superb pictures in no time at all. (See DVD 23.01.)

Know your terms

Throughout this chapter you will regularly come across common close-ups terms, such as 'reproduction ratio' and 'magnification'. They basically refer to the size of your subject on a frame of film compared to its size in real life, and are used to express the power of close-up equipment.

For example, if you photograph a caterpillar measuring 2 cm in real life so it measures 1 cm on a 35 mm frame of film or full-frame digital sensor, the reproduction ratio is 1:2, or half life-size, and the magnification 0.5✕. If the same caterpillar measures 5 mm on film or sensor, the ratio is 1:4, or one-quarter life-size, and the magnification 0.25✕. If it measures 2 cm the ratio is 1:1, or life-size, and the magnification 1✕.

If you use a digital SLR with a sensor that is not full-frame then apply the magnification factor that applies to lens focal length to calculate the effective repro-ratio. If you use a 1:1 macro lens at full 1:1 (life-size) reproduction on a digital SLR with a magnification factor of 1.4, for example, the effective reproduction ratio will be 1.4:1 or 1.4× life-size. This makes digital SLRs with smaller sensors ideal for close-up photography – because your subject is magnified even more.

Macro photography is a term used to describe pictures taken at reproduction ratios of life-size and above, whereas ratios between 1:7 and 1:1 fall into the close-up category.

Equipment for close-ups

There are more ways to shoot close-ups than there are to skin a cat, so it is worth sparing a little time to look at the various pieces of equipment you can use before deciding which ones to go for.

Macro zooms

The easiest method is to use the macro facility on your zoom lens (it should be called a close-up facility really). Many zooms offer a reproduction ratio up to 1:4, which is fine for flowers, small mammals and household objects.

Supplementary close-up lenses

These handy attachments fit to the front of your lens like filters, and reduce its minimum focusing distance so you can get much closer to your subject. The power of close-up lenses is measured in dioptres – the most common are +1, +2, +3 and +4. The bigger the number is, the greater the magnification obtained. A +4 dioptre lens used on a 50 mm standard lens with the focus set to one metre will give a reproduction ratio of 1:4, for example.

If you need extra power, more than one close-up lens can be used in combination. Image sharpness will suffer if you do this, though, because the optical quality of the lenses is not all that high. If you do need greater magnification, look at more powerful supplementary lenses – they are available up to +10 dioptres.

Reversing ring

This accessory allows you to mount a lens on your camera back-to-front, so it will focus much closer and allow you to take powerful close-ups. The advantage of reversing rings is they do not affect the optical quality of your lens because you are not adding any extra glass elements to the set-up. The main drawback is you lose all linkage between the camera and lens, so the metering system and automatic aperture stopdown no longer work.

All things considered, they are ideal if you are on a tight budget. Also, if you are using a bellows unit or extension tubes (see below) for reproduction ratios greater than life-size, image quality begins to suffer when the distance to the subject is less than the lens-to-film distance. By using a reversing ring to provide extra macro power this problem can be avoided.

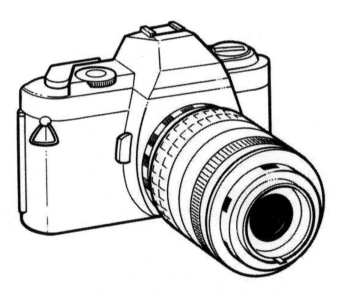

figure 23.1

Macro lenses

Specialist macro lenses provide the most convenient method of shooting powerful close-ups because they are designed for the job, making them quick and easy to use and capable of superb quality. The main advantage of using a macro lens is that you can obtain any reproduction ratio down to 1:2 or 1:1 (life-size) without the need of any other attachments.

There are two main focal lengths available – either 50/55/60 mm or 90/100/105 mm. The shorter lenses are small and light, but usually only offer a maximum ratio of 1:2 when used alone and require supplementary lenses to reach life-size repro. The longer versions allow 1:1 (life-size) reproduction. They also allow you to fill the frame from further away, which can be a real advantage when you are photographing timid subjects such as butterflies, and they double as an excellent portrait lens.

If you are serious about shooting close-ups, a macro lens is the best item to use for reproduction ratios up to life-size.

Extension tubes

These metal tubes fit between the lens and camera body, increasing the lens-to-film distance so greater image magnification is possible. The tubes normally come in sets of three, each a different size, so you can obtain different reproduction ratios. When all three are used together they normally give 80 mm or 90 mm of extension. The more expensive makes also retain links between the camera and lens, so automatic aperture stopdown can be achieved.

When the length of extension matches the focal length of the lens, the reproduction ratio obtained is 1:1 (life-size). So 50 mm of extension with a 50 mm standard lens or 85 mm with an 85 mm lens gives life-size images. Tubes can also be used in conjunction with a macro lens or reversing ring to achieve greater magnification.

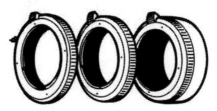

figure 23.2

Because the tubes do not contain any glass elements, image quality is again very high. However, the viewfinder image goes quite dark when using a lot of extension, so accurate focusing can be tricky. Also, the further you move the lens away from the camera to increase magnification, the more the exposure has to be increased. You do not have to worry about this when using a modern SLR as the integral metering system will adjust the exposure automatically.

Bellows unit

This system works on the same principle as extension tubes, but the cloth bellows are adjustable so you can obtain intermediate levels of magnification. Bellows also allow more extension – often up to 150 mm, which gives a reproduction ration of 3× with a 50 mm standard lens. In practice that means you can fill the viewfinder with a subject measuring little more than one centimetre in size, so for true macro images they just cannot be beaten.

Ideally, bellows must be used on a tripod as they are cumbersome and slow in operation. It is also worth investing in a focusing rail, which allows you to move the camera and bellows back and forth to achieve accurate focusing, rather than having to physically move the tripod.

For even greater magnification, reverse your standard 50 mm lens on the front of the bellows using a reversing ring.

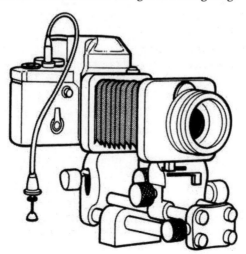

figure 23.3

As with extension tubes, bellows require an exposure increase which your camera's metering system will account for. (See DVD 23.02 and 23.03.)

The table below shows the reproduction ratio and magnification when using a 50 mm standard lens with different amounts of extension from bellows or tubes.

Extension	Reproduction ratio	Magnification
5 mm	1:10	0.1×
10 mm	1:5	0.2×
20 mm	1:2.5	0.4×
40 mm	1:1.2	0.8×
50 mm	1:1	1.0×
70 mm	1.4:1	1.4×
90 mm	1.8:1	1.8×
100 mm	2:1	2.0×
120 mm	2.4:1	2.4×
150 mm	3:1	3.0×

Controlling depth of field

The trickiest part of close-up photography is making sure your subject comes out sharp. Depth of field is severely restricted at close focusing distances, so you should always use the smallest lens aperture possible – usually f/16 or f/22 – to maximize what little depth of field there is and focus carefully on the most important part of your subject.

By doing this you encounter another problem – slow shutter speeds. Even in bright conditions you may a find a shutter speed of a quarter or even half a second is required when working at a low ISO of 50 or 100 and an aperture of f/16. This makes a tripod essential if you are to avoid camera shake. The shutter should also be tripped using a cable release and, if possible, your camera's mirror should be locked up prior to making the exposure, so vibrations are minimized which can lead to camera shake – when shooting close-ups the slightest movement is magnified and can ruin an otherwise great picture.

Subject movement can be equally troublesome and needs to be dealt with if you are to avoid blurred results. With flowers and other subjects that you can spend time photographing, a temporary windbreak can be erected from pieces of card and twigs pushed into the ground or by using a reflector to double as a wind shield. Unfortunately, if you try this approach with butterflies, insects and other timid subjects, they are likely to disappear before you are ready to take the picture. So the only option is to use flash. (See DVD 23.04.)

Using flash for close-ups

Electronic flash is the panacea of all ills when it comes to close-up photography. As well as giving you more control over the quality of lighting, the brief duration of the flash will freeze any subject movement so you can work at small apertures for maximum depth of field without worrying about producing unsharp pictures.

The best way to use flash for close-ups is by taking it off the camera's hotshot and mounting it on some kind of bracket, so you can position it close to the lens where it needs to be to produce the best results. There are numerous different brackets available for this purpose, though you could make your own, and for even illumination you should ideally use two guns, one either side of the lens and angled so they are pointing towards the subject.

Modern dedicated flashguns can be used for close-up photography and because they are linked to the camera's metering system you can expect perfectly exposed results every time – just leave everything to the wonders of technology and concentrate instead on composition and focusing.

If you are serious about close-up photography there are some very clever systems around that include wireless remote flash so you can position several flashguns around your subjects and trigger them all at once with full TTL flash control. Ringflash and macro flash units are also available that are specially designed for close-up photography (see figure 23.4).

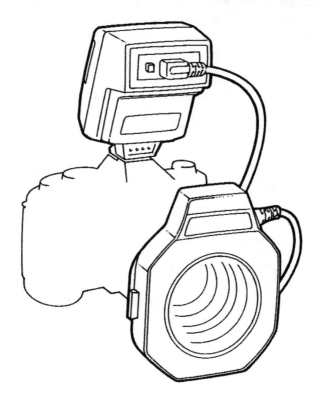

figure 23.4 Ringflash units like this model are designed to give correctly exposed and well-lit pictures when shooting at close focusing distances.

Close-ups in available light

If you decide to shoot close-ups in daylight, as many photographers do for more natural results, you will need to give the light a helping hand. The easiest way to do this is by using white reflectors to bounce light into the shadows and provide more even illumination – especially if you are working in shady areas, as is often the case.

Small pieces of white card or tin foil carefully positioned make ideal reflectors, or if you can afford it, buy a couple of small folding reflectors like those in the Lastolite range. It is also a good idea to shoot in slightly overcast weather rather than bright sunlight, so contrast is lower and the shadows are weaker. That said, if the light is harsh you can simply hold a

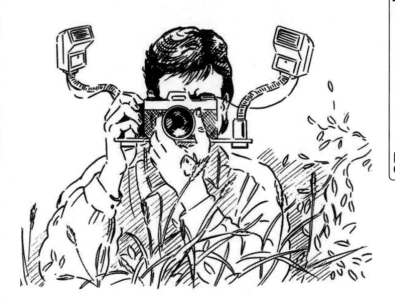

figure 23.5 An ideal set-up for close-up photography comprises two small manual flashguns mounted either side of the camera on adjustable arms, so you can vary the position of each gun to achieve the best possible results.

reflector or screen over your subject so that it is thrown into shade and the light is much softer. (See DVD 23.05–23.08.)

Close-up tips

- Be very quiet and cautious when photographing live subjects such as butterflies and insects. Make any slight moves and they will disappear in an instant.
- Choose the background to your close-ups carefully. Anything plain and neutral, such as green foliage, is ideal. It is also worth carrying a few pieces of card in your photo backpack, so they can be slipped behind your subject to create a suitable backdrop.

- Never damage plants and flowers in your quest to take perfect close-ups – treat nature with respect and you will be rewarded many times over.
- Many subjects, such as butterflies, flowers and plants are easier to photograph indoors than out because you will have more control over the lighting. Some photographers even breed their own butterflies especially.

24

photographing architecture

In this chapter you will learn:

- how to avoid converging verticals
- how to make the most of light
- how to shoot architectural details
- how to photograph interiors.

Buildings come in all shapes, sizes and designs, making architecture an exciting and challenging subject that can be enjoyed by beginners and experienced photographers alike. From crumbling old cottages and magnificent cathedrals to state-of-the-art skyscrapers and contemporary monuments, suitable subjects can be found literally everywhere you go. Even better, you do not need the communication skills of a portrait photographer, the expert knowledge of a nature photographer, or the lightning-quick reflexes of an action photographer to take stunning pictures of buildings – just an appreciation of light and composition.

Architectural photography is a very slow-moving, considered discipline. Professionals often spend hours, even days, waiting for the light to be perfect. They check weather reports and consult maps to discover the aspect of a building so they know when it will be well lit, and then put a great deal of effort into taking the best possible pictures of it. You need not go quite to those lengths, but if you want to do your subject justice a little effort is required. (See DVD 24.01.)

Finding the right viewpoint

The viewpoint you shoot from can make all the difference in architectural photography, so before firing away spend a little time looking at the subject building from different positions until you find the most successful one.

Pay particular attention to rivers, streams and ponds, which may feature a vivid reflection of the building, trees that can be used to frame it and hide unwanted sky, and flower beds or other features that can be used to add interest to the foreground.

Often your choice of viewpoint will be limited due to other buildings, street furniture, traffic and people getting in the way. The usual way around this is to use a wide-angle lens and shoot from close range, so you can exclude unwanted structures. Unfortunately, in doing so you immediately expose yourself to the biggest bane of any architectural photographer's life – converging verticals. (See DVD 24.02.)

Avoiding converging verticals

This annoying phenomenon makes buildings appear to be toppling over, and is caused when the back of the camera is tilted to include the top of a tall building in the shot. To prevent converging verticals the camera back must be kept parallel to the building. The trouble is, if you are using a wide-angle lens from close range, doing this means you lose the top of the building and gain a lot of unwanted foreground detail.

Luckily there are various solutions to this problem.

1 You could shoot from a slightly higher viewpoint, so you are looking across rather than up at the building. Architectural photographers often carry a step ladder in their car for this purpose. Shooting from a building opposite or standing on a wall are suitable alternatives.

2 If you back away from the building and use a short telephoto lens rather than a wide-angle you may find you will not need to tilt the camera to include the top of the building.

3 You can use a perspective control or 'shift' lens, which allows you to adjust the position of the front elements of the lens in relation to the film plane, so the camera back can be kept perfectly square but you are still able to include the whole building from close range. All the main camera manufacturers have one or more shift lenses in their range, usually with a focal length of 24 mm or 28 mm – although 45 mm and 90 mm versions are available too. They are very expensive though, and only worth buying if you shoot a lot of architecture.

4 A much easier option in this digital age is to correct converging verticals on the computer. Here's how:

- Open your image file in Photoshop then choose Select>All to place a dashed line around your image.
- Select View>Show>Grid to display a grid of lines over the image which will aid correction of the leaning verticals.
- Select Edit>Transform>Distort then click on the top left corner of the picture and drag the cursor out gently to the left – as you drag it the wall on that side of the picture will begin to straighten. Use the grid as a guide and stop when the vertical lines look OK.
- Repeat for the right side and tweak both sides until the verticals are vertical.
- Hit the return key on your keyboard to process the transformation then select View>Show>Grid and uncheck the grid so it disappears from your picture.
- If the image looks rather squat now, select Image>Image Size, uncheck the Constrain Proportions box and increase

the height of the image by between five and ten per cent. This should make it appear more normal. (See DVD 24.04–24.07.)

Of course, it isn't *essential* that you correct converging verticals – when used intentionally they can produce excellent results. If you look up the front of a tall building through a wide-angle lens, for example, the sides will converge dramatically to create a powerful, graphic composition. The key is to make sure the building is central in the frame, so each side converges equally. (See DVD 24.03.)

Architectural details

Do not get so wrapped up in capturing the whole building that you ignore the smaller but equally interesting details.

Old buildings in particular usually boast many ornate features, such as gargoyles, sundials, clock faces, weather cocks, carved stone archways, fluted columns and so on. Modern buildings are renowned for their symmetry and regimentation which make fantastic abstract images, so look for opportunities to exploit this. The patterns created by identical windows in a towering office block, precast concrete panels, roofing slates, rows of chimney pots, and reflections in glass-fronted buildings make eye-catching images. (See DVD 24.09.)

Using light

The quality of light is vitally important when shooting buildings, so it should be given just as much consideration as the viewpoint you choose. (See DVD 24.08.)

The best time of day to photograph a particular building depends upon its aspect, because this will determine whether or not it is in shadow. If you are lucky the light may be perfect when you arrive, but often you will have to wait for a while, or return the next day either earlier or later.

Low-angle side-lighting works well on older buildings because it reveals texture and form in the stone or brickwork. Stonework is also enhanced by the warm light of early morning or late afternoon, so these periods are ideal for photographing churches, cottages, castles and other old buildings.

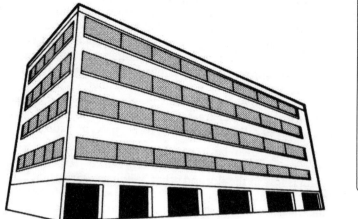

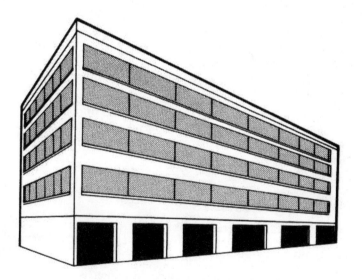

figure 24.1 Converging verticals look odd unless you exaggerate them for effect, so use one of the techniques outlined above to avoid the problem whenever possible.

Modern office blocks look more dynamic when they are bathed in bright sunlight against a deep blue sky, or at dusk when the ambient light is reflected from the sky so shadows are minimized. If you are photographing a glass-fronted building, wait until it is in shadow and the buildings opposite are well lit, so you can capture vivid reflections in the glass panelling. Avoid shooting around midday whenever possible – unless you are concentrating on abstracts and graphics – as the light is too contrasty and lacks character. Also, because the sun is overhead the façades of tall buildings tend to be in deep shadow.

Shadows can also be a problem when photographing street scenes, or buildings in a crowded city centre – especially when the sun is low in the sky and other buildings nearby block it out. One half of a street may be bathed in sunlight, for example, while the other half is shaded. In such situations your best bet is to wait until the whole scene is evenly lit or in shadow, so the contrast is reduced to a manageable level.

The only time shadows become an ally is if you want to record buildings as silhouettes – the ruins of an old castle or abbey at sunset, say. This is best achieved by shooting from a viewpoint that puts the building between the camera and the sun, so when you expose for the bright background the building is underexposed and records as a solid black shape. (See DVD 24.10.)

Finally, night-time presents many exciting opportunities to photograph buildings bathed in colourful artificial illumination. For more details refer to Chapter 21 on taking pictures at night. (See DVD 24.16.)

Shooting interiors

Although building interiors look simple to photograph, taking successful pictures demands rather more care and thought than you need to apply on the other side of the door.

The main problem you are likely to encounter is low lighting, which makes a tripod essential. Exposure times often run into many seconds when you are using a small aperture to provide sufficient depth of field and a low ISO for optimum image quality, so without a sturdy camera support you will be in trouble.

Interior lighting also tends to be very contrasty, particularly in old buildings that rely on window light for most of their illumination. In sunny weather light levels are high close to the windows, while everywhere else is dark and shady. So if you expose for the highlights most of the interior will come out too dark, while if you expose for the shadows the windows will burn out horribly.

Shooting in dull weather can help, because the difference in brightness between indoors and out will be reduced. Other than that all you can really do is bracket your exposures widely, then choose the frame that gives the best compromise between highlight and shadow detail.

Interior lighting is much better in modern buildings, so problems with contrast are more or less solved for you. Unfortunately, another obstacle presents itself – artificial lighting. Tungsten and fluorescent are the two most popular types of lighting used for interiors. If you take pictures under either type your pictures will come out with orange and green casts respectively unless you adjust the white balance of your digital camera or use colour-balancing filters when working with film.

The orange cast from tungsten lighting can be avoided using tungsten-balanced colour film or a blue 8OA filter on your lens. Fluorescent lighting is trickier to balance because the colour cast varies depending upon the age and make of the tube. For general use you can buy an FLD filter, which has a slight magenta colour to neutralize the cast. If you shoot film and scan the images, any colour casts can be removed digitally using software such as Adobe Photoshop, so do not worry if you lack the required filters.

If the interior is lit by mixed sources you cannot balance them all, so use colour negative film rather slide film as it tends to give better results. The colour balance can also be controlled more at the printing stage. Digitally, just see how you go using different white balance settings – or shoot on auto white balance and see how the sensor copes with the mixed lighting.

Finally, space is often restricted inside buildings, so a wide-angle lens of 24 mm or 28 mm will be required to include enough information in the frame. Converging verticals can again be a problem, so choose your viewpoint carefully. Small rooms are easy to cope with, but if you try to include the ceiling of a tall building, such as a cathedral, you may have no choice but to live with convergence if you do not have access to a shift lens or large-format camera. (See DVD 24.18.)

Using flash for interiors

Many architectural photographers overcome the problems of mixed light sources or poor lighting by using electronic flash to light interiors. This usually involves selectively lighting dark areas of the building so contrast is reduced and the illumination is balanced with the available light to produce evenly lit, natural results. To do the job properly you need powerful studio flash units, so it is only feasible if you have permission to photograph the building and can spend time setting everything up.

An alternative and more accessible technique for amateur photographers involves 'painting' the interior with the light from a portable flashgun. To do this, mount your camera on a tripod, lock the shutter open on bulb (B), then walk around the interior, firing the flashgun at dark areas by pressing the test button and gradually increasing the light levels. This technique is a little hit-and-miss, so experimentation is advised. You also need to make sure the flash is fired from behind walls and pillars, so you do not appear on the picture yourself.

Architectural tips

- A small hotshoe-mounted spirit level will come in handy for checking that your camera is perfectly square.
- Use a polarizing filter to saturate colours in sunny weather, deepen blue sky and reduce reflections in the windows of buildings.
- An 81 series warm-up filter is ideal for enhancing the richness of stone – especially when you are shooting in warm sunlight.
- Stick to a low ISO or slow film when photographing buildings, so you can capture every detail in razor-sharp clarity.
- If you are going to shoot a lot of architecture, a grid focusing screen with fine lines etched into the surface will help you check the building is perfectly square. (See DVD 24.17.)

25

sport and action

In this chapter you will learn:
- what equipment to use for sport and action photography
- about varying the ISO to cope with changing light
- how to keep your subject sharp
- how to choose the right shutter speed.

Capturing the thrills and spills of fast-moving action is an exciting and challenging task. At the same time, it is also one of the more tricky photographic disciplines, simply because it demands skills that are not required for most subjects.

Timing is the lynchpin in the whole mechanics of action photography. Often you only have a split second to take a picture, and if you hesitate the opportunity will be missed. As a result, it is essential you are completely familiar with your equipment so you can use it instinctively. You should be able to adjust the exposure without taking the camera from your eye if light levels fluctuate, know which aperture and shutter speed is set, and so on. Time spent fiddling around with buttons and dials is time wasted and shots missed forever.

A knowledge of the event you are photographing is also important, because it will enable you to predict the movements of your subject and prepare yourself to capture the action at its peak. If you are trying to photograph American football, for example, and you do not understand the flow of the game, many excellent opportunities will pass as you try to fathom out what is going on.

When you try shooting action for the first time the pace will seem quite daunting. There is so much to think about in so little time, and it is easy to start panicking. However, like all things in life, practice makes perfect. Driving a car for the first time is a frightening experience, but before long it becomes second nature and you wonder what the problem was. Action photography is much the same, and once you have mastered the techniques involved you will never look back. (See DVD 25.01.)

Lenses for action

As most sport and action takes place quite a distance from the camera, telephoto and telezoom lenses are usually required to fill the frame with your subject. Professionals tend to use a 400 mm or 500 mm telephoto as their standard, but that is mainly because access is restricted at large venues, even if you do have a press pass. By sticking to smaller venues, such as your local athletics track, football pitch or tennis courts, you can usually get much closer to the action, so a 70–200 mm or, even better, a 75–300 mm telezoom, will be long enough and often you will even be able to use shorter focal lengths.

Where a longer telephoto is required you can double the focal length of your lenses with a 2× teleconvertor. This is not an ideal solution, because the two stops of light lost when you do this restricts your use of fast shutter speeds, but you can overcome that problem by using faster film if necessary or setting your digital camera to a higher ISO.

Another approach is to photograph action that takes place close to the camera. If you buy a front-row ticket at Wimbledon, for example, you will have a better view of the tennis stars than the photographers in the press enclosure, so your 70–200 mm zoom will be perfectly adequate for filling the frame.

Rugby is another spectator sport that offers exciting photographic opportunities. At large grounds such as Twickenham a 75–300 mm telephoto will again be long enough to capture line-outs, scrums and touchline action from the stands – so much so that professionals often buy tickets themselves.

Finally, everyday action can be exploited by those of you with a limited lens system. Joggers in the park, kids racing around on their mountain bikes, motocross riders practising in the local quarry and city-centre cycle-racing can be photographed successfully using everything from a 28 mm wide-angle lens to a 70–200 mm telezoom. (See DVD 25.02.)

Useful accessories

The vast majority of modern cameras have a built-in motordrive that allows you to shoot at a rate of anything from two to ten frames-per-second (fps). Professional sports photographers tend to use the faster models so they can shoot rapid sequences of images. In fact, some digital SLRs are even made now specifically for sport and action photography, with ultra-fast motordrives and a lower pixel resolution so that much bigger bursts of images can be recorded before the camera's internal memory becomes full. Those images are written to the memory card more rapidly as the file sizes are smaller.

You do not need a shooting rate of 10 fps though; 2–4fps is more than enough. Also, do not be misled into thinking you cannot fail to capture the peak of the action by machine-gunning your subject. Perfect timing is still required, and the motor should only be used to speed up your response time.

When using long lenses some kind of support will also be required. A tripod is unsuitable because it is slow to use and restricts your movements, so most photographers opt for its one-legged cousin, the monopod, instead. The beauty of a monopod is it provides plenty of support when used properly, but gives you the freedom to move around and follow the flow of the action.

ISO for action

Most enthusiast photographers automatically assume that a high ISO – either in terms of film speed or digital camera setting – must be used for sport and action photography. However, often, nothing could be further from the truth.

In bright sunlight ISO 50 or ISO 100 will allow you to work at a shutter speed of 1/500 or even l/l000 sec with your lens set to a wide aperture, such as f/4. This is easily fast enough to freeze most action, so you might as well take advantage of the benefits a low ISO offers in terms of superior image quality.

If light levels suddenly drop, or you are shooting in cloudy weather, all you need to do is increase the ISO setting on your camera to 400 or 800, or in the case of film, load a roll of ISO 400. Indoors, an ISO of 800–1600 is more likely as light levels will be much lower. That said, always keep the ISO as low as you can because in film terms it means grain will be finer and images will be punchier while with digital cameras it will minimize noise (hot pixels).

If you are still a film shooter, remember that colour slide and black and white negative film can be uprated to a higher ISO and then push-processed. For example, if you rate a roll of ISO 400 film at ISO 1600 it must be 'pushed' two stops by the processing lab to compensate. Pushing is a handy technique to use in low light when you need to work at faster shutter speeds. (See DVD 25.06.)

Keep your subject sharp

Allied to perfect timing is the need for accurate focusing skills. There is little point in tripping the shutter at the right moment if your subject is not sharp. Also, when you are using telephoto lenses set to wide apertures depth of field is very shallow, so there is little or no margin for error.

Depending upon the type of event you are photographing, two completely different focusing techniques can be used – prefocusing and follow-focusing.

Prefocusing involves focusing on a point you know your subject will pass, such as a corner in a racetrack, a hurdle, a canoeist's slalom gate, or the crossbar in a high jump. All you do then is wait until your subject approaches and trip the shutter just before it reaches the point of focus. It is important to shoot just before your subject snaps into focus because the shutter takes a fraction of a second to open, so if you wait you will miss the shot.

The points generally chosen for prefocusing tend to be places where the pace of action is slowed down, so you stand a better chance of capturing a perfect shot and can use a slower shutter speed. Motorcyclists often travel at 150 mph on a straight section of track, for instance, but at a corner that speed will be halved.

Follow-focusing involves tracking your subject with the camera and continually adjusting focus to keep it sharp. That way, when something exciting happens you are ready to capture it. Before the days of auto focusing, sports photographers had to follow-focus manually, which is very difficult and takes years to master. These days, modern AF systems are amazingly quick and accurate and will do the job for you – just set the AF to Servo or Predictive mode and as you move the camera to track your subject the lens will automatically adjust focus to keep it sharp – providing the active focus sensor remains over your subject. (See DVD 25.04.)

Choosing the right shutter speed

The shutter speed you need to use to freeze action depends upon three important factors – how fast your subject is moving, how far away it is from the camera, and the direction it is travelling in relation to the camera.

If your subject is coming head-on, for example, you can freeze it with a slower shutter speed than if it is moving across your path. Similarly, a faster shutter speed will be required to freeze a subject that fills the frame than if it only occupies a small part.

A shutter speed of 1/4000 sec – the highest offered by most of today's SLRs – is fast enough to freeze any action.

Unfortunately, light levels will not always allow you to use such high speeds, even with your lens set to its maximum aperture, so you need to be aware of the minimum speeds required for certain subjects. Use the table below as a guide. (See DVD 25.03.)

Subject	Full frame across path	Half frame across path	45° to camera	Head-on
Person running (10 mph)	1/500 sec	1/250 sec	1/250 sec	1/125 sec
Cyclist/sprinter (25 mph)	1/1000 sec	1/500 sec	1/500 sec	1/250 sec
Car/bike (40 mph)	1/2000 sec	1/1000 sec	1/1000 sec	1/500 sec
Car/bike (70 mph)	1/4000 sec	1/2000 sec	1/2000 sec	1/1000 sec

Expressing movement

Of course, you need not always use a fast shutter speed. In fact, often doing so is counter-productive, because by freezing all traces of movement you can easily lose the drama and excitement of the event. A high jumper caught in mid-air over the crossbar is obviously in motion, for example, but a racing car frozen on the track might as well be stationary when totally frozen.

This can be avoided by intentionally introducing some blur into your pictures. If you use a slow shutter speed – anything from 1/60 to 1/2 sec – and keep the camera still, your subject will simply blur as it passes, while the background remains sharp. Runners at the start of a marathon or a canoeist passing through a slalom gate are two subjects that could benefit greatly from such an approach.

A technique which works even more successfully, and can be used for just about any action subject, is panning. Again, a slow shutter speed is used, but instead of keeping the camera steady you track your subject with it by swinging your body, and trip the shutter while you are moving. This produces an image where your subject comes out relatively sharp but the background blurs. The effect can look stunning.

The amount of blur created depends upon the smoothness of the pan and the shutter speed used. If you want your subject to be pin sharp you need to pan evenly, so it remains in exactly the same part of the frame throughout the exposure – this takes practice to master. If the pan is uneven or your subject is moving unevenly – such as a runner with his arms and legs swinging – you cannot avoid creating blur. But do not worry as this often leads to more powerful results, and extensive blurring of both the subject and background can produce eye-catching impressionistic images.

As a starting point, use a shutter speed of 1/250 or even 1/500 sec with motor racing, 1/60 or 1/125 sec with cyclists and 1/30 sec with joggers. Once you gain confidence and your panning improves you will be able to keep your subject sharp in the frame when using shutter speeds down to half a second or slower. (See DVD 25.08–25.10.)

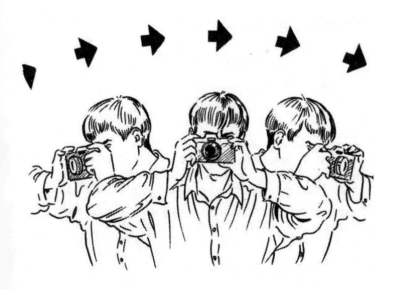

figure 25.1 The key to success with panning is swinging the camera in a smooth, even motion so your subject comes out sharp but the background blurs to add a feeling of action and excitement.

Using flash for action

Another way of adding excitement and drama to your action picture is by using a technique known as slow sync flash. This can be practised using an ordinary portable flashgun or your camera's integral flash, and involves combining a burst of electronic flash with a slow shutter speed, so you get a blurred and frozen image of moving subjects on the same frame of film.

Sport and action photographers often use slow sync flash because it helps to capture the feeling of speed and action that tends to be lost by using a fast shutter speed to freeze all traces of movement. However, you can use it on any moving subject, from your kids racing around the park on their bicycles, to people having fun on fairground rides.

Many modern SLRs and compact cameras now have a slow sync flash mode which allows you to use the technique automatically. If your camera does not, chances are your flashgun will. This means that if you set the camera to aperture priority mode, it will not automatically set the shutter to the recommended flash sync speed – which is too fast to capture any blur – and instead sets a shutter speed that is correct for the ambient (existing) light. Ideally you need a shutter speed around 1/15 or 1/8 sec to get sufficient blur in the picture.

To make your flashlit subject stand out from the background it is a good idea to underexpose the ambient light by one stop, so set your camera's exposure compensation to ×1 stop. To balance the flash with the ambient light you also need to underexpose the flash by one stop. You may find that your camera or flashgun does this automatically when set to slow sync mode. If not, set the flash exposure compensation to ×1 stop or set your flashgun's variable output to half power.

For the best results, focus on a spot your subject will pass, track it towards that point with the camera and trip the shutter while moving so the background blurs. It takes a little practice to master, but before long you will be producing stunning slow sync flash pictures. (See DVD 25.11.)

Event advice

Different types of sporting events demand a completely different approach, so the more you know about them the better. Here are a few hints on how to make the most of some common sport and action subjects. (See DVD 25.05.)

Football Go to local matches so you can shoot from the touchline. Rather than running up and down throughout the match, stay in one place and use different lenses to home-in on the action. Most photographers position themselves close to one of the goals, as that is where the best opportunities tend to lie. Lenses of 300 mm and above are required for distant shots, while a 70 × 200 telezoom will be long enough for closer action.

Motor racing Ideally you need a press pass, so you have access to all areas. If you are lucky enough to obtain one, watch where other photographers tend to gather – some spots are better than others. Use straight sections for panning and corners for prefocusing. Lenses of 300 mm and above are required for track shots, while shorter telephotos and wide-angles can be used successfully in the pits.

Tennis Local tennis tournaments provide lots of exciting opportunities, but even Wimbledon and other major gatherings are not out of the question for amateurs. Buy a ticket for one of the three front rows, where you can capture frame-filling action with a 70–200 mm or 75–300 mm zoom.

Athletics The options are almost limitless here, with a wide range of events to cover. A head-on position is useful for long jumpers, hurdlers or runners reaching the finish line, and a 300 mm or 400 mm lens will take you into the heart of the action. From trackside or near jumps, techniques such as slow sync flash and panning can be employed to great effect. Access is better at smaller venues.

Motocross You can usually get close to the action, so all you need to fill the frame is a short telephoto lens or a telezoom. Position yourself near a bend or jump, pre-focus and capture the rider airborne. Panning and slow sync flash can also be used effectively. If you do not have a racetrack nearby, find out if there is a quarry where riders practise – they will usually cooperate by performing stunts for your camera, so you will have more control over the pictures taken.

Cricket Because the action takes place miles away from the boundary, a long telephoto lens is essential. For shots of individual players you will need a 600 mm or even 800 mm lens. Cricket matches go on for hours, so you can take your time and wait for the most exciting incidents, such as players being bowled or caught out.

Action tips

- Practise your focusing techniques on cars driving down the street or on your children playing in the park.
- Never be afraid to shoot lots of frames when covering a sporting event – the fast nature of the subject makes it a little hit and miss.
- Learn about new events by watching them on TV or talking to people who are regular followers.
- Do not be misled into thinking you need press passes for large venues to take successful action pictures – your local Sunday afternoon soccer or rugby match can be just as rewarding.
- Analyse your pictures and try to learn from your mistakes. You may find the same problem keeps cropping up, such as poor timing or inaccurate focusing. The only way to solve it is by recognizing it in the first place.

26

still life

In this chapter you will learn:
- how to come up with great still-life ideas
- about using the right equipment
- how to master composition
- how to choose suitable backgrounds.

Still-life photography is perhaps the least popular subject among enthusiast photographers, mainly because it lacks the excitement of action or the natural beauty of landscape, and also because it demands a great deal of patience, care and imagination.

With most disciplines – landscape photography being a perfect example – the subject matter is already there. All you have to do is select an interesting portion of it, compose the picture and fire away. Still-life photography is more like painting, in that you start out with an empty canvas and the subject matter has to be built up from scratch. In other words, you have to create the picture before you can take it, and the success of the final image is dependent on your imagination, creativity, and skill. Tripping the shutter is usually the last step in a time-consuming process that may take anything from a few minutes to several hours. (See DVD 26.01.)

Picture ideas

There are many ways of approaching still-life photography and the one you choose will depend upon the amount of equipment at your disposal, the time you are willing to dedicate, and the type of results you wish to produce.

Professionals are renowned for spending days in their studio, carefully creating intricate compositions and using countless powerful lights to produce immaculate illumination. No expense is spared. If one apple is needed, an assistant will be duly dispatched to the local market to buy a whole crate so the best specimen can be selected, wine is purchased by the case, in the hope that one bottle will be perfect, and so on.

You need not go to such extremes, of course. Simple household items can be used as props in your still lifes, such as a bowl of fruit, fresh vegetables, garden implements, or an artist's brushes, paints and palette. Collections also make ideal subject matter – coins, stamps, old bottles, cameras, china and porcelain are popular examples. Alternatively you could devise a theme, such as Christmas, the swinging sixties, your favourite colour or a specific shape, and then look around for suitable objects. The options are limited only by your imagination.

The great outdoors or other locations such as your attic, garden shed or basement can be an equally rewarding source of 'found' still lifes, which are photographed *in situ* using natural light for the illumination. An old pair of muddy boots in a corner of the garage, the pattern created by terracotta plant pots stacked behind your greenhouse, an old cartwheel or piles of building materials; cobweb-covered bottles, tins and tools on the shelves in your garden shed, a rusting plough or abandoned car covered in vegetation, the texture of peeling bark on an old tree, fishing tackle laid out on the riverbank, seashells and pebbles on the beach, and autumn leaves carpeting the ground... These are just a few examples of what you are likely to discover as you search around.

The beauty of shooting 'found' objects is that you do not need to spend so much time creating each picture, so it combines the best of both worlds. That said, there is nothing to stop you re-arranging the items you find to make a more pleasing composition, or taking them indoors so you have more control over the lighting used.

Still-life photographers are like magpies. They hoard all sorts of bits and pieces that are picked up from the side of the road, in rubbish skips, or at car boots sales, so there is always a selection of props at hand for new creations. (See DVD 26.04.)

Equipment for still life

Although large- and medium-format cameras are the mainstay of professional still-life photographers, the 35 mm or digital SLR is equally suitable. In fact, digital is ideal really because you get to see the results immediately and can adjust the composition, lighting and exposure accordingly until everything is just right.

In terms of lenses, a 50 mm standard or 28–70 mm standard zoom will serve you well for classic tabletop still-life work because you will have the control to move as close to or as far away from the set-up as you like. A telezoom covering 70–200 mm will also come in handy for some shots, plus a macro lens or close-up attachment for taking pictures of small objects. Wide-angle lenses tend to be avoided for still-life work because they distort shapes and exaggerate perspective.

The only other items you need are a sturdy tripod to keep your camera steady, a cable release, plus a selection of reflectors. Filters do have their uses, but mainly to add creative effects. ISO settings should ideally be kept low for optimum image quality and resolution of fine detail – ISO 50–100 is ideal.

If you are shooting film, there is also a place for using fast, grainy stock to produce more painterly, atmospheric images – when combined with a soft-focus filter, fast film can produce beautiful, delicate images. Digitally, you can add grain and soft focus later. Black and white can also be very effective for still-life images.

Composition and background

The key word here is simplicity. Most photographers over-complicate their still lifes by trying to cram too many things into the frame. The end result is usually a confusing muddle, where the viewer cannot work out what is going on.

A far better approach is to start off with one or two key props and concentrate on creating an interesting composition from those alone, by experimenting with different lighting set-ups and varying the position of the items in relation to one another. Further objects can be added, but only if the composition will benefit.

With found still lifes, try a variety of compositions rather than opting for the most obvious one. Do not worry too much about whether or not the subject matter is identifiable as it is the aesthetic quality of the final picture that counts. Using different lenses and shooting from different angles can alter the meaning of a shot immensely.

The background should be given careful consideration as it can make all the difference between the success and failure of a well-composed still life. Again, plain, simple backdrops tend to work best. A sheet of black card or velvet pinned to the wall will make an uncluttered background that emphasizes the objects in the still life. To create a seamless background, bend the card or fabric so it forms a smooth sweep, and stand the props on it. This can be achieved using a tabletop or chest of drawers placed against a wall, so the background sweeps down onto the flat work surface.

For still-life shots of small objects all kinds of background materials can be used. Oiled slate works well with jewellery or shiny ornaments because it emphasizes the smoothness of the props, while black Perspex is ideal for creating perfect reflections. Old canvas, sackcloth, the back of your leather jacket, a rusting metal sheet and aged timber such as the panels inside an old chest of drawers are also suitable. Or you could paint card, plywood or canvas to create an original backdrop – splattered or mottled patterns look superb and add texture to the shot. Many photographers hoard old tins of emulsion paint for this purpose. Cans of spray paint are also ideal. (See DVD 26.02.)

Lighting a still life

This is the area where many photographers come a cropper, because the quality of light used can make all the difference between success and failure. The type of lighting you use depends upon your needs and what you have at your disposal. But rather than spending a fortune on expensive studio lighting, first look at the sources you already have.

Daylight flooding in through the windows or skylights of your home can be used to produce all sorts of lighting effects – all you need to do is place a table close to a large window and arrange your props on it. If you shoot during the late afternoon, warm, low-angle side-lighting will cast long shadows that reveal texture and form in your still life. Or you could reduce the size of the window opening using black card, so a more directional shaft of light is created. (See DVD 26.03.)

The diffuse light of an overcast day is perfect for atmospheric still lifes. Use a north-facing window, which only receives reflected light, and pin a sheet of tracing paper over the window to soften the light even further. Any shadows can be controlled using white, silver or gold reflectors made from cardboard.

When using window light you are limited to the daylight hours, but most of you will have access to another handy source of illumination – your portable flashgun. If you connect the gun to your camera with a sync cable it can be used in different positions around the props to create a range of lighting effects. To simulate window light, construct a diffusion screen from a timber frame and tracing paper, place it a metre or so away from the side of your still life and fire the flashgun through it. Bouncing the flash off a white reflector board positioned above or to one side of the still life will also produce attractive illumination.

The action-stopping ability of your flashgun is also worth exploiting. If you position it behind the still-life set-up and pointing towards the camera, the brief burst of light can be used to freeze water being poured from a bottle, or the splashes created when ice cubes are dropped into a glass.

Finally, a slide projector can be used to create dramatic lighting effects. Because the lens acts like a powerful spot you can direct the light on specific items. Try arranging small props on the ground, using a sheet of course art paper or board as the background, and then shine the light across it so long shadows are cast and the texture is revealed. This simple technique can be used to create stunning abstract images from everyday objects, and you can put filters on the projector lens or even place colour slides in the projector to create weird and wonderful effects.

Experimentation is the key to success. (See DVD 26.08 and 26.09.)

Studio still lifes

Tungsten lamps or studio flash units provide unlimited flexibility, allowing you to control the direction, harshness and intensity of the light to create exactly the result you have in mind. Pictures can also be taken at any time of day, or night, whereas with window light you are restricted to the daylight hours.

You do not need a purpose-built studio or lots of lights to achieve professional quality results. A corner of your lounge, a spare bedroom or garage can be converted into a temporary studio by clearing a suitable space, and one light plus a selection of reflectors will allow you to experiment with a range of lighting effects.

The type of lighting you choose will depend upon the items you are photographing. Shiny objects such as silverware, bottles and jewellery need to be treated carefully because their reflective surfaces tend to create hotspots which look unattractive. One solution is to construct a 'light tent' from a white sheet and then direct the light through it. This produces an all-encompassing, shadowless form of light that adds an overall sheen to shiny surfaces and reveals their shape perfectly. Alternatively, you could surround your subject with white reflectors and bounce light onto them, or use large softbox attachments from close range.

So you can gauge the effect of the light, black out the windows in the room and use the modelling lamps on the flash heads. You may need to spend several hours adjusting the position of the lights, adding reflectors, taking them away and so on, but eventually you will obtain the perfect result.

Where hotspots are not a problem you can be more adventurous and light your props from different directions to create various effects. Frontal lighting is ideal for revealing the colour of an object, but because shadows fall behind it the results tend to look flat and lack modelling. Shadows become more evident as you move the light to the side.

Sidelighting produces very bold, dramatic results. Shadows become an integral part of the composition, revealing texture and form to give your still lifes a strong three-dimensional feel. One light diffused with a soft box and placed to the side of the still life will produce an effect similar to window light on an overcast day. To fill in the shadows and lower contrast simply place a reflector on the opposite side.

Backlighting a still life by positioning the light source behind the props and pointing it towards the camera will render solid objects as silhouettes, while translucent or transparent materials such as glass or plastic take on a wonderful luminosity that emphasizes pattern and colour.

Attractive rim-lighting can also be obtained with the light source behind your subject. If you backlight a bottle of red wine, for example, very little light will pass through the wine itself, but the outline of the bottle will be revealed as a fine white line.

To obtain an even tone in the background when backlighting, the flash unit or tungsten spot should be placed behind a sheet of opal Perspex or fired through several layers of tracing paper.

Top lighting is another popular technique used by still-life photographers to produce evenly lit pictures of a wide range of objects. Usually the light is diffused using a large softbox attachment which is suspended above the tabletop set-up. You could make one using a wooden frame with two or three sheets of tracing paper stapled to it. If you do not want any obvious shadows in the picture, stand the props on a white or light-toned surface, so the light is reflected upwards.

Still-life tips

- Choose your props carefully so they relate to each other and form an attractive composition.
- Still-life photography has no time limit, so never rush a shot. You can leave the props in position for days if necessary, while you experiment with different compositions and lighting set-ups.

- Keep your eyes peeled for any interesting objects while you are out and about, or browsing through junk shops and car boot sales, and build up a collection of props that can be used in future still lifes.
- Remember to keep things simple. If you over complicate a composition is will lose impact and create confusion.

(See DVD 26.10.)

glossary

There are dozens of words and phrases used by photographers, many of which you will come across in this book. To avoid confusion, here are explanations for the most common terms.

Adjustment layer A layer in a digital image created so you can make adjustments to it without affecting the main image.

Adobe Photoshop Image manipulating software The standard choice among photographers for digital imaging.

Ambient light Available light, such as daylight, tungsten room lighting or window light.

Aperture Hole in the lens through which light passes en route to the film. Each aperture is given an f/number to denote its size. Large apertures have a small f/number, such as f/2.8; small apertures have a large f/number, such as f/16.

Artifacts By-products of digital processing, like noise, which degrade image quality.

Aliasing Square pixels make curved shapes look jagged when viewed close up. This problem can be solved using anti-aliasing software and filters.

ASA Old method of measuring film speed (American Standards Association).

Attachment File, such as a digital image, sent with an email.

Backlighting Term used to describe shooting towards a light source, so your subject is lit from behind.

Beam splitter Mirror or prism which reflects and transmits light, used in cameras with autofocusing or spot metering.

Bit Smallest unit of data representing on or off, 0 or 1, black or white.

Bit depth Also known as colour depth, it describes the size of colour palette used to create a digital image, such as 16bit

Brightness range. The difference in brightness, often measured in stops, between the highlights and shadows in a scene.

B setting A shutter setting which allows you to hold your camera's shutter open while the shutter release is depressed. Handy for night photography, when the exposure time required runs outside the shutter speed range on your camera.

Blending mode A setting in Photoshop that allows you to merge two layers so the pixels in one affect the pixels in the layers beneath. Different blending modes create different effects.

Blown out Term used when the highlights in an image are overexposed to the point that no details are recorded and they appear white.

Burning Copying images onto recordable and re-recordable CDs.

Burning-in Darkroom technique where more exposure is given to certain areas of the print, to darken them down or reveal detail.

Byte A small unit of computer memory (see kilobyte, megabyte and gigabyte). Eight bits make a byte.

C-41 process Chemical process used to develop colour negative/print film.

Calibration The process of adjusting computer monitors, printers and scanners so they all work consistently together.

Card reader A small unit that connects to your computer and has small slots that accept memory cards from digital cameras so you can download the images on the card to your hard drive.

Catchlight The reflections created by highlights or bright objects which appear in your subject's eyes and make them look more lively.

CCD (Charged Couple Device) Arrangement of electronic sensors that are used in autofocus cameras to aid accurate focusing, and digital cameras and scanners to resolve images.

CDR (Compact disc recordable) Blank compact discs used to store digital images, music and large text files. They usually have a capacity of 750MB. The least expensive way to store and archive digital images.

CDRW Compact disc that can be used more than once. CDRs can only be used once.

CD writer Hardware unit that lets you copy files onto blank recordable and re-recordable CDs – an ideal way to store digital images.

Channel The colours in a digital image. RGB image files have three channels – red, green and blue.

Chromogenic film Colour film that forms dyes during processing. Ilford XP2 is the only mono type available.

Cloning The practice of copying pixels from one part of a digital image and pasting them over pixels in another part to get rid of dust spots, hairs, skin blemishes, telegraph wires and other unwanted elements.

CMYK An image mode used to print images in books and magazines. Stands for cyan, magenta, yellow and black (K).

Colour contrast Use of colours which clash when in close proximity to each other, such as red and blue.

Colour harmony Use of colours which look attractive together and produce a soothing result, such as green and blue.

Colour management Process of ensuring all devices in a digital workstation – computer, scanner, printer – are all calibrated so what you see on the computer screen looks the same as what comes out of the printer.

Colour sensitivity How well film responds to light of different wavelengths – some films are more sensitive to certain wavelengths, particularly red and blue.

Colour space RGB, CMYK and LAB are all kinds of different colour space with their own characteristics.

Colour temperature Scale used to quantify the colour of light. Measured in Kelvin (K).

Compact flash One of a number of removable and reusable memory cards for digital cameras.

Compound lens Lens made up of different elements.

Compression Process that reduces the size of a digital image file so that it requires less storage space, transmits faster by email and downloads faster from the internet. This is done using computer algorithms to create 'recipes' for groups of pixels so the actual pixel size remains unchanged.

Contrast The difference in brightness between the highlights (the brightest parts) and the shadows (the darkest parts) in a scene. When that difference is great, contrast is high; when it is small, contrast is low.

Contre-jour French term which means shooting into the light, or 'against the day'.

Converging verticals Problem common in architectural photography which makes buildings appear to be toppling over. It is caused when the camera back is tilted to include the top of a building.

CPU Central processing unit, another name for a microprocessor.

Crop To remove parts of an image that are not required, usually to improve the composition.

Curves A useful tool in Photoshop for adjusting contrast, colour and brightness in a digital image in individual channels or all together.

Custom profile A special profile created for inkjet printers so that the printer settings are optimized for a specific paper and ink combination to achieve the best possible print quality.

Cut-off Darkening of the picture edges, caused when a lens hood or filter holder is too narrow for the lens, or too many screw-in filters are used together. Also called vignetting.

Data back Camera back that allows you to print the time and date on your pictures.

Daylight-balanced film Film for normal use which is designed to give correct colour rendition in light with a colour temperature of 5500K.

Default The standard settings used by an application until they are changed by the user.

Depth of field The area extending in front of and behind the point you focus on that also comes out acceptably sharp.

Depth-of-field preview Device which stops the lens down to the taking aperture so you can judge depth of field.

Depth of focus The distance the film plane can be moved from the lens without losing sharp focus.

Dialogue box A window or box that appears on your computer screen when using an application that allows you to change settings.

Diaphragm Name given to the series of blades that form the lens aperture.

Digital zoom Optical zooms actually magnify your subject so it looks bigger in the picture but digital zooms merely enlarge a section of the image so image quality is reduced – rather like enlarging part of a negative.

DIN German method of expressing film speed, still used today along with the ISO scale.

Double exposure Technique used to combine two images on the same piece of film.

Downloading Moving data from one device to another, such as digital images from a memory card to a computer hard drive.

dpi (dots per inch) An indication of resolution of a scanner or printer. The higher the number the better the quality. With scanners, dpi refers to the number of dots per inch it can resolve (though the correct term is ppi – pixels per inch). With printers it is the number of separate ink droplets per inch that are deposited on the printing paper.

Duotone An image constructed from two different colour channels, normally used to tone an image.

Dynamic range A measure of the brightness range in photographic materials and digital sensing equipment such as scanners. The higher the number the greater the range and the better the quality.

Dye sublimation A type of printer that uses a CMYK pigment-impregnated ribbon.

E-4 Old colour slide film process replaced by E-6. Now only used to process Kodak Ektachrome colour infrared film.

E-6 Process used to develop just about all colour slide film except Kodachrome.

Emulsion The light-sensitive layer on film and printing paper.

Enprint Standard size of print used by processing labs, usually measuring 6 × 4 inches.

Exposure latitude Amount of over- and underexposure a film can receive and still yield acceptable results. Colour print film has a latitude of up to three stops over and under.

Feathering Making the edges of a selection in a digital image softer so the joins are not visible.

Field camera Type of large-format camera which folds down for easy carrying.

File format The way in which an image is saved and stored (see **Tiff** and **jpeg**).

Film speed Scale used to indicate the sensitivity of film to light. An ISO rating is used. The higher the ISO number, the more sensitive the film is and the less exposure it requires.

Film scanner Scanner designed to digitize slides and negatives. Limited to the size of film format it will accept.

Filter factors Number indicating the amount of exposure compensation required when using certain filters.

Firewire A fast data transfer system now common on computers and associated equipment.

Flare Non image-forming light which reduces image quality by lowering contrast and washing out colours.

FlashPath Adaptor which allows SmartMedia cards to be fitted into a standard floppy disc drive.

Flash sync speed Fastest shutter speed you can use with an electronic flash to ensure an evenly lit picture. Varies depending upon camera type – can be anything from 1/30 to 1/250 sec with most SLRs.

Flatbed scanner Scanner designed mainly to digitize flat artwork such as drawings and photographic prints, but can also be used for slides and negatives.

Focal length Distance between the near nodal point of the lens and the film plane when the lens is focused on infinity. Also used to express a lens's optical power.

Focal plane shutter Type of shutter found on all SLRs and many medium-format cameras.

Focal point Point where light rays meet after passing through the lens to give a sharp image. Also used to describe the most important element in a picture.

Fogging Accidental exposure of film or printing paper to light.

F/stop Number used to denote the size of the lens aperture.

Gigabyte (GB) One thousand megabytes or one million bytes. Most commonly used to express the capacity of a storage device such as a memory card or computer hard drive.

Grey card A sheet of card equivalent to the 18 per cent grey reflectance for which photographic light meters are calibrated.

Greyscale A mode used to save black and white images. There are 256 steps from black to white in a greyscale image.

Ground glass screen Type of focusing screen found in many cameras.

Guide number Indicates the power output of an electronic flashgun and is expressed in metres for ISO 100 film.

Hard disc/drive (HD) Computer storage device used to store all data on a computer from software applications to text, music and digital images. It can either be built-in or separate.

High key Type of picture where all the tones are light.

Highlights The brightest part of a subject or scene.

Histogram A graph that displays the range of tones present in a digital image as a series of vertical columns

Hyperfocal distance Point of focus at which you can obtain optimum depth of field for the aperture set on your lens.

Incident light reading Method of measuring the light falling onto your subject rather than the light being reflected back. Incident readings are taken using a handheld light meter. Compare with 'reflected metering'.

Infrared filter Opaque filter that only transmits infrared light. Used with infrared film.

Inkjet printer Common type of printer that sprays ink droplets of varying sizes and can be used to create high quality prints.

Interpolation System of adding new pixels to a digital image by copying other pixels nearby so the output size can be increased without losing image quality.

Iris Another name for the lens aperture.

ISO Abbreviation for International Standards Organisation, the internationally recognized system for measuring film speed.

Jpeg Stands for Joint Photographic Expert Group and is a common file format that compresses images for easier storage and quicker transmission. Image quality is reduced slightly each time you copy a jpeg file.

Kelvin Unit used to measure the colour temperature of light.

Key light The main light in a multi-light set-up which provides the illumination on which the exposure reading is based.

Kilobyte One thousand (well, 1024 to be precise) bytes, often written as KB.

Layered image A digital image created in Photoshop by combining several layers with each layer contributing something to the appearance of the final image. A popular and effective way of manipulating digital images.

Layer opacity The strength or transparency of a Photoshop image layer – you can adjust opacity from 0 to 100 per cent to control how much of the layer beneath is visible.

Leaf shutter Type of shutter found in many medium-format and all large-format cameras. The shutter is in the lens rather than the camera body.

Levels Set of tools in Adobe Photoshop that allows you to control image brightness and contrast.

Life-size Term used in close-up photography when the subject is the same size on film as it is in reality.

Line film High-contrast black and white film which eliminates almost all intermediate grey tones.

Lith film High-contrast black and white film which eliminates grey tones to produce stark black and white images.

Lith print A traditional printing technique where a print is heavily overexposed under the enlarger then underdeveloped in weak lith developer to produce high-contrast prints with unusual image colour. The effect can be mimicked in Photoshop.

Lossy format A file format that compresses an image by losing information. Jpeg is the most common lossy format.

Lossless format A file format that does not lose information. The Tiff format is the most common example of this.

Low key Picture which has mostly dark tones to give a dramatic, moody effect.

Magnification ratio Also known as reproduction ratio. Refers to the size of a subject on a frame of film compared to its size in real life.

Marquee A Photoshop tool that allows you to select part of an image with great precision before applying changes.

Masking Selecting part of an image then blocking it off so that it is not affected by changes you make to the rest of the image.

Masking frame Also called an enlarging easel. Used to hold printing paper flat during exposure and allows you to create borders around the print.

Medium-format Type of camera using 120 roll film. Image sizes available are 6 × 4.5 cm, 6 × 6 cm, 6 × 7 cm, 6 × 8 cm and 6 × 9 cm.

Megabyte One thousand kilobytes of data (1024 to be precise). Written as MB, it is the common unit of measurement used to express the size of a digital file and also computer memory.

Megapixel One million pixels. Digital cameras now have sensors containing several megapixels – the higher the number, the higher image quality is.

Metamarism The strange phenomenon where black and white prints can take on a colour cast when viewed in certain lighting conditions. Quite common among inkjet papers.

Mid-tone The average tones in an image – in a black and white print mid-tones are mid-grey tones.

Mirror lock Device found in some cameras which allows you to lock up the reflex mirror prior to taking a picture, to reduce vibrations and the risk of camera shake.

Monochromatic Means 'one colour' and is often used to describe black and white photography or colour photography when a scene comprises different shades of the same colour.

Monobloc Type of studio flash unit with its power source and controls built-in – as opposed to units that are powered by a separate generator.

Monopod Camera support with one leg.

Multi-coating The delicate coating applied to most lenses and some filters to prevent flare.

Multiple exposure Technique where the same frame of film is exposed several times to create unusual effects.

Neutral density filter Filter which reduces the amount of light entering the lens without changing the colour of the original scene.

Neutral density graduate filter Filter that is clear on the bottom half and neutral graduate on the top half. It allows you to tone down the brightness of the sky and even out contrast when shooting landscapes so correct exposure can be achieved in both the sky and landscape. Various densities are available, from 0.3 (1 stop) to 1.2 (4 stop) to give you control.

Newton's rings Patterns caused when two transparent surfaces come into contact – such as a negative in a glass negative carrier.

Noise Looks like grain in a normal photographic image and appears on digital images as brightly coloured pixels in dark areas. Most common when you are using a high ISO setting and shooting in low light.

One-shot developer A type of film developer which has to be discarded after one use only.

One-touch zoom lens Zoom design which allows you both to focus and zoom the lens using a single barrel.

Open flash Technique where the camera's shutter is locked open, usually on the B setting, and the flash is fired at the required moment.

Optical viewfinder Direct viewing system found on some digital cameras.

Orthochromatic film Film which is insensitive to red light so it can be processed under a safelight, for example, lith film.

Oxidation Process by which photographic chemicals become exhausted due to exposure to oxygen – one reason why they should be stored in full and tightly capped bottles.

Panchromatic film Type of film or printing paper sensitive to all colours in the spectrum. Normal colour film is panchromatic.

Parallax error Problem encountered when using rangefinder and twin-lens reflex cameras. Because the viewing and taking systems are separate what you see through the viewfinder is not exactly the same as what the lens sees. It is most noticeable at close focusing distances, but modern compacts are corrected for it.

Paste The process of placing part of a digital image over another to change its appearance.

PC socket Socket on camera body which accepts a flash sync cable.

Peripherals Any hardware item than can be added to a computer – printers, scanners, CD writers and so on.

Photoflood Tungsten studio light with colour temperature of 3400K.

Photopearl Tungsten studio light with colour temperature of 3200K.

Photoshop The world's most popular and sophisticated image editing software, produced by Adobe for both Mac and Windows.

Pigment inks A type of ink used in modern inkjet printers that has much better archival (lasting) qualities than dye-based inks.

Pinhole camera Simple camera which uses a tiny pinhole to admit light to the film inside instead of a lens.

Pixel Made up from the words Picture Element – it is a tiny square of digital data, like a single tile in a mosaic.

Pixellation Unwanted effect in digital images where pixels are so large they are visible to the human eye.

Plug-in A program that works alongside an application from a different manufacturer. There are many plug-ins available to photographers that work in Photoshop.

Polarizing filter Type of filter that blocks out polarized light so colour saturation is increased, glare removed and reflection eliminated in non-metallic surfaces.

Predictive autofocusing Autofocus mode found on some SLRs which predicts how fast the subject is moving and automatically adjusts focus so when the exposure is made your subject is sharp.

Primary colours Colours which form white when combined. Red, green and blue are the three primary colours of light.

Prime lens Any lens with a fixed focal length, such as 28 mm, 50 mm or 300 mm.

Profile The colour reproduction characteristics of an input or output device. This is used by colour management software to maintain colour accuracy in digital images when they are viewed on other computers or output as prints.

Push-processing Technique where film is rated at a higher ISO, then processed for longer to compensate.

RAM Random Access Memory – the part of a computer than holds data while work is in progress, such as when you are working on a digital image in Photoshop. The more RAM you have, the better – 1GB is not uncommon.

RAW A file format used by many digital cameras which allows you to record every detail the camera takes – rather like a negative. The image file must then be processed afterwards.

RAW converter Software used to process images captures in the RAW file format.

Red-eye Problem caused by light from a flashgun reflecting back off the retinas in your subject's eyes so they record as red spots.

Reflected metering System of light reading used by a camera's integral meter, which measures the light reflecting back off your subject. Compare with 'incident light reading'.

Resolution Refers to image quality. High resolution images are big files that contain millions of pixels and can be output as large prints. Low resolution images make much smaller files but contain fewer pixels and can only stand small reproduction – such as images on websites.

RGB An image mode for colour photographs comprising red, green and blue. Each separate colour has its own channel of 256 steps.

Ring flash Flashgun with a circular tube surrounding the lens to provide even illumination of close-up subjects.

Rule of thirds Compositional formula which is used to place the focal point of a shot one-third into the frame for visual balance.

Scanner Item used to digitize images – slides, prints or negatives.

SCSI (Small Computer Systems Interface) An older means of connecting peripherals to computers, now mainly superseded by USB and Firewire.

Scratch Disc A portion of a computer's free hard disc that acts as an overflow RAM.

Selection Isolating part of an image so that it can be worked on without affecting other parts of the image.

Selenium cell Type of cell found in light meters which is sensitive to light and does not need a battery to work.

Selenium toner A toner which makes black and white prints archivally safe by converting remaining silver salts into a stable compound. Can also add a subtle colour depending upon the paper type used.

Shadow The darkest part of an image.

Sharpening Processing filter which makes an image look sharper by increasing contrast between pixels.

SmartMedia Type of removable and reusable memory card for digital cameras.

Snoot Conical attachment which fits to a studio light so you can direct the beam of light to where it is needed.

Softbox Attachment which fits over a studio flash unit to soften and spread the light.

Split toning Toning a black and white image with more than one colour – such as sepia in the highlights and blue in the shadows.

Stop Term used to describe one f/stop. If you 'close down' a stop you select the next smallest aperture. If you 'open up' a stop you select the next largest aperture.

Thumbnail Low-resolution image, often used for reference purposes.

Thyristor Energy-saving circuit in many automatic and dedicated flashguns which stores unused power to reduce recycling time.

TIFF (Tagged Image File Format) The most common file format used for digital images as it allows high resolution, is compatible with all operating systems and can be copied as many time as you like with no loss of data or image quality.

Toning Adding colour to a black and white image.

Transparency Another name for a slide.

Tungsten-balanced film Film designed to give natural results under tungsten lighting.

TWAIN Cross-platform interface that allows you to acquire images from scanners and digital cameras from within your graphics application. Stands for Toolkit Without An Interesting Name.

Universal developer Type of developer that can be used to process both black and white film and printing paper.

Unsharp mask A sophisticated sharpening filter found in many digital image software applications.

Upload Sending images and files to a remote computer, usually to go on a website.

Uprating Rating film at a higher ISO, then 'push-processing' it to compensate.

USB (Universal Serial Bus) A computer connectivity system which allows easy connection of peripherals to your computer.

Vanishing point Point where converging lines in a picture appear to meet in the distance, such as furrows in a ploughed field.

Variable contrast paper Black and white printing paper that can produce contrast grades from 0 to 5 with the aid of filters.

Vignetting see **Cut-off**.

Waist-level finder Type of viewfinder used on many medium-format cameras which you look down on with the camera held at waist level.

White balance Control found on digital cameras that allows you to correct colour casts, such as when shooting under artificial lighting, so your pictures look natural.

Windows The world's most popular and widely used operating system for PCs (personal computers), created by Microsoft. The other is Mac for Apple Macintosh Computers.

Zone system A system devised by the late Ansel Adams which involves pre-visualizing how you want the final black and white print to look at the time of taking the picture, so you can choose the exposure carefully. The scene is divided into zones – black is zone 1 and pure white zone 9, with various densities of grey tones falling in between the two extremes.

index

teach® yourself

From Advanced Sudoku to Zulu, you'll find everything you need in the **teach yourself** range, in books, on CD and on DVD.

Visit **www.teachyourself.co.uk** for more details.

Advanced Sudoku and Kakuro
Afrikaans
Alexander Technique
Algebra
Ancient Greek
Applied Psychology
Arabic
Arabic Conversation
Aromatherapy
Art History
Astrology
Astronomy
AutoCAD 2004
AutoCAD 2007
Ayurveda
Baby Massage and Yoga
Baby Signing
Baby Sleep
Bach Flower Remedies
Backgammon
Ballroom Dancing
Basic Accounting
Basic Computer Skills
Basic Mathematics
Beauty
Beekeeping
Beginner's Arabic Script
Beginner's Chinese Script
Beginner's Dutch

Beginner's French
Beginner's German
Beginner's Greek
Beginner's Greek Script
Beginner's Hindi
Beginner's Hindi Script
Beginner's Italian
Beginner's Japanese
Beginner's Japanese Script
Beginner's Latin
Beginner's Mandarin Chinese
Beginner's Portuguese
Beginner's Russian
Beginner's Russian Script
Beginner's Spanish
Beginner's Turkish
Beginner's Urdu Script
Bengali
Better Bridge
Better Chess
Better Driving
Better Handwriting
Biblical Hebrew
Biology
Birdwatching
Blogging
Body Language
Book Keeping
Brazilian Portuguese

Bridge
British Citizenship Test, The
British Empire, The
British Monarchy from Henry VIII, The
Buddhism
Bulgarian
Bulgarian Conversation
Business French
Business Plans
Business Spanish
Business Studies
C++
Calculus
Calligraphy
Cantonese
Caravanning
Car Buying and Maintenance
Card Games
Catalan
Chess
Chi Kung
Chinese Medicine
Christianity
Classical Music
Coaching
Cold War, The
Collecting
Computing for the Over 50s
Consulting
Copywriting
Correct English
Counselling
Creative Writing
Cricket
Croatian
Crystal Healing
CVs
Czech
Danish
Decluttering
Desktop Publishing
Detox
Digital Home Movie Making
Digital Photography
Dog Training

Drawing
Dream Interpretation
Dutch
Dutch Conversation
Dutch Dictionary
Dutch Grammar
Eastern Philosophy
Electronics
English as a Foreign Language
English Grammar
English Grammar as a Foreign Language
Entrepreneurship
Estonian
Ethics
Excel 2003
Feng Shui
Film Making
Film Studies
Finance for Non-Financial Managers
Finnish
First World War, The
Fitness
Flash 8
Flash MX
Flexible Working
Flirting
Flower Arranging
Franchising
French
French Conversation
French Dictionary
French for Homebuyers
French Grammar
French Phrasebook
French Starter Kit
French Verbs
French Vocabulary
Freud
Gaelic
Gaelic Conversation
Gaelic Dictionary
Gardening
Genetics
Geology

Lithuanian
Magic
Mahjong
Malay
Managing Stress
Managing Your Own Career
Mandarin Chinese
Mandarin Chinese Conversation
Marketing
Marx
Massage
Mathematics
Meditation
Middle East Since 1945, The
Modern China
Modern Hebrew
Modern Persian
Mosaics
Music Theory
Mussolini's Italy
Nazi Germany
Negotiating
Nepali
New Testament Greek
NLP
Norwegian
Norwegian Conversation
Old English
One-Day French
One-Day French – the DVD
One-Day German
One-Day Greek
One-Day Italian
One-Day Polish
One-Day Portuguese
One-Day Spanish
One-Day Spanish – the DVD
One-Day Turkish
Origami
Owning a Cat
Owning a Horse
Panjabi
PC Networking for Small
  Businesses
Personal Safety and Self
  Defence

Philosophy
Philosophy of Mind
Philosophy of Religion
Phone French
Phone German
Phone Italian
Phone Japanese
Phone Mandarin Chinese
Phone Spanish
Photography
Photoshop
PHP with MySQL
Physics
Piano
Pilates
Planning Your Wedding
Polish
Polish Conversation
Politics
Portuguese
Portuguese Conversation
Portuguese for Homebuyers
Portuguese Grammar
Portuguese Phrasebook
Postmodernism
Pottery
PowerPoint 2003
PR
Project Management
Psychology
Quick Fix French Grammar
Quick Fix German Grammar
Quick Fix Italian Grammar
Quick Fix Spanish Grammar
Quick Fix: Access 2002
Quick Fix: Excel 2000
Quick Fix: Excel 2002
Quick Fix: HTML
Quick Fix: Windows XP
Quick Fix: Word
Quilting
Recruitment
Reflexology
Reiki
Relaxation
Retaining Staff

Romanian
Running Your Own Business
Russian
Russian Conversation
Russian Grammar
Sage Line 50
Sanskrit
Screenwriting
Second World War, The
Serbian
Setting Up a Small Business
Shorthand Pitman 2000
Sikhism
Singing
Slovene
Small Business Accounting
Small Business Health Check
Songwriting
Spanish
Spanish Conversation
Spanish Dictionary
Spanish for Homebuyers
Spanish Grammar
Spanish Phrasebook
Spanish Starter Kit
Spanish Verbs
Spanish Vocabulary
Speaking On Special Occasions
Speed Reading
Stalin's Russia
Stand Up Comedy
Statistics
Stop Smoking
Sudoku
Swahili
Swahili Dictionary
Swedish
Swedish Conversation
Tagalog
Tai Chi
Tantric Sex
Tap Dancing
Teaching English as a Foreign
    Language
Teams & Team Working
Thai

Thai Conversation
Theatre
Time Management
Tracing Your Family History
Training
Travel Writing
Trigonometry
Turkish
Turkish Conversation
Twentieth Century USA
Typing
Ukrainian
Understanding Tax for Small
    Businesses
Understanding Terrorism
Urdu
Vietnamese
Visual Basic
Volcanoes, Earthquakes and
    Tsunamis
Watercolour Painting
Weight Control through Diet &
    Exercise
Welsh
Welsh Conversation
Welsh Dictionary
Welsh Grammar
Wills & Probate
Windows XP
Wine Tasting
Winning at Job Interviews
Word 2003
World Faiths
Writing Crime Fiction
Writing for Children
Writing for Magazines
Writing a Novel
Writing a Play
Writing Poetry
Xhosa
Yiddish
Yoga
Your Wedding
Zen
Zulu